EMMA KENNY

THE
SERIAL KILLER
NEXT DOOR

Chilling true stories of the killers hidden among us

SPHERE

SPHERE

First published in Great Britain in 2024 by Sphere

3 5 7 9 10 8 6 4

Copyright © Emma Kenny 2024

The moral right of the author has been asserted.

A CIP catalogue record for this book
is available from the British Library.

ISBN 978-1-4087-3191-8

Typeset in Sabon by M Rules Ltd
Printed and bound in Great Britain by
Clays Ltd, Elcograf S.p.A.

Papers used by Sphere are from well-managed forests
and other responsible sources.

Sphere
An imprint of
Little, Brown Book Group
Carmelite House
50 Victoria Embankment
London EC4Y 0DZ

The authorised representative
in the EEA is
Hachette Ireland
8 Castlecourt Centre
Dublin 15, D15 XTP3, Ireland
(email: info@hbgi.ie)

An Hachette UK Company
www.hachette.co.uk

www.littlebrown.co.uk

THE
SERIAL KILLER
NEXT DOOR

Contents

Prologue

In the still of the night, just beyond the veil of ordinary existence, there is a realm where shadows shift, and what was once familiar becomes an emblem of dread. The stories we are about to embark upon are not for the faint-hearted. They delve into the most sinister enigmas of humanity: serial killers. You might want to lock your doors, but what if the danger has already seeped through your walls and into the fabric of your seemingly normal, everyday existence?

Every morning, as you collect the newspaper from your porch, or wave to the elderly woman tending to her roses, you're living alongside a plethora of stories. Most are benign: tales of ordinary lives, of loves lost and found, or of dreams nurtured or broken. But some tales are crafted in the darkest corners of the human psyche. These are stories that, when told, make us question our sense of safety and shatter our belief in the inherent goodness of humanity.

Who lives next door to you? Perhaps a friendly postman with a perennial smile, a teacher who shapes young minds, or a businessman in a sharp suit? They are faces you recognise, people you've exchanged pleasantries with, individuals as 'ordinary' as you or me. But it's in the very depths of this ordinariness that a frightening anomaly could lurk. For within some of these seemingly normal souls lie desires so dark, they are almost impossible for the majority of us to comprehend.

The allure of the serial killer in popular culture combines both fascination and repulsion. What drives a person to not only take a life, but to do it repeatedly, ritualistically and without a shadow of remorse? To dwell on this question is to toy with a madness that lies hidden beneath the surface of civility. These aren't monstrous creatures displaying outward signs of their depravity for everyone to see. Often, these demons are indistinguishable from the rest of us; masters of disguise, concealed behind masks of normality. Perhaps that's what terrifies us the most. It's the notion that someone you know, someone you've invited into your home, laughed with, or maybe even loved, could be leading a dual life: part light and part unspeakable darkness.

How many times have neighbours of captured serial killers uttered in disbelief, 'He was so normal' or 'I would never have suspected her'? Well, evil doesn't always appear as we expect it to. It doesn't announce itself; instead, it sidles up quietly next to us, sometimes even sharing our bed. It exists by our side because that is exactly where it feels safest and most powerful. It is, in fact, in these very shadows of normality that these frightening predators wait for their unsuspecting and often trusting prey.

As you turn these pages, you will be brought face to face with humanity's darkest side. You will venture into the chilling, methodical minds of individuals who committed heinous acts, often while being integral parts of their communities. From the infamous to the lesser known, the stories herein will challenge your perceptions, test your understanding of human nature, and make you question every casual interaction you've taken for granted. By the end of this journey, you may find yourself watching a little more closely, listening a little more intently, and wondering: Do I really know who lives next door to me?

It is precisely this enigma, this idea of seemingly ordinary people leading horrifying secret lives, that sparked my interest in serial killers. Reading account after account of apparently gregarious, friendly, intelligent and socially functioning members of society leading heinous double lives made me question how and why this horror can often metastasise almost right in front of us. I soon discovered I wasn't alone in this contemplation and that there was a whole community of like-minded individuals out there asking the same questions.

Unravelling the minds of serial killers requires a fortitude to delve into the darkest recesses of human nature. My foray into this chilling realm was not a product of mere curiosity, but rather a path shaped by years of engagement with young offenders and victims As a psychological therapist my time working closely with individuals who have committed crimes served as the crucible within which my fascination and determination to understand serial killers was formed. Each chapter of this book will journey into the minds of enigmatic and terrifying figures who slipped under the radar, not to glorify their heinous actions but to attempt to understand their psyche, their motivations, and perhaps to recognise the signs of a potential perpetrator before it's too late.

In the confines of my therapy room and the projects I ran, I was granted a rare and invaluable perspective, witnessing first-hand the complexities and paradoxes that define these individuals. These encounters demanded a departure from the black and white perceptions that often dominate public discourse, pushing me to grapple with the grey areas and the nuanced realities of their existence.

Engaging with young offenders on a human level, striving to comprehend their motivations, triggers and vulnerabilities, I was confronted with the daunting task of reconciling the seemingly irreconcilable. How does one make sense of the coexistence of banality and brutality? What drives an individual to repeatedly commit acts of unspeakable violence? I found myself grappling with the fundamental question of nature versus nurture, contemplating the extent to which these individuals were products of their environment, genetics, or a confluence of both.

These questions became the fuel for my relentless pursuit of understanding, driving me to delve deeper into the psychological, sociological and biological underpinnings of serial murder. The process has been punctuated with moments of profound disquiet, as well as breakthroughs and insights that illuminated the factors contributing to extreme criminal behaviour.

The depth of my engagement with offenders laid the groundwork for a nuanced appreciation of the human capacity for violence and the potential for redemption. It instilled in me a conviction that understanding serial killers is not an exercise in glorifying their actions, but rather a necessary endeavour to prevent future atrocities and honour the legacy of their victims.

I have also had the privilege of working for many years with victims. Engaging with those who had endured unspeakable pain and loss provided a vital counterpoint to my interactions with perpetrators. It offered a stark reminder of the human cost of crime, grounding my quest for understanding in a deep-seated commitment to justice and empathy.

Speaking to victims and their families introduced me to resilience in its purest form, showcasing the strength of the human spirit in the face of adversity. It underscored the importance of providing a voice to those who had been silenced, ensuring that their stories were heard and their experiences validated.

This work also sharpened my awareness of the long-lasting impact of these crimes, highlighting the ripple effect of trauma that extends beyond the immediate aftermath. It underscored the significance of fostering healing and support networks, as well as the imperative to advocate for change and accountability.

As I transitioned into the world of television, presenting shows about true crime, the insights gleaned from my years of immersive experience served as an invaluable foundation. I found myself in a unique position to bridge the gap between the public's fascination with true crime and a nuanced, informed perspective on serial murder.

My commitment to giving a voice to the voiceless has been further amplified by the incredible community that has rallied around my work in the television and digital space. The gratitude I feel for the people who have followed my true crime shows, subscribed to my YouTube channel and engaged with the stories I bring to life is truly immeasurable. Their passion for justice and empathy for the victims has created a space where these stories are not just told, but are heard and felt, fostering a sense of collective responsibility and awareness.

As this book unfolds, I carry with me the stories of both the victims and the perpetrators, as well as the voices of the community that has supported this journey. Together, we explore the complexities of serial murder, and the unwavering belief that every story deserves to be told and heard.

1

Parker Ray: Twisted desires and the toy-box terror

We will begin our journey looking at some of the most deviant criminals in America: a place where, although death is often the punishment for murder, the worst of humanity are not deterred from committing the most heinous acts.

Here, in the shadows of the American Southwest, amid the breathtaking landscapes and the serene beauty of the open skies, there lies a haunting, twisted tale.

Within the barren expanse of the New Mexico desert, the town of Elephant Butte held a monstrous secret. Among its inhabitants was a man who would become the embodiment of nightmarish fantasies: David Parker Ray, notoriously dubbed the 'Toy-Box Killer'. But to understand the beast, one must first delve into the tragic journey of the boy.

Every story has a beginning, and Ray's early years were a tapestry woven with violence, abuse and psychological torment. On 6 November 1939, in a world at war, David Parker

Ray was born to unstable parents Nettie Opal Parker and Cecil Leland Ray. His younger sister, Peggy Pearl Ray, would arrive three years later, and the two unfortunate children would experience a difficult and draconian childhood in the desert. Horrifyingly, one of them would emerge a demon.

The dysfunctional Ray home lacked love and comfort, and the children found themselves in a household dominated by a controlling, abusive, alcoholic father and a drug-addicted mother. Even when Cecil divorced Nettie, taking custody of his two children, things didn't improve. It wasn't long before he abandoned them to the care of their grandparents, where they found themselves at the mercy of a cold and cruel grandfather: a strict disciplinarian and fundamentalist. Any dissidence resulted in physical punishment, and tactility was seen as a weakness. Nettie had abandoned them, and the children's formative years certainly lacked the nurture of a mother's love.

Although their father had left them in the hands of their grandparents, Russell and Dolly, who were first-generation ranchers, he would still continue to visit his children. A perverse and cruel man, these visits were something his children must have dreaded and were undoubtedly the root cause of his only son's twisted and deviant psyche. Cecil was a violent, misogynistic drunk and would bring Ray horrifying 'gifts' each time he visited: collections of violent and pornographic S&M magazines that would help shape this horrifyingly impressionable young man's view of women and catalyse his metamorphosis into a monster.

Little is publicly known about Ray's parents or sister, but fragments of his childhood stories speak of unfathomable horrors. It is said that Ray's father meted out unspeakable acts of abuse on him, a torment that sometimes had sadistic sexual overtones. The lessons this ruthless father taught his son are beyond comprehension for normal parents and included killing and having sex with animals. One can only shudder at the thought of what little David saw and experienced. These were the formative years that perhaps instilled in him a perverse understanding of pleasure, pain and power.

Unsurprisingly, Ray was not popular among his peers. Shy and introverted in others' company, especially around girls, he was often teased and bullied by his classmates. Despite this, and his horrendous background, he was not known to be a troublemaker. As a teenager, however, he began to abuse alcohol and drugs, and developed an unhealthy fetish for broken bottles, which he kept in a hideaway he had built in the woods.

Such traumatic experiences during these crucial, impressionable years often leave scars that are far too deep to heal. Ray's experiences, unfortunately, planted the seeds of a perverse curiosity. This was the foundational bedrock upon which the future 'Toy-Box Killer' would build his empire of terror.

One thing Ray excelled at, from an early age, was building and fixing machinery, a skill he would later use for evil, rather than good. After a short stint in the US Army, he became a maintenance man for the New Mexico Parks Department, where these skills would be honed in preparation for the horrors to come.

As he grew into a man, Ray's life was unsettled at best. He married multiple times and, although he had children, he never really settled down; spending a few years on the road, enjoying a hippie lifestyle, before finally returning home to his third wife, where he lived as an apparent 'family man' for a decade. This, however, was a facade, because as he matured, so did his sexual desires. But these weren't the typical yearnings of a young man. No, these were dark, insatiable urges that merged pain with pleasure. Sexual paraphilia, a condition involving atypical sexual desires or behaviours, manifested strongly within him. And Ray's predilections bordered on the macabre. He didn't merely crave the act but was obsessed with the very idea of domination and control. Cries of pain, pleas for mercy – they were music to his ears. His veneer of respectability, therefore, hid a sordid reality; his love of S&M had morphed into something monstrous and he was probably torturing and murdering women for years without detection.

The true depravity of this demon's capabilities would only begin to come to light on 22 March 1999, by which time he had almost reached the age of sixty. The horrors that would unfold after residents of Elephant Butte reported a naked woman, covered in blood and wearing a metal slave collar and six-foot chain padlocked around her neck, running along a dirt road, would be incomprehensible to even the most disturbed minds.

The woman turned out to be twenty-two-year-old Cynthia Jaramillo, who was desperately running for her life, having escaped the clutches of Ray. Working near her home in Albuquerque, she had been approached by Ray when he offered her twenty dollars for oral sex. She had then naively agreed to go back to his RV with him; a decision she would live to regret for the rest of her life.

At this point, Ray's fourth marriage had ended in divorce and he was in a relationship with Cindy Lee Hendy, a woman with desires as malevolently perverse and depraved as her partner's: she too enjoyed raping and humiliating women. On arrival at his RV, Cynthia would come face to face with this second monster after Ray produced a police badge and advised her that she was under arrest for soliciting. As he proceeded to cuff and gag her, the horrifying truth began to dawn on Cynthia: this was no police sting, it was a kidnapping. Even in those moments of utter fear and panic, as he drove the 150-mile journey away from the safety of her home, however, she could never have imagined the grotesque horrors that awaited her.

As his desires had intensified, Ray had begun to cultivate a haven for his twisted fantasies: the 'toy box'. This chilling trailer was a chamber of horrors equipped with an array of tools and devices designed for torture and murder. It was a testament to Ray's meticulousness and epitomised the depths of his depravity. Inside, victims would find themselves in a world of pain.

The euphemism and childish innocence of 'toy box' was a deliberate juxtaposition, a mocking nod to the childhood games and innocence that Ray himself was robbed of. This trailer was his perverted playground, and the savage nightmares that unfolded within its walls were the games he played. The residents of Elephant Butte, a quiet town with just 1,300 residents, where nothing interesting ever happened, had no idea that a monster was walking among them in plain sight.

On arrival at their gruesome destination, Cynthia was taken into the back of the twenty-five-foot-long, windowless trailer and chained to a post. If she was wondering what fate awaited her there, she would not have to wait long, because the diabolical demon had a recording set to play that would reveal her terrifying fate in all its gory detail. All she could do was listen to the words of a depraved monster and anticipate the horrors to come with dread as he recounted her sickening fate . . .

'Hello there, bitch. Are you comfortable right now? I doubt it. Wrists and ankles chained. Gagged. Probably blindfolded. You are disoriented and scared, too, I would imagine. Perfectly normal, under the circumstances. For a little while, at least, you need to get your shit together and listen to this tape. It is very relevant to your situation. I'm going to tell you, in detail, why you have been kidnapped, what's going to happen to you and how long you'll be here . . . Now, you are obviously here against your will, totally helpless, don't know where you're at, don't know what's gonna happen to you. You're very scared or very pissed off. I'm sure that you've already tried to get your wrists and ankles loose and know you can't. Now you're just waiting to see what's gonna happen next. You probably think you're gonna be raped and you're fuckin' sure right about that . . . '

Ray made a number of horrifying tapes during his reign of terror that he would play to his terrified and helpless victims. The pleasure he derived from his victims' knowledge of the horrors to come was despicable and his foul plans were certainly inspired by his cruel father's twisted lessons. Cynthia would have been under no illusion about the fate that awaited her, as she listened to his chilling words:

'I'm going to rub canine breeder's musk on your back, the back of your neck, and on your sex organs. Now I have three dogs. All of 'em's male, 'cause I don't need any fuckin' pups. One of 'em is a very large German shepherd that is always horny, and he loves it when I bring him in the house to fuck a woman. After I let

him in the house, he'll sniff around you a little bit and, within a minute, he'll be mounting you. There's about a fifty–fifty chance which hole he'll get his penis into, but it doesn't seem to bother him whether it's the pussy or the asshole. His penis is pretty thin. It goes in easy, but it's about ten inches long and when he gets completely excited, it gets a hell of a knot right in the middle of it. Now I've had slaves tell me that it feels like they got a baseball inside of 'em.'

Cynthia would later tell police that Ray had treated her like a dog, making her eat from the floor and even bathing her like a dog. On one occasion, he had even inserted gravy into her vagina, while she was restrained, so that his dogs could remove it against her will.

Exactly how long Ray had been kidnapping, raping and torturing young women is still unknown but what is certainly clear is that his victims' fates became even worse after he met the diabolical Cindy Lee Hendy and introduced a number of his 'select' friends into his warped games.

From capture, every moment of his victims' time in the 'toy box' would be monitored and recorded. Every victim would be raped multiple times a day, and would be expected not only to satisfy Ray, but also his deviant friends and girlfriend. A particular fetish was the use of dildos, and all his victims knew exactly what to expect, because his cruel recordings would leave them in no doubt:

'The dildos are gonna be used a lot, more than anything else, and consequently, what you're going to have the most trouble with. Many of them are long, very large in diameter and very painful while they're being forced in. Your mistress will use them in your pussy and I like to use them in both holes.'

While being held prisoner in the 'toy box', Ray's victims were expected to be subservient and show total respect to both him and Cindy – they were required to start every sentence with 'master' or 'mistress'. The narcissist particularly enjoyed the title 'Dungeon Master'. Any failure to follow the rules would be punished in a variety of ways, from whipping to the use of electric shocks, horrifyingly articulated in the recording he would play them:

'Each time you fuck up, I'm gonna press a little button and send a few thousand volts of electricity through your nipples, right down into your tits. You are in training, so it will just be a quick blast. I'm not going to hold it down and torture you. But each time you screw up, it's gonna be a little bit worse.'

Surprisingly, perhaps, Ray did not kill all of his victims. The tapes callously explained how, once he was finished with them, their bodies would be thoroughly cleaned to remove any DNA evidence, then his prey would then be plied with a cocktail of drugs designed to confuse them and create a state of amnesia. This would ensure that they would be unable to implicate him to the police. Again, this was chillingly explained in his own words:

'I get off on mind games. After we get completely through with you, you're gonna be drugged up real heavy, with a combination of sodium pentothal and phenobarbital. They are both hypnotic drugs that will make you extremely susceptible to hypnosis, auto-hypnosis, and hypnotic suggestion. You're gonna be kept drugged a couple of days, while I play with your mind. By the time I get through brainwashing you, you're not gonna remember a fuckin' thing about this little adventure.'

Cynthia would later divulge the horrifying depths of the torment she faced under the ministrations of this deranged demon. After capture, she was tortured for several days, continually raped and humiliated with a range of horrifying sex toys, medical instruments and an electric-shock machine. Then, having been threatened that things were going to get even worse, and that she was going to be taken to another secure room, where the pain and degradation would be magnified, she became determined to escape. Surely nothing could be worse than remaining where she was, waiting for the next horrifying ordeal? Incredibly, Cynthia would tell police, just as she was losing hope, an opportunity to escape presented itself.

It transpired that, leaving Cynthia chained to a pole in his trailer, Ray had left for work. In an act of brash stupidity, he left the keys to Cynthia's slave collar nearby and, seizing her chance, she managed to reach them and unlock her padlock. Noticing a nearby phone, she even managed to call 911, before Cindy returned, disconnected the call and smashed her over the head with a table lamp. A struggle ensued, where Cynthia fought for her life, finally managing to stab Cindy with an ice pick and make a desperate bid for freedom.

Blood pouring from her head injury, naked and still wearing her chain and collar, Cynthia miraculously managed to escape. Convinced her captors were in hot pursuit, she desperately attempted to flag down passing cars. Yet drivers were unwilling to help this naked, hysterical and bloody woman. Salvation finally showed itself, however, in the shape of Darlene Breech. Regularly leaving her trailer home unlocked, in this quiet town, she was shocked and appalled when a wounded and weeping Cynthia burst through her door and pleaded for help. Finding her a robe and trying to calm the distraught young woman, Darlene called the police, who were already en route, having received Cynthia's earlier 911 call. Although she had been cut off, the vigilant operator had heard the ensuing struggle and immediately acted upon it.

When Cynthia recounted her personal horror story, the police in this sleepy neighbourhood were sceptical; talk of a horror chamber, a sex slave and bestiality seemed fantastical to say least. They obtained a search warrant, though, and were horrified by what they found: a fifteen by twenty-five-foot horror chamber, kitted out with implements of sexual torture, from cattle prods and shock sticks to giant dildos and whips. Chains and pulleys adorned the walls and there was even a coffin-sized box that Ray would sometimes cruelly encase his victims in.

Ray's innocuous-looking trailer turned out be a horrifying prison of torture. Inside its claustrophobic, windowless walls, its victims would remain permanently restrained, either suspended on pulleys or strapped to a frame, their legs straddled in irons, while Ray and his girlfriend satisfied their perverse and grotesque desires. There was even a gynaecological examination table with a mirror fixed above it, so that his powerless prey had to watch the horrors that were inflicted upon them.

Despite the overwhelming evidence against Ray, the bespoke torture chamber and Cynthia's testimony, the police knew it would be difficult to prove that she was an unwilling victim. She was a sex worker and Ray was well known within the community as a polite man who had held down a full-time job and was respected as a mechanic. He also had a clean record.

Fortunately for Cynthia, however, her case was strengthened when the police found a video-tape recording of an unknown victim suffering similar abuse. Police managed to trace the victim after they released footage from the video and it was recognised by her mother-in-law. The unknown woman turned out to be Kelli Garrett and her mother-in-law recalled her going missing for several days. When she was found unconscious on the side of the road, she was described as dishevelled and confused. Having tried to explain to the police and her family exactly what had happened, no one had believed her. Instead, they had assumed she had been unfaithful, got high on drugs and tried to cover up her actions. As a result, she was asked to leave by her family and her husband subsequently filed for divorce. Ray had not only raped, humiliated and abused her, but he had also destroyed her life as she knew it.

Kelli had been telling the truth all along. Ray had kidnapped her and raped and tortured her for several days, then drugged her, driven her to a remote location, slashed her throat and left her to die. In spite of having been drugged, she was able to corroborate many of the details of Cynthia's story. She also confirmed that Ray's daughter, Glenda Jean 'Jesse' Ray had been responsible for drugging her at a local bar, taking her to Ray's trailer and helping to restrain her.

News of this kind was unheard of in Elephant Butte, and the appetite of the press was insatiable. Not long after the story broke, another victim, a woman named Angelica, came forward to say she too had been abducted, raped and tortured by Ray and Cindy after she had called at their house to borrow cake mix. After days of captivity, during which time she was raped, humiliated and degraded, she managed to persuade her captors to release her. They agreed, then drove her to a remote area of the desert and dumped her there. Shockingly, after Angelica reported the horrific ordeal to the police, they had decided not to take action against Ray and his girlfriend. Once Cynthia's ordeal made headline news, however, police finally realised they had a serial rapist and potentially a serial killer on their hands.

Faced with mounting evidence and witness statements against her, Cindy began to panic and, aiming for a plea deal and a reduced sentence, began to cooperate with police. It transpired that she had moved to New Mexico to avoid being prosecuted for a number of offences, including drug possession, where she had embarked on a relationship with Ray, who was twenty years her senior. It was then that the sordid and horrifying details of his reign of terror fully emerged.

Cindy claimed that Ray had horrifically tortured and murdered a minimum of fourteen women, dismembering their bodies and discarding them in various rivers and ravines around the local area, including in Elephant Butte Reservoir. She also implicated Ray's daughter in these heinous crimes, as well as one of his friends, Dennis Roy Yancy, claiming they both played a part in the disappearance of twenty-two-year-old mother of two Marie Parker.

During questioning, Yancy proved extremely cooperative, revealing exactly what had happened to Marie. He alleged that Ray and Cindy had abducted the young mother, then raped and tortured her for several days, before calling him. He alleged that, on his arrival, Ray had ordered him to strangle Marie with a rope, and that he had acquiesced because he was terrified of Ray. He also asserted that Ray photographed the whole sordid murder. Later Yancy would try, unsuccessfully, to lead police to her body. Tragically her remains, like so many victims of heinous predators, would never be found. Justice prevailed, though, and Yancy was found guilty of second-degree murder and conspiracy to commit first-degree murder and sentenced to thirty years in prison.

Jesse, Ray's daughter, was found guilty of kidnapping and criminal sexual penetration, and sentenced to just thirty months in prison, with an additional five years to be served on probation. Cindy had the charges against her reduced to five counts of being an accessory, because she cooperated with police, and she was given a sentence of thirty-six years.

The courts decided to put Ray through three separate trials: one for each of his surviving victims. He had a number of health problems and suffered a heart attack just as his first trial was beginning, while police were searching for more victims. Staggeringly, in his trial for crimes against Kelli Garrett, two jurors thought her story was unbelievable, and believed that any sex acts she experienced had been consensual. Nevertheless, he was eventually found guilty on all twelve counts of kidnapping, sexual abuse and conspiracy in a retrial in 2000. Inconceivably, though, he was never convicted of murder.

Ray's next trial was cut short when he agreed a plea deal with prosecutors. In return for a lenient sentence for his accomplice daughter, he pleaded guilty to all charges. He was sentenced to 223 years but, in a cruel twist of fate that meant true justice for his innocent victims would never be realised, he had another heart attack, which killed him, in May 2002. He was sixty-two years old.

Tragically the truth of the Toy-Box Killer's victims was taken to the grave with him as, although he had agreed to show authorities where he had buried many of his victims, his untimely death prevented this from happening. Following his death, the infamous 'toy box' was opened up to the public, and hundreds of items belonging to alleged victims, mostly jewellery and clothes that had been taken as mementos, were displayed in the hope that they would be recognised, and their owners identified. Sadly, this was not the case, and, with no new leads, the case came to an end.

It is clear that the world will never know the true extent of this heinous murderer's reign of terror or how many innocent young women never lived to tell the tale and escape the horrors of this depraved psychopath's 'toy box'. Ray had miles of abandoned land to dump his bodies in, and he had his choice of sex workers and drifters at the local Blue Waters Saloon bar, where it is believed he targeted many of his victims. Although he had admitted to police, before his death, that he had made money selling videos of his raping and torturing of victims online, this has never been verified.

Indisputably, Ray epitomised a sexual sadist and personified evil in his paraphiliac behaviour. For a diagnosis of sexual sadism disorder, patients have to have been repeatedly and intensely aroused by the physical or psychologic suffering of another person, and to have specifically expressed this in fantasies, intense urges or behaviours. Patients also have to have acted on their urges with a non-consenting person. The condition also has to have been present for at least six months. In extreme cases, like that of Ray, sexual sadism can become criminal due to an overwhelming desire to find unwilling victims, leading to rape and murder. For this monstrous individual, it became a way of life.

Ray enjoyed the feelings of power and control gained through the infliction of physical and psychological pain and humiliation, allegedly spending one hundred thousand dollars on his torture chamber alone. Although he meticulously diarised his nefarious activities, and allegedly told his first wife that he had kidnapped, tortured and murdered his first victim as a teenager, we will never know the full extent of his crimes.

It actually transpired that one of his first victims was an ex-business partner, Billy Bowers, who was found in Elephant Butte Reservoir, with a bullet hole in his head, by two fishermen. Later, Cindy would tell authorities that it was after this incident that Ray had learned to slit the bodies of victims and fill them with cement, to avoid them floating to the surface. No doubt this is why his victims' bodies have never been recovered. It is believed he murdered over sixty people in his lifetime, all the while living a double existence as a respected member of his community.

What turns a boy into a depraved monster? To say that Ray's childhood experiences directly led to his crimes would be a simplistic assertion. Many endure childhood traumas without turning to a life of crime. On the contrary, many lead determinedly better lives as a result. But, in Ray's case, the fusion of his early life experiences and an inherent predisposition towards sexual paraphilia created a deadly concoction. Ray didn't just seek sexual gratification; he yearned for power. This was not just about physical dominance, but also about psychological control. His victims weren't merely bodies to him; they were souls to be broken and spirits to be crushed. Every scream, every tear, every drop of blood was a trophy, a validation of his omnipotence.

One can't help but wonder how such a monster was born from the womb of humanity. Was he a product of his environment, a child scarred beyond salvation, or was there an inherent darkness, a lurking beast waiting for the right moment to unleash its fury? In the end, one is left pondering the fragility of the human psyche. How fine is the line between man and monster? And how easily can it be crossed? David Parker Ray's story serves as a chilling reminder of the depths to which humanity can sink, given the right – or rather, wrong – set of circumstances.

2

Jerry Brudos: Shadows of a disturbed childhood

Against the backdrop of mid-century America, in the bustling neighbourhoods of Portland, Oregon, lurked a killer. Not just any killer, but one with a dark fetish and a thirst for power and control.

To understand the mind of such a frightening individual, one must travel back in time, to a world where family dynamics, societal expectations and personal desires tragically converged to give birth to a monster. Delving deeply into Brudos' psychology, there is an undeniable link between his childhood experiences and the horrific crimes he committed as an adult.

Born to Henry and Eileen Brudos on 31 January 1939, in Webster, South Dakota, Jerome Henry Brudos was the younger of two sons. From the earliest days of his life, young Jerome, who became known as Jerry, was caught in a tumultuous relationship with his mother. His birth had not been planned and she had always hoped for a daughter. This unexpected pregnancy cemented her desire for a girl, and her desperation for a daughter grew throughout her baby's gestation. Tragically, the birth of another son created a chasm of disappointment, as she now faced the knowledge that this yearning would remain forever unfulfilled.

This longing for a daughter did not subside over time and, instead, played out in both subtle and overt ways. She would sometimes dress infant Jerry in feminine clothing; a gesture that, to many psychologists, seemed to underline her rejection of him as a son and would certainly have confused the impressionable young man, making him feel both different and an outcast.

Young Brudos knew his place; he was fully aware that he was an unwanted baby and felt unloved and unworthy from the outset. Cruelly, his mother made no attempt to hide her disappointment about bearing a second son and failing to conceive the daughter she craved. From the moment he was born, he was denied his mother's love and affection, and her selfish feelings of resentment would come to frame his world. As a boy, he faced both physical and emotional abuse from the person who should have loved, protected and nurtured him the most. His father, often away with work, was unable to redress this emotional deprivation and cruelty, and left him at the mercy of this uncaring woman. Even more devastatingly for Brudos, though, was that this maltreatment did not extend to his brother, whom she showered with love and attention. This would have been a further blow to his low self-esteem and must have exacerbated his feelings of inadequacy.

Added to his unhappy and tumultuous family life, Brudos

faced the instability of his family moving around the country for several years, before settling in Salem, Oregon. As he grew, the deep-seated need for his mother's approval intertwined with his emerging identity. By the age of five, Brudos had developed an unusual fetish for women's shoes, especially high heels. Finding a pair while playing on a rubbish tip in Portland, he took them home, fascinated by them. When his mother discovered him wearing them, she cruelly reprimanded him, said that he was 'wicked' and demanded that he take them back to the dump. Disobeying her command and desperate to keep the thing he most coveted, he hid them. She soon discovered their hiding place and burned them in a fire, humiliating her young son both verbally and emotionally.

Undoubtedly her callous and unempathetic response unlocked something in Brudos. Instead of accepting his unusual behaviour as childish curiosity, she treated him as disgusting and depraved. Considering her previous dressing of him in feminine clothing, this seems ironic at least, and must have further confused his impressionable young mind. For this cold and callous mother, though, anything sexual was aggressively disapproved of, and this would certainly come to influence Brudos' development into a man, as well as his evolving attitude towards women.

As Brudos grew older, his family continued to move, and when he was around seven they settled in Riverton, California. His fixation with women's shoes was unabated, and he attempted to steal a pair of his first-grade teacher's shoes; he was thwarted when another child informed her. At this time, he also began taking his mother's shoes and was consistently punished verbally and physically on discovery.

Unsurprisingly, because of his eccentric behaviour, Brudos' school years were plagued with isolation. A socially awkward child obsessed with his own internal world, his peers saw him as an oddball. He'd often be caught stealing women's shoes, further alienating him from his classmates and ensuring that they would mercilessly tease him. These initial instances can be seen as the embryonic stages of what would become a horrifying obsession.

Brudos' troubled childhood and sad home life was further exacerbated by two more moves between the ages of eight and twelve: first to Grants Pass, then to Wallace Pond, Oregon. Here, as puberty struck, his desires escalated, and he began breaking into homes and stealing not only shoes but also the underwear of his neighbours' teenage daughters. On one occasion, he even tried to remove and steal a pair of shoes from a sleeping teenage family friend. She awoke to catch him in the act and the consequence was humiliation once again.

As Brudos experienced puberty, his mother's disapproval of sex became clear, and her treatment of her son became even more cruel and unsympathetic. After experiencing a wet dream, he was reprimanded and forced to scrub his sheets by hand. Being forced to associate shame and guilt with a completely natural occurrence helped mould Brudos into the monster he became.

Understandably, Brudos' aberrant behaviour resulted in him being sent to psychiatric hospitals during his teenage years, where he was diagnosed with 'adolescent adjustment disorder', meaning he had a difficult time transitioning from childhood to adulthood: a fact that was clear to anyone who observed his actions and inclinations. This was unsurprising, given that his mother constantly emasculated him and filled him with feelings of shame. It is likely that no treatment would ever have been able to undo the lasting damage caused by his abusive upbringing at the hands of his cold and heartless mother.

As he grew, Brudos' behaviour became more alarming and began to foreshadow the horrifying path he would choose. In his neighbourhood, he gained a reputation as a peeping Tom, often hiding and watching women undress, then breaking into their homes to steal their shoes and underwear, which he kept in a personal collection at home. As his behaviour escalated from offences against property to offences against people, he began stalking local girls, knocking them unconscious or choking them until they passed out, then stealing their shoes. He would later admit that even at the tender age of seventeen, he had developed a fantasy of abducting a woman, forcing her to obey him and having her beg for mercy.

When his family moved to Corvallis, Oregon, he made this sickening fantasy a reality. First, he prepared his lair, digging a hole in a hillside where he planned to keep his 'sex slaves'. Then, wearing a mask and armed with a knife, he attacked and abducted his first victim. Threatening to stab her if she did not satisfy his sexual demands, he forced her to strip naked while he took photos of her. He wore a mask for the entirety of her confinement and, when he eventually let her go, he approached her, unmasked, claiming he had been abducted and held captive by the same perpetrator. Fortunately, his story failed to convince authorities and, following his arrest, he was sent to the Oregon State Hospital for nine months.

Here he shared details of his warped sexual fantasies,

discussing his desire to keep sex slaves and his fantasy of freezing dead bodies into different sexual positions. Unsurprisingly, it became clear that these fantasies centred around his hatred of his mother and, subsequently, women in general. He was diagnosed with borderline schizophrenia.

In spite of the months spent in hospital, Brudos managed to graduate from high school in 1957 and went on to join the military in 1959, at the age of nineteen. He was discharged after only one year, as it was deemed his character was unfit for service. Having failed in the military, he was forced to return home, further undermining his self-esteem. Once there, he was cruelly made to sleep in a barn, like an animal, and continued to be treated as the family outcast and deprived of the help he so clearly needed.

Somehow, however, amid all the chaos, there were glimmers of normalcy in Brudos' life. He managed to become a skilled electronics technician and began working at a radio station where he met his future wife, seventeen-year-old Darcie Metzler. He married her in 1961, and they moved to Portland, Oregon. Here he fathered two children and held down regular jobs, finally becoming a fully functioning member of the community and hinting at the man he could have been had his dark desires not overpowered him. Sadly though, beneath this veneer of respectability, Brudos' darker desires never really waned, and his sexual fetishes pervaded their family life. He would often make Darcie do the housework wearing only high heels and take voyeuristic photographs of her. She also caught him wearing lingerie and found photos he left around the house of himself wearing women's clothing. Although Darcie found this strange, she tolerated his unusual behaviour.

Brudos appeared to be a respectable family man to the neighbours, who thought they knew him so well; but despite having a son and a daughter, being softly spoken and neither drinking nor smoking, his paraphilias were driving him to become violent and would soon come to control him. In fact, the basement of his family home had become a personal sanctuary where his dark fantasies were allowed free reign. Here he collected troves of stolen shoes and lingerie. His wife, bound to obey her husband by the societal norms of the time, was instructed never to enter this underground lair without first notifying him via an intercom.

By now, Brudos had begun experiencing crippling migraines and blackouts. Controlled by his aberrant urges, he would often use these as an excuse to leave the house at night, falsely claiming that the fresh air helped to relieve the pain. The reality was, however, horrifyingly different. Rather than using the time to recuperate, he spent it prowling the streets, looking for opportunities to steal women's clothes and underwear. This escalation in his behaviour coincided with difficulties in his marriage, as his wife had become intolerant of his peculiarities and began focusing her time and attention on their children. As his relationship deteriorated, he was left free to pursue his darkest desires. He was not shocked to find himself virtually alone again, as it mirrored his childhood experiences. However, it likely magnified his hatred of women; the two people he felt should have loved and supported him, the most significant female figures in his life, had both let him down.

By 1967 his paraphilias had overwhelmed him and he began stalking a woman in Portland because he was attracted to her shoes. He followed her home, waited until she had gone to bed, broke in, strangled her until she passed out, raped her and stole her shoes. Although he took his victims' shoes home with him, and slept with them, he was not connected to the crime straight away. What is certain, though, is that the arousal he felt when confronted by the limp and helpless body of his victim would play out in his fantasies after the event and foreshadow worse that was to come. For Brudos, this was the prelude to even more heinous acts. His subsequent victims would not escape with their lives.

In 1968, Brudos' dark fantasies took an even more sinister turn. His shoe fetish merged with an urge to dominate, and this marked the beginning of his transition to serial killer. His first innocent victim was nineteen-year-old Linda Slawson. Living with her mother and siblings in Aloha, Oregon, Linda was earning money selling encyclopaedias door to door. On 26 January 1968, she made the fatal mistake of choosing Brudos' door to knock on.

Luring Linda inside by feigning interest in her wares, Brudos then brutally attacked her and strangled her to death, all while his wife and children were inside the house. Once he had murdered Linda, he was able to play out the warped fantasies that had been building to a crescendo throughout his life. He took her to his lair, had sex with her corpse, then dressed her up in items of underwear and mementos he had previously stolen from women he had stalked. After photographing her body, he then mutilated it, cutting off her left foot and keeping it as a trophy; the first of several he would keep from murdered victims. He would later assert that he kept the foot in a freezer, so that he could use it to model shoes. He then dumped her body in the Willamette river and, like so many innocent victims before her, it would never be found.

The monster later told authorities that, after his first murder, he dressed up in high heels and masturbated. This is a ritual that would be repeated after his subsequent murders.

Later that year, a stroke of misfortune sealed the fate of twenty-three-year-old Jan Whitney. While driving from Salem to Albany after celebrating Thanksgiving with her family, her car broke down. Spotting her at the side of the road, Brudos offered her a lift to his house, where he assured her she would be able to contact a garage. She naively accepted this apparent good Samaritan's offer and did not live to tell the tale. As with Linda before her, Brudos strangled her to death, had sex with her body and took her to his lair. There he had sex with her corpse before hanging her from a pulley on his ceiling. Over the next few days, he returned to molest and photograph her body. He even placed a mirror beneath the pulley, something he would live to regret.

This time the gruesome trophy was one of Jan's breasts. He removed it, filled it with resin and had the audacity to use it as a paperweight. He then stuffed Jan's mutilated chest with brown paper towels before callously disposing of her body in the Willamette river. To ensure she would not be found, he attached a piece of metal from a railway track to her corpse. By now Linda's foot was so badly decomposed that he disposed of that too. Jan's abandoned car was discovered later at a rest stop along Interstate 5.

Just over a year after taking the life of his first victim, on 27 March 1969, at the age of thirty, Brudos claimed his third. Police had received reports of a man dressed in women's clothing acting suspiciously outside the Meier & Frank department store in Salem earlier that day, but sadly had not found him. This would prove fatal for nineteen-year-old university student Karen Sprinker, who was due for a lunch date with her mother later that day. Sadly, she would never make it, as Brudos, dressed as a woman, abducted her at gunpoint just after she had parked and exited her vehicle. Her locked and abandoned car was later found on the store's rooftop car park.

Tragically for Karen, her ordeal was not short-lived, as Brudos kept her alive in his workshop lair, raping her and forcing her to dress in shoes and underwear from his morbid collection. As with Linda and Jan, he photographed her throughout her ordeal, enjoying every moment of her suffering. Her murder, too, was prolonged and even more callous, as he hung her from a pulley and left the room, cruelly allowing her to strangle to death. He returned later to have sex with her corpse before removing her breasts to make resin moulds from them. Like his earlier victims, her body was dumped in the Willamette river.

On 21 April 1969, Brudos' sick campaign of violence and murder finally began to unravel. He attempted to abduct his fourth victim, twenty-four-year-old Sharon Wood, at gunpoint from a basement floor car park in Portland. While dragging her into a green Volkswagen (a car that belonged to his mother), she screamed to attract attention and managed to escape. Shockingly, this failed abduction did not deter him, however, and he attempted to abduct fifteen-year-old Gloria Gene Smith on her way home from school the following day. Although he threatened her with a gun, she managed to pull free and escape with her life, as Brudos panicked and fled the scene.

The insatiable predator's fourth and final victim, twenty-two-year-old Linda Salee, a secretary from Beaverton, was not so lucky. Just one day later, on 23 April 1969, she was confronted by Brudos, dressed as a police officer, in Portland's Lloyd Center shopping mall. Linda was seen leaving a jeweller, after buying her boyfriend's birthday present, before her disappearance.

Brudos abducted her, took her back to his lair and sexually assaulted her while strangling her to death. Rather than mutilating her corpse, he attempted to galvanise her body by passing an electric current through it. When this failed, he resorted to necrophilia, then attached her body to a car transmission with copper wire and nylon cord and sunk it into the Willamette river. Law enforcement officers searched for the four missing women, but it was fishermen who discovered Linda Salee's body on 10 May 1969, in the Long Tom river: a tributary of the Willamette. Karen Sprinker's body was later discovered by police just fifty feet from where Linda was found. A murder investigation was launched.

Because Karen had been a university student, police began to interview her peers about her disappearance. Many began describing a man acting suspiciously, dressed as a Vietnam veteran, roaming the grounds of Sackett Hall, a girls' dormitory at the Oregon State University. He had been pestering women for dates, telling them he was a lonely veteran. Some of the girls had even felt sorry for him and agreed to go on dates. Police felt certain this was their man.

One of the women who was lucky enough to survive a date with the monster had refused a second because she had become suspicious of his behaviour. Instead, she had phoned the police. A golden opportunity that could not be missed, they managed to persuade the potential witness to arrange a date with him so that they could set up a honey trap. When

Brudos arrived, they arrested him and charged him with the armed assault of fifteen-year-old Gloria Smith. She subsequently managed to identify him from a police line-up.

Five days later, Brudos was back in police custody. They obtained a warrant to search his property and discovered his gruesome lair. The evidence was incontestable. They found the copper wiring that had been used to tie Linda Salee to the car transmission before dumping her body, a nylon rope used to strangle some of his victims and a list of potential female victims' names, addresses and phone numbers. Even more horrifyingly, they discovered the grisly photographic evidence of his brutal murders; images of his victims before and after death, some of them even hanging from the pulley dressed in items he still owned. In one photograph, investigators found an image of his face reflected in the mirror he had placed underneath the pulley. They also found the grotesque paperweights. In the face of insurmountable evidence, Brudos confessed to the murders of four women and the press branded him 'The Shoe Fetish Slayer'.

Initially, Brudos pleaded not guilty by reason of insanity to the murders. After evaluation by court psychiatrists, however, it was established that, although he had antisocial personality disorder, he was not suffering from mental illness. So, three days before his case went to trial, he changed his plea to guilty. Tragically for Linda Slawson's loved ones, though, Brudos was never tried for her murder, despite his earlier confession. Her body was never found and, frustratingly, there was no evidence to prove he had ever abducted her.

Justice was finally served for his other innocent victims when Brudos was sentenced to three consecutive life sentences without the chance of parole. As Oregon did not have the death penalty at that time, he was incarcerated at the all-male maximum security Oregon State Penitentiary.

Many found it difficult to believe that Brudos' wife, Darcie, could have known nothing of his horrifying double life, particularly as his murders took place under her own roof. He even kept the bodies of victims in their house for days. As a result, she was charged with aiding and abetting, but insisted on her innocence and was ultimately acquitted. She divorced him soon afterwards, changed her name and began a new life with her children away from Oregon.

Even in prison, Brudos' foot fetish continued, and he ordered catalogues from women's shoe companies to satiate his desires. Although he tried to appeal on many occasions, even bizarrely claiming one of the photos used at his trial was of a different dead woman, he failed. The reality was that prison offered him more than the outside world had; he was given seventeen years of psychological treatment that left him feeling 'more stable than he ever had'. He even successfully completed degrees in general sciences and counselling, going on to do a master's in the latter.

Despite his long sentence, Brudos attempted to secure parole many times. This was always denied, largely due to his callous refusal to discuss his crimes. In 2005 he claimed this was 'an act of vengeance' and that his legal rights had been removed. Little did he know that his time was running out and that cancer was slowly devouring his sick body. On 28 March 2006, he died in prison. He had been the longest incarcerated inmate in the Oregon prison system, having served thirty-seven years: significantly longer than each of his victims' short lives.

Brudos' crimes were indisputably horrific and gruesome,

but to fully grasp their significance, it's important to consider the broader psychological picture. Many experts believe that his childhood played a critical role in shaping the killer he became. His mother's overt yearning for a daughter, coupled with her repeated emotional rejections, may have instilled in him a twisted perception of femininity. The stolen shoes and underwear were not just objects of sexual fascination, but symbols of a feminine world from which he felt perpetually excluded; a world he came to lust after and despise in equal measure.

In the world of true crime, Jerry Brudos certainly stands as a chilling testament to the profound effects that childhood experiences can have on the adult psyche. His life, from his tumultuous relationship with his mother to his violent crimes, serves as a stark reminder that while the human mind is capable of greatness, it is equally susceptible to the darkest of deviations. The shadows of a disturbed childhood, when left unexamined, can lead to a legacy of terror.

Sexual paraphilias are intense and persistent sexual interests outside of the realm of what's considered typical or normative. For Jerry Brudos, his paraphilias manifested predominantly in fetishism, especially towards women's shoes. It is certainly worth exploring the depth of Brudos' particular paraphilia and the possible factors that might have driven these desires.

Brudos' paraphilic tendencies did not end at fetishism, however. He also displayed sexual sadism, a disorder characterised by deriving pleasure from the physical or emotional suffering of others. This was evident in the brutal way he murdered his victims, often strangling them. Beyond the act of murder, Brudos would dress up his victims, post-mortem, in stolen underwear and high heels, taking photographs of them to relive the act and satisfy his deviant desires. His actions demonstrated a need to exert control and dominance over women, turning them into lifeless objects of his fetishistic desires. His misogyny undoubtedly stemmed from his childhood experiences.

It's challenging to pinpoint an exact cause for paraphilias. In many cases, a combination of biological, psychological and environmental factors come into play. Brudos' relationship with his mother was fraught with complications and likely introduced a deep-seated sense of rejection in Brudos from a very young age. His mother's act of dressing him in girls' clothing could have been a pivotal moment, fusing feelings of humiliation and rejection with the symbolic representation of femininity (in the form of clothes). Given his history, it is plausible to suggest that Brudos might have felt emasculated or rejected in his formative years. As a response, his crimes can be seen as attempts to reclaim power and control. By turning his victims into mere objects, he could exert ultimate control over femininity without the fear of rejection.

Developmental factors also played a pivotal role: the onset of Brudos' shoe fetish at a young age indicates that his paraphilic interests might have roots in early developmental stages. Childhood experiences, especially those that merge with sexual development during puberty, can lay the groundwork for adult sexual preferences and fixations. Brudos' act of stealing a teacher's shoes during childhood, an action both bold and transgressive, suggests an early onset of his fetishistic disorder.

Some research has indicated that individuals with certain paraphilias may have variations in brain structure or function, although concrete evidence remains sparse. It's unclear if Brudos had such neurobiological deviations, but it's a factor that can't be entirely ruled out.

In the realm of forensic psychology, Brudos' case offers a glimpse into how personal histories, intertwined with psychological and possibly biological factors, can lead to the development of severe and dangerous paraphilias. The reasons behind these paraphilias can be as complex and multifaceted as the human mind itself. No matter how he was created, though, Brudos was a perverted sexual predator that was evolving by the day. The young women he murdered had their whole lives ahead of them and their futures were brutally destroyed by a monster that enjoyed humiliating them as much as murdering them. In just fifteen months, while living a seemingly normal life, he tortured and murdered four women and attempted to abduct two more. His appetite was insatiable and his paraphilias came to dominate his life.

Whether he was broken by a cruel and heartless mother or was born broken doesn't change the fates of Linda Slawson, Jan Whitney, Karen Sprinker and Linda Salee, or the devastation of their suffering families. Brudos was a ruthless, sadistic serial killer and the world is a better place without him in it. The words of one of the detectives who apprehended him sum him up best: 'he was a true monster.'

3

Ted Bundy:
Unmasking the monster

Theodore Robert Bundy, who became infamously known by the hypocorism Ted, remains an enigmatic and horrifying figure in the annals of American criminal history, almost half a century after his murderous rampage. From 1973 to 1978, he orchestrated a reign of terror, preying primarily on young women. While he ultimately confessed to the horrific murders of more than thirty women, many experts and authorities believe the actual toll is likely to be far greater. His heinous crimes were not limited to murder; he committed acts of rape, mutilation and even necrophilia. Despite being incarcerated, Bundy's cunning and resourcefulness allowed him to escape from custody twice before his eventual capture in 1978, when the justice system finally saw to it that he was executed via electric chair in Florida on 24 January 1989.

Bundy's early life may have foreshadowed the dark paths he later took. Residing with his mother and grandparents on the outskirts of Philadelphia, a young Bundy faced a family dynamic shrouded in deception. In 1946, at the age of twenty-two, his biological mother, Eleanor Louise Cowell, gave birth to Bundy at a home for unwed mothers. To circumvent the societal scorn of having a child out of wedlock, his grandparents presented themselves as his parents, leading him to believe that his real mother was his elder sister. He only discovered this unsettling truth at the age of fourteen. Reports of exactly how this transpired differ: some say he found a birth certificate, others that his cousin teased him for being illegitimate. Whatever the truth, it is clear that his early family environment was far from nurturing. His grandfather, who he felt close to, was known for having an unstable temperament and authoritarian attitudes, and relished cruelty to animals, authoritarian attitudes and extreme pornography. This tumultuous upbringing was compounded by Bundy's struggles in school; although he showed academic prowess, his introverted nature made him a target for bullying.

The intricacies of Bundy's psychological make-up have been the subject of much speculation and analysis. Established psychological paradigms, such as the attachment theories postulated by Ainsworth and Bowlby, Piaget's moral development framework, and Erikson's psychosocial stages, offer some lenses through which to examine his twisted psyche. In the months following his birth, Bundy was placed in the Elizabeth Lund Home and denied the crucial maternal bonding typically expected during this period. Such early-life disruptions can result in a skewed emotional development, leading to insecure and muddled attachments.

Erikson's theory posits that children, especially in their infancy, require consistent and dependable caregiving to foster trust. By around eight months, the majority of infants tend to exhibit clear attachment behaviours, usually leaning towards their mothers. However, Bundy's recollections revolve predominantly around his authoritarian grandfather, and with his grandmother's documented struggles with depression and agoraphobia, his emotional foundation was shaky at best.

The excuses found to explain the deviant behaviour of many serial killers, though, really can't be made for Bundy. Hs childhood experiences were certainly better than many. When he was just four years old, his mother took him to Washington state, where she met Johnny Culpepper Bundy. They were married on 19 May 1951, Johnny formally adopted Ted, and the couple went on to have four more children. Relocation to Washington certainly strained Bundy's already fragile familial ties, though, and he struggled to connect with his stepfather, Johnny, despite the latter's attempts to foster a bond.

This sense of alienation was exacerbated by the family's financial woes, which heightened Bundy's feelings of inadequacy and resentment. His mother was a secretary and his stepfather a hospital cook. Although Bundy never respected him, considering him unintelligent and working class, he helped provide stability in his life. As a family, they attended church and Bundy attended kids' clubs and camps and even became the Methodist Youth Fellowship's vice president.

In spite of this, Bundy was socially awkward and, although he liked to claim he had always been 'one of the boys', it simply wasn't true. He had a speech impediment for many years, which made it difficult for others to understand him and caused him to be teased. He increasingly withdrew, immersing himself in radio broadcasts and edging into the world of explicit content. Such patterns of isolation, combined with a hyperactive imagination, are traits that have been observed in other serial killers.

As Bundy navigated his adolescent years, a more sinister side to his psyche began to surface. He enjoyed hurting animals; he tortured frogs and apparently even once hung a stray cat from a clothesline, doused it in lighter fluid and set it alight. He also tormented mice, killing some and letting others live; an early indication of the thrill he got from power and control, and a foreshadowing of the horrors to come. It's also claimed he took children into the woods, stripped them and took their clothes, which reveals his enjoyment of humiliating others. He also cultivated a disturbing interest in violent pornography and was an avid reader of crime literature, particularly that focusing on sexually motivated offences.

Paradoxically, Bundy showcased an ability to function seemingly normally in society, excelling in his studies at the University of Washington, where he read psychology, and even taking a stab at law school. During these academic pursuits, he became involved with Diane Edwards (who is often referred to under the pseudonym *Stephanie Brooks* in the media), a student from a well-to-do Californian family. This relationship was significant for Bundy, as Diane's world represented everything he desired: affluence, recognition and societal acceptance.

Although Bundy always knew Diane was out of his league, his feelings of inadequacy were confirmed in 1968, when she ended their relationship because she felt he had few prospects. He claimed, 'She expected more of me than I was capable of giving.' Many believe this was a catalyst for Bundy's cruel murders, asserting that this event pushed him over the edge and drove him to target victims who bore a physical resemblance to her. Bundy would later challenge such a theory, stating that he simply went for attractive young women 'who caught [his] eye' but admitting that he had always had an overwhelming fear of rejection.

Surprisingly, their relationship rekindled in 1973, while he was on a trip to California. Diane was thrilled to witness Bundy's transformation; he was attending law school and was on the verge of a promising political career. Some claim the couple even got engaged before Bundy vanished from her life without explanation. Later he coldly admitted, 'I just wanted to prove to myself that I could have married her.' It transpired he had deliberately rekindled the relationship with the sole intention of ending it in an act of vengeance.

In spite of him being a vicious, deviant psychopath, Bundy is known the world over as the poster boy of serial killers and has gained a truly undeserved glamorous reputation, largely due to a multitude of film portrayals of his life. As a result of this romanticised image, the truth of his crimes has been diluted and, horrifyingly, although many of his victims' names have been forgotten, his infamy lives on. Yet each and every one of his victims deserves remembrance; each had families and friends who loved them, each had hopes and dreams for the future, each had lives that were cruelly and viciously snuffed out by a predator that personified evil. He may have been portrayed by some as charming, attractive and exceptionally clever, but the reality is that Bundy was a cold-blooded monster: a rapist, murderer, paedophile, necrophile, thief and con man.

Bundy had proved himself to be cold and calculating in his

relationship with Diane, but the depths of his depravity were yet to be realised. His campaign of terror began on 4 January 1974, when he was just twenty-eight years old and would change eighteen-year-old Karen Spark's life irrevocably. She became the first known victim of this demon and, like each and every one that came after, deserves to be remembered. A dancer at the University of Washington, it appeared Bundy had been stalking her for some time. She had seen him at the local laundromat; he'd been staring at her, then looked away. In the early hours of that bleak January morning, Karen had been reading and thought she saw a man's face peering through her window. She lived with male friends, and naively felt safe. After she fell asleep, however, Bundy broke into her basement apartment and beat her brutally with a bed post, then savagely sexually assaulted her with it, causing devastating internal damage and completely splitting her bladder. It appears he left before he could kill her, because he heard one of her male housemates close by.

Although Karen somehow survived the horrendous ordeal, she wasn't discovered until seven o'clock the following evening and remained unconscious in hospital for ten days. His brutal attack left her with permanent disabilities, including hearing and sight loss, and destroyed her dancing career. Sadly, she remembered nothing of the attack, and was unable to help police in the search for their perpetrator.

Just weeks later, on 1 February 1974, Bundy claimed his next innocent victim, and she would not live to tell the tale. Twenty-one-year-old Lynda Ann Healy was an attractive, successful psychology student and talented musician, who gave daily weather and ski reports on local radio, when her life was so cruelly cut short. Like Karen, she had been chosen by Bundy long before she knew it; her roommate, Monica Sutherland, would later recall an incident at the local laundromat, when Bundy had entered without any washing, messed around with a machine and left after checking the back door. The incident had unnerved Lynda. Monica also remembered once looking out of the front door because a neighbour's dog was barking, to find a man standing on her step shaking the dog. When more neighbours appeared, he fled the scene.

Tragically for Lynda, Bundy broke into her basement apartment on that bleak February night, beat her, dressed her and, after making her bed and hanging her blood-stained nightdress in her wardrobe, carried her away. Part of her skull would later be found on Taylor Mountain, and Bundy would finally confess to her murder before his execution in 1989.

During the first half of 1974, college students began disappearing from the Pacific Northwest area. It appears that, as his MO developed, he stopped the home invasions and instead used lies and cunning to deceive young women. Feigning injury and asking for help, Bundy would lure victims to his car where he would incapacitate them using a crowbar and handcuff them. He had already removed the front passenger seat of his car to accommodate their bodies. He would then take them to a preselected secondary location, where he would remove their clothes and brutally rape and strangle them. During this time, two students reported encountering a man with his arm in a sling, driving a VW beetle, trying to carry books and asking for help. Unfortunately, the police failed to make any connection to the previous killings or disappearances, so Bundy remained free to continue his bloody campaign and many more women would fall prey to this monstrous predator.

On 12 March 1974, a conscientious English student at Evergreen State College in Olympia, Donna Gail Manson, went missing on her way to a jazz concert. She was not reported as missing for six days, as she often hitch-hiked and disappeared for several days without notice. Although Bundy confessed to her murder before his execution, he cruelly kept her resting place a secret and her remains were never discovered.

On 17 April 1974, eighteen-year-old Susan Elaine Rancourt disappeared. A straight-A student studying at the University of Central Washington, she left a meeting on her university campus and never made it back to her dormitory. Vanishing without a trace, she did not leave a shred of evidence. Unlike most of his victims, Susan was blonde.

Bundy's next known victim was twenty-year-old Roberta Kathleen Parks, who disappeared when she was at a low point in her life. She had rowed with her father, who had then had a heart attack. Kathleen was also having boyfriend issues and had consumed alcohol on the night she disappeared. Bundy later admitted that after he abducted her from the campus of Oregon State University, he forced her to undress, broke her neck while raping her, then drove her to Taylor Mountain. Still conscious, she endured the five-hour trip before Bundy raped her again and beat her to death before decapitating her.

Although by now police had recognised an obvious pattern to these disappearances, they had no physical evidence to connect them to the perpetrator. Bundy was simply coined 'The Campus Killer' by the press. So he was free to continue his cruel campaign, and, on 1 June 1974, Bundy's next known victim was Brenda Carol Ball. Described as a free spirit by friends, she vanished after drinking and listening to music at the Flame Tavern. She was last seen talking to a man with brown hair and his arm in a sling. Like Donna, her disappearance wasn't reported immediately. In fact, it was over two weeks, on 17 June, before police were alerted, by which time eighteen-year-old Georgann Hawkins had also been abducted.

Described as happy and much loved by her friends, Georgann had been named a daffodil princess at high school and travelled the state, meeting children and attending charity events. On the evening of 11 June 1974, she had left a party and was returning to her lodgings. After speaking to a friend at her window, Georgann only had fifty feet to walk to her dormitory, yet she never made it back. Bundy later claimed he lured her to his car, feigning a broken leg and having dropped his briefcase. He then hit her with a crowbar, drove her to another location and strangled her. Afterwards, he spent the night with her body. In a stroke of pure arrogance, he returned to the scene of abduction while the police were there, to retrieve her earring and shoe. Witnesses would later report seeing a man on crutches, with his leg in plaster, in the vicinity where Georgann vanished. Apparently, the depraved monster revisited her corpse on three occasions.

The insidious double life of this reportedly charming man is exemplified by the fact that Bundy was working as assistant director of the Seattle Crime Prevention Advisory Commission during this time, and even wrote a pamphlet on rape prevention. Shockingly, he would go on to work at the Department of Emergency Services: an agency involved in the search for the very women he had abducted and murdered. It was here that he met and dated Carole Ann Boone, emphasising how he lived two seemingly incompatible existences. How could a man maintain a relationship while murdering women? Undoubtedly, his good looks and amiable facade fooled those who moved in his circles and thought they knew him well.

By now the public were terrified. At the advice of law enforcement, hitch-hiking dropped sharply, and the police found themselves under pressure to find the perpetrator. Without any physical evidence, though, this was proving onerous. The only thing police had to go on was the similarities in each case: the disappearances all took place at night, often near ongoing construction work, and there had been multiple reports of a man wearing a cast or sling driving a brown or tan Volkswagen Beetle.

On 14 July 1974, however, these similarities were undermined, as brazen Bundy abducted two women from a busy beach at Lake Sammamish State Park. He even had the hubris to introduce himself as *Ted*! Here, arm in a sling and loudly revealing himself, he asked for help unloading a sailing boat from his car. Three witnesses would later recount seeing him approaching and leaving with twenty-three-year-old Janice Anne Ott, who lived in Issaquah and worked as a case worker at the Youth Services Centre. Astonishingly, four hours later, nineteen-year-old Denise Marie Naslund disappeared from that very beach. Living in Seattle, she was studying to be a computer programmer. Described as kind and helpful by those who loved her, she had been at the beach with her boyfriend. She went for a toilet break and was never seen again. This vile monster would later cruelly claim that he made one of these innocent victims watch while he killed the other.

As more women began disappearing, and Bundy became less vigilant in his approach to abduction, police were able to release a description of their suspect. By now this sadistic killer's double life was at its pinnacle; he was in a relationship with Elizabeth Kloepfer, whom he claimed to have 'loved so much it was destabilising'. Both she and a former work colleague, Ann Rule, gave Bundy's name as a suspect. Kloepfer told police she had found a bag of women's underwear, a bowl of keys and a knife in his car. She even asserted that Bundy had left their home the night Brenda Ball had gone missing.

Exasperatingly, police were inundated and unable to deal effectively with the hundreds of names they were being given each day, and charmed Bundy was quickly ruled out as a likely suspect because he was a law student with no convictions and simply appeared 'like one of them'. Seven witnesses from Lake Sammamish would also claim the perpetrator did not match the photo police showed them of Bundy. These grave errors would seal the fate of many more innocent victims and give Bundy an even greater sense of omnipotence, as police now admitted they would only catch this heinous killer if he committed another crime and got caught.

In August 1974, Bundy moved to Salt Lake City, Utah to study law, where he would date a number of women. His poor results in Washington meant he hadn't made it into his university of choice and had had to settle with a night-school course. Describing this as one of the greatest disappointments of his life, it would certainly have reinforced the feelings of inadequacy that had previously plagued him. His place at the University of Utah was secured through recommendation letters from the governor of Washington, whose re-election campaign he'd worked on. While there, he became a much-loved member of the Mormon church, which again emphasises the extent to which he constructed a double life for himself. Rather than putting an end to his killing spree, however, he murdered just as prolifically in his new life, beginning by raping and strangling a still-unidentified hitch-hiker in Idaho on 2 September 1974.

His next known victim was Nancy Wilcox. A happy sixteen-year-old and one of six children, she loved cheerleading, attended church and had an active social life. All that tragically changed on 2 October 1974, when she made a decision that would cost her her life. She left school to buy some gum and vanished into thin air. Witnesses would later report seeing her in a light-coloured Volkswagen but, frustratingly, police weren't sharing information across jurisdictions at that time and authorities were unaware that their predator had moved to a new hunting ground. Further, her disappearance was initially considered a run-away. Although her remains were never found, Bundy later admitted to abducting her, then burning and burying her body two hundred miles away.

Just over two weeks later, ruthless Bundy stalked his next victim. On 18 October, seventeen-year-old Melissa Anne Smith, daughter of the Midvale police chief, caught the eye of this monster. A caring young girl who was returning home after plans to stay at a friend's house fell through, she disappeared like so many young women before her. Her badly beaten, raped and sodomised body was found nine days later, in a nearby mountain area, by two deer hunters. The postmortem would harrowingly reveal she had been kept alive for up to seven days before being strangled with a nylon stocking. Thirteen days later, on Halloween, sevente-year-old Laura Ann Aime disappeared near Lehi. Her naked body was found nine miles away and had also been beaten beyond recognition, raped, sodomised and strangled with a nylon stocking.

With each murder, Bundy's arrogant sense of invincibility grew, and he began to pass himself off as an authority figure to gain his prey's trust. This would be confirmed by eighteen-year-old Carol DaRonch, who was lucky enough to escape Bundy's callous clutches with her life. On 8 November 1974, Bundy approached Carol in a shopping centre and told her someone had tried to break into her car. Asking her to ac-company him and check for damage, she obliged, believing him to be a police officer. On confirming nothing had been taken, he asked her to go with him and fill in a complaint form. When she became suspicious and asked to see his ID, he quickly flashed a silver badge at her. Despite her growing sense of unease, she got into his car where he eventually managed to handcuff her left hand and, holding a gun to her head, threatened to kill her. Carol proceeded to fight for her life, breaking all her nails. She ran into the road and a car stopped for her and took her to the police station. Later, she would pick him out of a police line-up, remembering his appearance and distinctive walk. Her lasting memory of him was his 'blank lifeless eyes'.

Unsatiated, Bundy was still hungry for a kill and, this time, he was determined to succeed. Seventeen-year-old Debra Jean Kent, who was later described as a 'mother hen' to her four younger siblings, had been watching a play at Viewmont High School that same evening. She left at around 10.30 to pick up her brother from a nearby skating rink. Witnesses would report hearing loud screams from the school car park and seeing a light-coloured Volkswagen speeding away. Investigators found a key where she vanished, and it chillingly opened the handcuffs that had been removed from Carol DaRonch's wrists. Debra's body was never found.

In November 1974, Bundy's girlfriend, Kloepfer, contacted King County police a second time, having read about women disappearing around Salt Lake City. She was interviewed, but no action was taken. She called the Salt Lake County Sheriff's Office in December of that year, giving Bundy's name but again, because information wasn't shared between jurisdictions, the police failed to make connections and he remained at large. Surprisingly, considering her suspicions, Kloepfer continued to see Bundy, later asserting that their relationship was 'complex' but that she had loved him.

As 1975 dawned, Bundy's voracious appetite for murder remained unsatiated. Twenty-three-year-old Caryn Eileen Campbell was his next victim. On vacation with her fiancé in Snowmass Village, Colorado, she went to get a magazine and completely disappeared. Her frozen, naked body was found over a month later, next to a dirt road just outside the resort: she had been killed by multiple blows to her head by an object that had left distinctive grooved depressions on her skull. Her body had also endured deep lacerations from a sharp weapon.

As 1975 continued, so did Bundy's murderous rampage and Julie Cunningham was his next known victim on 15 March. Living one hundred miles northeast of Snowmass, twenty-six-year-old Julie was a popular, gregarious young woman who had recently broken up with her boyfriend. Feigning injury and on crutches, Bundy asked Julie to help carry his skis to his car. Once there, he clubbed and handcuffed her, then took her to his kill site, where he assaulted and strangled her. Grotesquely, he continued to visit her remains for weeks after the murder. Sadly, for her family, her body was never found. Twenty-five-year-old Denise Lynn Oliverson was the next to fall into his clutches, after going on a bike ride following a row with her husband near the Utah–Colorado border.

By May 1975, Bundy sunk to even more depraved depths when he abducted an innocent child: Lynette Dawn Culver. Living in Pocatello, Idaho, she was happy and doing well at school. On 6 May 1975, the grotesque monster abducted her and took her to a hotel room, where he sexually assaulted her. He then drowned her and disposed of her body in a river. Like so many of his victims, her body would remain undiscovered. Susan Curtis vanished from Provo, Utah, at the end of the following June, having left a ball at university to brush her teeth; again, her body would never be recovered.

Meanwhile police in Washington state were puzzled that their murder spree had apparently ended so, using new database technology, they sifted through the mass of data they had collected and managed to pinpoint twenty-six persons of interest: unsurprisingly, Bundy's name was on that list. On 16 August 1975, he was finally arrested by Utah highway patrol officer Bob Hayward, who had observed his VW Beetle cruising around a residential area in Granger at 2.30 a.m. A short chase ensued until Bundy stopped his car, claiming he'd panicked because he'd been smoking dope, but Hayward could not smell it. Instead, he noticed a crowbar and the fact that the front passenger seat had been removed. A thorough search also revealed a ski mask, a second mask made from tights, handcuffs, bin bags, rope and an ice pick.

In spite of the fact that Bundy's car matched the description from Carol's attempted kidnapping in November 1974, and that Kloepfer had given his name in December and that there was a variety of evidence found at his apartment – a guide to Colorado ski resorts with a checkmark by Wildwood Inn, where Carol Campbell disappeared from, and a brochure from Viewmont High School, where Debra Kent had vanished from – it was considered circumstantial and Bundy was, frustratingly, released on bail. He would later assert that investigators were incompetent and had missed a hidden stash of Polaroid photographs of his victims, which he destroyed immediately after his release. He also sold his VW Beetle in 1975 in an attempt to destroy evidence.

Bundy was placed under twenty-four-hour surveillance while investigators interviewed Kloepfer. She told them about the unexplained objects in his apartment: the crutches, the bag of plaster of Paris, the meat cleaver that he had never used for cooking, the surgical gloves, the oriental knife he kept in his glove compartment and the sack full of women's clothing. She also disclosed the fact that he made her wear her hair long and parted in the middle and that she sometimes caught him examining her body under the covers at night. She also divulged the damning fact that she had not been with Bundy on the dates that the Pacific Northwest victims had vanished.

Managing to trace Bundy's car, police found hairs similar to that of Caryn Campbell. Devastatingly, though, this still wasn't enough to charge him with murder, so authorities had to make do with the far lesser charge of kidnapping and assault. Bundy was found guilty in June 1976, and sentenced to fifteen years. In prison, he was placed in solitary confinement after being discovered with an 'escape kit' that consisted of road maps, airline schedules and a Social Security card.

By October 1976, Bundy was finally charged with Caryn's murder. In a truly arrogant display of narcissism, Bundy chose to represent himself. This proved to be a clever move, as he was not required to wear shackles and was shockingly given permission by the judge to conduct research in the library. Here he jumped from the second-floor window, injuring his ankle, but still managing to evade police for six days. He was caught after driving erratically in a stolen vehicle. Police discovered maps in the car that suggested the location of Caryn's body.

Once back in prison, Bundy was permitted to view the prosecution's evidence, and it appeared their case was falling apart, and that Bundy might be free after serving his sentence. Bundy devised a plot to escape a second time: acquiring a hacksaw blade, a prison floor plan and losing sixteen kilograms in weight so that he could saw a hole in the ceiling, crawl through the space and break into the chief jailer's apartment. Here he stole clothes before arrogantly walking out of his front door, having previously stuffed his bed with books and files to avoid detection. He was so successful that his escape wasn't discovered for seventeen hours. Prison staff had been negligent and offered Bundy the head start he needed; he made it to Chicago. He had five hundred dollars, believed to have been smuggled in by prison visitors, one of whom was Carole Ann Boone. Rather than lay low, Bundy couldn't resist the urge to hunt, and the inconceivable incompetency of authorities would devastatingly result in the deaths of more innocent women.

On 14 January 1978, Bundy rented a room at the Oak boarding house in Tallahassee, near Florida State University, in the name of Chris Hagen. He was seen at a bar close to Chi Omega sorority house. Later that evening, Kathy Kleiner returned to that same sorority house, after attending a friend's wedding. She shared a room with fellow student Karen Chandler and the two women fell asleep at around 10.30.

At 2.45 a.m. Bundy approached their sorority house. After picking up a log, he broke in and crept upstairs to the second-floor landing. The first room he entered belonged to twenty-one-year-old Margaret Bowman, who was alone. Bundy callously struck her with so much force that he split her skull, then strangled her to death with a pair of tights. He then crossed the landing into the room of Lisa Levy where he brutally beat and raped her, sexually assaulting her with a hairspray bottle, tearing one of her nipples and biting her, before strangling and killing her. The bite mark would prove crucial in future evidence against him. Bundy then crossed the landing again and entered Kathy and Karen's room. Tripping over a trunk, he woke Kathy up and brutally attacked her, lacerating her shoulder and breaking her jaw in three places. He then turned and struck Karen.

At that moment, in a stroke of fortune, another sorority sister, Nita Neary, returned from a date. This undoubtably saved the lives of her friends. As car headlights shone into Karen and Kathy's room, Bundy fled downstairs. Hearing someone running, Nita spotted a man exiting the house, holding a log in his right hand. She woke her roommate and was unsure whether she should call the police, when Karen emerged covered in blood. While helping her, they discovered Kathy, whose facial injuries were so devastating, paramedics thought she had been shot in the face. The four attacks had taken just fifteen minutes.

Undeterred by his close call, Bundy then broke into the basement apartment of another student, Cheryl Thomas. When neighbours heard banging from her apartment, they called the police, who found her severely beaten with a dislocated shoulder, broken jaw and fractured skull. Although, like Karen and Kathy, she was lucky to survive her injuries, they permanently ended the dreams she had of a dancing career. The frenzied viciousness of these attacks reflected Bundy's state of mind at that point in time: he was on the run, unable to plan his kills, and left incriminating evidence.

Almost a month later, Bundy was still on the run. Driving a stolen white van, he approached fourteen-year-old Leslie Parmenter in a shopping centre car park in Jacksonville but was spooked by the arrival of her older brother, which undoubtedly saved her life. The following morning, on 9 February 1976, he abducted twelve-year-old Kimberly Dianne Leach from Lake City Junior High School. Having been asked to collect her teacher's purse, Kimberly left her class and never returned. The last person to see her alive was Clarence Anderson, who saw her being led to a van by a man who he presumed was her father. Kimberly was crying. By the time her mummified body was discovered seven weeks later, forty-five miles away in a tin shack, next to a hog pen in Suwannee river, Bundy was back in custody. She had been raped and her throat had been cut. The position of her body suggested the callous monster had slit her throat while raping her.

Bundy was re-arrested on 15 February 1976, just six days after the heinous killing of Kimberly. Stopped while driving a car that he had stolen from near Chi Omega House, he violently attempted to evade arrest. Shots were fired, and Bundy was tackled to the ground. On searching the vehicle, police found three sets of IDs belonging to female FSU students, twenty-one stolen credit cards and a stolen television. On the way to custody, he told officers he wished they had killed him.

Facing questioning, Bundy initially claimed to be twenty-nine-year-old Ken Misner. When this was proved false, he refused to give police his real name and was thankfully denied bond because of it. The media reported him as a 'mystery man' and, even though they published photos of him, he wasn't recognised as the escaped convict he was. Officers quizzed him on the co-ed deaths, but still didn't realise he was the monster currently being hunted. Resources were so limited then that information was mainly passed on using phones or mail. He eventually agreed to divulge his true identity on his own terms: in exchange for a phone call with Elizabeth Kloepfer. During the call, he chillingly told her he was sick and consumed by something he did not understand and could not contain.

In June 1979, Bundy finally faced trial for the murders of Margaret Bowman and Lisa Levy, plus three counts of attempted murder for the assaults on Kathy Kleiner, Karen Chandler and Cheryl Thomas. It would be the first trial in the US to be televised nationally and, to his detriment, the psychopath would still insist on representing himself. He was offered a guilty plea that would avoid the death penalty, but narcissistically refused, despite the strong evidence against him, which included the bite mark and Nita Neary's eyewitness testimony. Perhaps he didn't want the world to know the depravity of his true nature.

On 24 June 1979, after less than seven hours' deliberation, the jury found Bundy guilty on all counts and the judge imposed two death sentences for the murders. Yet this still left many victims without justice. Six months later he went on trial for the abduction and murder of Kimberly Leach and another death sentence was imposed, after the judge described his crime as 'shockingly evil, vile and with utter indifference to human life'.

Bundy's astonishing hubris was evident throughout his trial, epitomised when he proposed to one of his prison visitors, Carole Ann Boone, while she was giving evidence. She believed herself to be 'Ted's advocate' and, although she accepted his offer of marriage, and managed to become pregnant with his daughter, she was shocked when he eventually confessed to his horrific crimes. Always having believed in his innocence, like so many other women who would avidly follow his trial, Boone moved to Washington with her daughter and refused his call on the morning of his execution after discovering the harrowing truth. She was devastated that she could have been so mistaken. After his trial, Bundy confessed to even more crimes in interviews, speaking in the third person, possibly in an attempt to disassociate himself from his guilt. What became clear in these was his intense hatred of women, perhaps stemming from the lies about his true parentage.

Even on death row, Bundy courted attention and his narcissism was on display: he offered assistance in hunting the Green River Killer, but this proved unproductive as it was another seventeen years before he was eventually caught.

When Bundy was finally executed, on 24 January 1989, his last words were, 'I'd like you to give my love to my family and friends.' Repetition of the possessive determiner 'my' and the complete failure to mention his victims or their families cruelly conveyed his complete lack of remorse and his shockingly self-absorbed nature. Even when he was facing death, and had nothing more to lose, he wasn't humane enough to offer closure to his victims' families. His narcissistic, uncompassionate nature meant he didn't even contemplate them or their feelings as relevant or important.

Looking back at Bundy's reign of terror, it is hard to understand how he could murder so prolifically and remain on the loose for so long. One of the main reasons was that he was an intelligent and organised serial killer who knew police procedure well. This enabled him, until he began to unravel psychologically when he was on the run, to leave crime scenes virtually devoid of any evidence. This was aided by the fact that he offended in the days before DNA profiling. No doubt, if he'd committed the same crimes a decade later, he would have been caught and many lives would have been spared.

Bundy also killed over a large geographical area, across seven states. Planning meticulously, he would research the area first, establishing secluded places where he could take and kill his victims. He would also leave their bodies in remote and vast locations, which made them harder to discover. He used blunt trauma to incapacitate victims, which largely prevented any form of defence, and murder by strangulation also meant there would be little evidence left behind.

Certainly, the incompetence of authorities also aided and abetted this monster, as it took too long for police departments in different states to realise that they were hunting the same killer. The freedom he was given once on trial was also indefensible. Even the sentencing comments from the judge beggared belief; he told Bundy to 'take care of himself'. A greater act of disrespect to his innocent victims is hard to imagine.

Indisputably, Bundy killed prolifically because he never felt satiated; he was driven by obsessive homicidal fantasises that were never truly satisfied, even by his most sadistic killings – the anticipation of the kill proved more satisfying than the reality. He found himself compelled to continue his depraved rampage in order to achieve the unobtainable. Many consider him a 'lust killer', because he raped his victims and engaged in sexual activity with their corpses. Also, typical of 'lust killers', as time went on, Bundy became more violent and left less time between murders. Sex was not his main motivation, though; Bundy was a serial killer obsessed with power and control. The sexual assaults were simply a way of dominating his victim, of making him feel omnipotent. As he would later boast, 'You feel the last bit of breath leaving their body. You're looking into their eyes. A person in that situation is God!'

Bundy viewed his monstrous murders as giving him God-like power, rather than recognising them as the epitome of his deviancy; he was a necrophiliac, paedophilic psychopath who had no respect for human life. He would abuse and kill victims, then continue to desecrate their bodies after death, revisiting corpses and indulging in sexual activity with them until decay, putrefaction and animal predation made it impossible. This post-mortem sexual activity perpetuated his feelings of power and control as, avoiding any chance of rejection, he could violate the bodies at his discretion. Like many serial killers, he also took trophies. It's believed he decapitated at least a dozen of his victims, taking their heads home and indulging in sex acts with them. Bundy also took clothes, jewellery and other personal possessions belonging to his victims, sometimes giving them to women he met; no doubt to reinforce the thrill of the murders and his feelings of power. He even photographed women he murdered. When asked why, he coldly replied, 'When you work hard to do something right, you don't want to forget it.'

Exactly when Bundy began his murderous campaign will always be shrouded in uncertainty. Before he was arrested, however, he was on the verge of a promising political career and was well thought of by those who worked with him. He had seemingly got away with his previous crimes and had the woman of his dreams, acknowledging, 'there it was, a life that had been missing for me'. Yet he threw it all away in order to satisfy his deviant desires. Even during his confessions, he failed to divulge when and why this occurred. Perhaps he was telling Kloepfer the truth when he claimed that he was consumed by something he couldn't contain. He alleged he began his 'predator stage' in the mid-1970s, when he was twenty-seven. Prior to this he asserted he was an 'amateur' and therefore refused to give details of those murders, perhaps because they didn't live up to his later 'standard' or maybe because even a monster like him could feel some shame. He once stated that he would never talk about 'some murders' because they were 'committed too close to home, too close to family or involved victims who were very young'.

Common among serial killers, Bundy's MO developed over time. In the early days he would consume alcohol to diminish his inhibitions. His deviancy began at a young age with acts of voyeurism: looking through windows, watching women undress and rummaging through neighbours' bins in the hope of finding explicit pictures. Later he would break into properties and beat sleeping victims, like Karen Sparks, before he evolved into the heinous predator he eventually became. As his killings mounted, he became more confident:

abducting women in public places, driving a distinctive car with a missing seat and kill kit in the boot, returning to crime scenes and even introducing himself to victims as 'Ted'.

Although, horrifyingly, he has often been romanticised in the media as a confident, smooth-talking charmer, Bundy was full of neuroses, believing himself inadequate, struggling to articulate when in stressful situations, and he was a habitual nose picker and nail biter. He was a paradox in many ways: claiming not to understand human social behaviour, while mimicking it perfectly. In fact, it was his ability to recognise how people *should* behave that made him so dangerous. He was the 'wolf in sheep's clothing', fooling everyone around him, even the police who, in spite of being given his name on numerous occasions, ruled him out. When Ann Rule worked with him on suicide prevention, she described him as 'kind, solicitous and empathetic', which leads one to understand how, in being able to mimic empathy, he would come to cruelly exploit it against the women he would murder after feigning injury.

Pathologically, Bundy has been diagnosed with a number of different conditions: from bipolar to dissociative identity disorder, and there is agreement on the fact that he had some form of antisocial personality disorder. He scored a frightening 39/40 on the Hare Psychopathy Checklist. But the true reason for Bundy's reign of terror will never be known. Shortly before his execution he claimed in an interview that pornography and true crime stories had triggered his murderous behaviour. However, the interviewer was a critic of pornography, and some believe it was an attempt at manipulation. He also contradicted this in other interviews. The reality is, as his final words confirmed, Bundy never accepted responsibility for his horrific crimes, always point-ing the finger of blame elsewhere: at society, at the police (for planting evidence), at TV for brainwashing him, even at the victims themselves.

In fact, Bundy never understood the enormity of his crimes, or experienced feelings of guilt because of them, claiming, 'I am in the enviable position of not having to feel any guilt. And that's it. Guilt is this mechanism we use to control people. It's an illusion. It's this kind of social control mechanism and it's very unhealthy.'

Horrifyingly, many young women expressed dismay after Bundy's execution and, in a phenomenon known as hybris-tophilia, felt they belonged to him, epitomising the bizarre global fascination with this vile criminal. Perhaps his own misogynistic words need recounting to emphasise the ab-horrence of this idea: 'Women are possessions. Beings which are subservient, more often than not, to males. Women are merchandise.'

Although no humane person will ever be able to under-stand Bundy's motivations, one thing is paramount: his victims, each and every one of them, must be remembered. By refusing to share their final resting places, Bundy exacer-bated their loved ones' suffering, while reminding us of the monster he truly was. The world is certainly a better place without this demon in it and it is sad that it took as long as it did for justice to prevail. It is even sadder, perhaps, that through portrayals of him in the media, the lie of 'Bundy the charmer' still exists. This lie devalues every innocent victim and every hurting family: it needs to be exposed for justice to truly prevail. Bundy was no charmer: he either attacked and abducted women whist they were sleeping and vulnerable, appealed to their feelings of sympathy, feigning injury, or took innocent children from their places of education, where they should have been at their safest. Bundy was a vicious, heinous predator and paedophile and, if he has to be remembered at all, it should be in those terms only. A personification of evil, he truly exemplified the depths a human being can sink to. This ugliness can be masked by an attractive exterior, and Theodore Robert Bundy truly is proof that monsters can exist in plain sight and walk among us every day.

4

Richard Trenton Chase: The thirst for blood; the Sacramento nightmare

In the annals of criminal infamy, the story of Richard Trenton Chase, the ominous 'Vampire of Sacramento', stands as a chilling testament to the labyrinthine depths of human depravity. This tale is not for the faint of heart; it delves into the shadows, unravelling the intricate, dark tapestry of one of history's most perplexing killers. A symphony of sinister whispers, psychological disturbances and morbid fascinations played in the theatre of his mind, leading to a macabre dance of death that would haunt the inhabitants of Sacramento, California for generations. Unbeknown to them, a demon would evolve and walk among them, irrevocably changing the landscape of the place they called home.

Most of us have a childhood fear of the bogeyman. For the people of this Californian city, that fear became a reality when, in the span of just one month, between December 1978 and January 1979, a heinous and bloodthirsty serial killer murdered six of their own. These killings would soon become notorious for the shocking carnage left at the crime scenes. It was a time when communities felt safe and people left doors unlocked; for the 'Vampire of Sacramento', this was an invitation to a blood-fest.

Born on 23 May 1950, in Santa Clara, California, the world was a hostile and chaotic canvas for young Chase. Finding himself in the volatile confines of an abusive and dysfunctional family, the seeds of darkness found fertile ground in his vulnerable psyche. His father was an abusive drunk, who frequently beat him and his younger sister. Sadly, his wilfully blind and ineffectual mother exacerbated these cruel behaviours. His parents' relationship was explosive, with his mother constantly accusing his father of being unfaithful and trying to poison her. The anger and frustration born out of his wife's accusations would then be inflicted upon his innocent children.

This trauma and instability twisted and contorted Chase's burgeoning mind, laying the foundation for antisocial behaviour and a twisted moral compass. The paranoia exhibited by his mother would later manifest itself in young Chase's behaviours and it was in these shadows that the whispers of his future first began to emerge. By the age of ten, Chase was already exhibiting signs of the MacDonald triad: bed wetting, torturing animals (particularly neighbourhood cats) and starting fires. In spite of this tumultuous start to life, though, young Chase did not cause problems at school. Described as quiet and withdrawn by his peers, many suspected he was taking drugs in his final years there, but he still managed to graduate high school in 1968.

Chase did indeed become addicted to both drugs and alcohol during his teenage years. As his dependency grew, so did his strange and erratic behaviour and he became involved in petty crime. According to girls he dated at the time, he was unable to maintain an erection during sex. It would soon transpire that regular sex could not arouse him and that a living, warm-blooded, consenting partner would never satisfy his deviant and disturbed desires.

Concerned about his inability to consummate relationships, at the age of eighteen, Chase sought the advice of a psychiatrist who concluded that he was likely to be suffering from a mental illness. He suggested his impotence could be a result of suppressed anger and suggested therapy. Although hospitalisation and treatment for his addiction was also recommended, Chase discharged himself. Unchecked and alone, his behaviour soon spiralled out of control, and he began to develop hypochondria, further exacerbating his issues. It is sobering to imagine how differently the future may have turned out if Chase had been forced to take the advice he was given in those early days, when his damaged mind could have been soothed by a caring professional and his abuse could have been acknowledged by someone who could have potentially made a difference.

Tragically, this did not happen and, by the age of eighteen, Chase had been thrown out of his parents' home and, exacerbated by alcohol and psychotropic drugs, his mental health had deteriorated even further. By now he found himself living in a shared apartment. This did not last long, however, as his erratic and bizarre behaviour would soon alienate his housemates and seal his fate as an odd and solitary loner for ever.

Constantly under the influence of drugs like marijuana and LSD, Chase would often be found walking around naked. When asked to move out by his unnerved flatmates, he refused, leaving them no option but to vacate the property themselves. Left alone, his condition worsened and ensured that no one would ever tolerate living with him again. Instead of craving the company of others, Chase sought solace in the corrosive embrace of drugs and alcohol. These twin demons played a sinister symphony within him, intensifying his mental turmoil, eroding his judgement and blurring the lines between impulse and restraint. The dance with narcotics steered him ever closer to the precipice of darkness and destruction.

By 1972, Chase was left with no choice but to move back home to his cold and unempathetic mother, who had recently divorced from his father. Here, with little to do but worry about himself, his mental state continued to decline, and his hypochondria began to overwhelm him, as he became more and more convinced that he was dangerously ill. At times he thought his heart had stopped beating, that someone had stolen his pulmonary artery and that he was a walking corpse. He even believed his skull had broken into pieces that were shifting beneath his skin. This caused him to shave his head so that he could track the movement of his cranial bones. Now convinced that his mother was trying to poison him, he left her home and moved into an apartment paid for by his father.

Clearly suffering from mental illness, Chase would try and improve his physical health by pressing oranges to his forehead, believing the nutrients would be absorbed via diffusion. Later, believing himself to be Jewish, he would claim the Nazis were turning his blood to powder and had planted poison beneath his soap dish. A river of darkness began to flow through Chase's mind, fed by his grotesque fascination with blood and gore. He was ensnared by the belief that his very life essence was drying up, and the only salvation lay in consuming the blood of the living. This obsession became the pulsating heartbeat of his existence, a siren song drawing him deeper into the abyss.

Overpowered by these uncontrollable feelings, Chase began killing and gutting rabbits then blending their internal organs with Coca-Cola and drinking this foul concoction. Neighbours would also witness him taking neighbourhood pets into his apartment, which would never be seen again. On one occasion, he confessed to one of them exactly what he had done to their beloved dog, which reveals the deterioration in his psyche and his inability to understand any kind of human empathy.

At the age of twenty-five, Chase's aberrant behaviour would reach a crescendo. After killing a rabbit, he injected its blood into his body, infecting his own blood in the process. Finally, it was acknowledged that he was a danger to himself, and he was admitted to Beverly Manor Psychiatric Hospital. Here, the cacophony within Chase's mind reached a fever pitch with the diagnosis of paranoid schizophrenia. Reality became a shifting, distorted kaleidoscope, with hallucinations and delusions painting grotesque images on the walls of his consciousness. Though most who share this diagnosis never tread the path of violence, in Chase, the disorder was a dark catalyst, fuelling the fires of malevolence and birthing a monster from the ashes of sanity.

At first, doctors did not believe his grotesque claims of

killing and drinking the blood of animals. This would be proved true, however, when he was discovered with his mouth covered in blood. Staff would subsequently find two dead birds on his windowsill with broken necks. It transpired that he had drunk their blood, and, on further investigation, it was also discovered that he had stolen syringes and been extracting and drinking blood from the hospital's therapy dogs. This earned him the frighteningly inappropriate nickname 'Dracula' among the staff and would foreshadow the nightmarish horrors to come.

Despite numerous unsuccessful escape attempts, twenty-seven-year-old Chase was finally discharged after over a year of institutionalisation. Doctors erroneously believed society was safe and that he did not pose a threat to the community in which he lived. The truth was shockingly different, however, and it would soon become clear that his rehabilitation had failed. Returning to his mother's home, she aided and abetted the disintegration of his already fragile mind by weaning him off his medication, asserting that he did not need it. Her unforgivable and senseless actions would help seal the fate of those who would fall into his clutches, and the lack of any subsequent care would ensure the complete destruction of his already fragile mind.

Soon after, Chase moved into his own apartment and his new housemates, like the last, were unable to tolerate his odd behaviour, and quickly moved out. Wrapped in the cold embrace of social isolation yet again, Chase was bereft of human warmth and connection. The frigid tendrils of loneliness twisted his perceptions, magnified his inner demons, and created a breeding ground for malevolent desires. In the echoing silence of his isolation, the sinister whispers grew ever louder, ever more insistent. As his mental health declined further, his appearance deteriorated and he stopped bathing, grooming himself and brushing his teeth. He also stopped eating and became emaciated and withdrawn.

Chase's mother refused to accept the severity of his condition, refusing to acknowledge his worrying change in appearance. In fact, her denial was so great that when he arrived at her house with a dead cat and began to eviscerate it in front of her, smearing himself in its blood and entrails while screaming hysterically, she simply closed her door on him. Perhaps aware of the damage her foolish intervention had caused, she shunned him instead of recognising his cry for help and let him down once again. Even more horrifyingly, in spite of his physical state and the neuroses he clearly exhibited, he was able to purchase a gun and practised using it obsessively, completely unchecked.

Perhaps Chase's final chance at salvation offered itself on 3 August 1977, after his mother had helped him plan and finance a trip to Nevada. Here, state police officers found his Ford Ranchero lodged in a sand drift near Pyramid Lake. On further inspection, they would make the grim discovery of two rifles and a bucket filled with blood and liver. When they discovered Chase himself, he was naked, covered in blood and hysterical. He insisted the blood was his own and that it had leaked through his skin. The blood was later confirmed as cows' blood, not his own and, despite police concerns, he was released. One wonders at the sense of this unfortunate decision considering his past and his overtly poor mental health. This mistake would prove fatal for those who would be unfortunate enough to fall prey to him in the coming months.

The doors of institutions opened and closed for Chase, but the care he received was fragmented, inconsistent, a tragic tapestry of missed opportunities and failed interventions. The inadequacies of his treatment allowed the darkness within him to fester and grow, transforming him into a ticking time bomb of violence, waiting to explode. Dancing precariously on the edge of sanity, Chase externalised blame, attributing his actions to unseen forces and external entities. This dance of deflection masked any semblance of remorse, allowing him to justify the unspeakable acts that he was inching ever closer to committing.

As Chase's mental health spiralled out of control, his desire to own weapons grew and, on 2 December 1977, he bought himself a .22 calibre semiautomatic pistol. By late December, his mental state had deteriorated even further. His sense of isolation and rejection had been exacerbated by his mother's refusal to allow him home for Christmas and, as his fascination with guns and blood developed, a new fixation began to permeate his mind: the case of 'The Hillside Strangler' (who eventually turned out to be two cousins working together). Kenneth Bianchi and Angelo Buono Junior kidnapped, raped and strangled to death at least ten women in a four-month period, between October 1977 and February 1978. In Chase's damaged mind, he began to feel an aberrant empathy with 'The Hillside Strangler', believing they were both victims of a Nazi UFO conspiracy.

The mixture of these heinous and very dangerous obsessions culminated in his first murder, on 29 December 1977. An opportunistic killing, Chase fired two shots at fifty-one-year-old Ambrose Griffin, who was helping his wife bring in groceries after a shopping trip. Although one shot missed, the second hit him in the chest and he did not survive. The usually safe and neighbourly community was shocked by this callous and senseless murder. Although witnesses described a man fleeing the scene, no arrests were made, and Chase would remain free to pursue his deviant desires. This first opportunistic murder would serve as the prelude to the horrors that were to come.

During the police investigation, they would discover that a woman in the neighbourhood had reported a man shooting at her home two days previously. A bullet from a .22 calibre pistol was discovered, and it was determined to have come from the same gun that had been used to kill Ambrose; he had intended to kill her. A disorganised offender with no victim profile, Chase would prove difficult to find.

Less than two weeks after the shooting, Chase asked a neighbour, Dawn Larson, for a cigarette, then forcibly restrained her until she gave him the whole pack. Just two weeks after that, he tried to break into the home of Jeanne Layton. Luckily for her, her doors were locked, and her windows secured. Coming face to face with him through the glass of her door, she later recounted how he had menacingly looked into her eyes, lit a cigarette and walked away. At the time she had no idea just how lucky she was. In front of her locked door stood a monster. She had escaped the clutches of the man who would soon become known as the 'Vampire of Sacramento'.

Chase's next unfortunate victim would not be so lucky, and their trust in their neighbours would seal their devastating fate, as Chase would later confess that he considered an unlocked door an open invitation. On 23 January 1973, he entered the home of pregnant Teresa Wallin. She and her husband, David, had their future neatly mapped out and were excited at the prospect of a son, whom they had planned to name Dane. Tragically, as David left for work that morning, he had no idea that their kiss goodbye would be their last, and that their dreams of a family and a future together would be so brutally shattered.

After entering her home armed with his .22 rifle, Chase shot Teresa several times, killing her almost instantly. Once murdered, her innocent body fell victim to the full extent of his grotesque and twisted desires. Dragging her to her bedroom, he mutilated and sexually assaulted her corpse, raping her while continually stabbing her with a butcher's knife. During this barbaric attack, he punctured her lungs, liver, stomach and breasts before disembowelling her and removing her internal organs. Leaving her intestines spilling from her body, he used a yoghurt pot to drink her blood. Before fleeing the scene, he cruelly desecrated her body even further, stuffing dog faeces down her throat and smearing her blood on the walls.

Her husband discovered this horrifying and macabre scene after returning home late because his car had broken down. Arriving home after dark, he found his house in complete darkness and heard a stereo playing. Noticing stains on the carpet, he followed them to their bedroom where he made the harrowing and life-changing discovery. Forever haunted by the horror of it, he would later state: 'I had no idea where I was, or who or what I had seen. It was just beyond all comprehension. All I know is the noise I was making; I was screaming and screaming, so much that my neighbours raced over to help me.'

David's parents would arrive before the police, and the

horror of witnessing her daughter-in-law's desecrated and brutalised body would break David's mother permanently. In court later, Chase's cold and callous mother would heartlessly ask Teresa's family, 'Why didn't your dog protect you?' To which her heart-broken husband would reply, 'Why didn't you protect us, you sick individual? You raised that! You raised that!'

Because of the disorganised nature of the brutal murder, police were quickly able to identify a footprint in the blood and establish that the same gun had been used to kill Ambrose Griffin. It also turned out that, a few days earlier, he had entered the home of Robert and Barbara Edwards. They had discovered him leaving through a window and, although Robert had chased him, he had escaped. They later discovered he had defecated in their son's bed and urinated in his drawer. Disgusted by this foul act, they could never have realised how close they had come to a much more barbaric fate.

Two days after Teresa's murder, Chase bought two puppies from a neighbour, killed them and drank their blood, then cruelly left their bodies close to her home. It seems his bloodlust was insatiable and more innocent victims would soon fall prey to his sickening appetite.

On 27 January 1978, just four days after Teresa's brutal murder, Chase discovered another unlocked door. This time it belonged to thirty-eight-year-old Evelyn Miroth. Inside the house were her son, six-year-old Jason and her twenty-two-month-old nephew, David Ferreira, whom she was babysitting, as well as her fifty-one-year-old neighbour and friend Dan Meredith. It was in this unfortunate home that Chase graduated to mass murder.

Watching the children while Evelyn bathed, Dan was

killed first, with a single shot to the head, when he went to investigate a noise. It is believed that Evelyn's terrified son ran into his mother's room for protection, after hearing the fatal gunshot. Chase followed him and shot this innocent young boy twice in the head. He then shot Evelyn's baby nephew before killing Evelyn in the bathroom. He then dragged her lifeless form into her bedroom and onto her bed, where he desecrated her body, cutting open her stomach and removing her organs. He also stabbed her in the anus, vagina and neck before trying to remove one of her eyes. It is believed the monster then drained and drank her blood, before sodomising her multiple times, leaving a large amount of semen on her body. Stealing Dan's car keys, he then fled the scene in his red estate car, which was later found abandoned only a few hundred yards from Chase's house. The demon took the body of twenty-two-month-old David with him.

Police were alerted to this devastating scene when a friend of Jason's called for a play date. They entered the house and discovered the massacre, as well as the missing toddler. They would also find the aftermath of a frenzied and disorganised killing spree that included bloody foot and handprints throughout the house.

Once home with his prey, demonic Chase cruelly decapitated and castrated baby David and used his genitals as a straw to suck blood from his tiny body. He then blended his internal organs before drinking this foul cocktail. It would be months before his decapitated body would be discovered, dumped in a car park behind a church close to Chase's apartment.

The chaos within Chase mirrored the chaos without, painting a grisly picture of a man driven by dark urges, unburdened by forethought or remorse. These heinous crimes were the physical manifestation of the storm raging within his psyche, a stark reminder of the potential for darkness that lies at the intersection of mental illness, trauma and isolation. His killings were characterised by a chaotic, frenzied nature, earning him the classification of a disorganised killer in criminal profiling. His crime scenes were erratic, with evidence of frenzied attacks, lack of planning, and little effort to conceal his atrocities. This disorganised modus operandi reflected the chaotic symphony within his mind, and the unrelenting turmoil that drove him to act on impulse rather than calculation.

At last, and far too late, authorities realised they had a depraved serial killer on their hands and called for the help of the FBI. Using crime scene evidence, they created an astonishingly accurate profile of their suspect:

White male aged twenty-five to twenty-seven; thin, undernourished appearance; single; living alone in a location within one mile of abandoned station wagon owned by one of the victims. Residence will be extremely slovenly and unkempt, and evidence of the crimes will be found at the residence. Suspect will have a history of mental illness and use of drugs. Suspect will be an unemployed loner who does not associate with either males or females and will probably spend a great deal of time in his own residence. If he resides with anyone, it will be with his parents. However, this is unlikely. Suspect will have no prior military history; will be a high school or college dropout; probably suffers from one or more forms of paranoid psychoses.

They were certain the monster would kill again.

Although law enforcement spoke to many witnesses, little evidence was given, other than the fact that the perpetrator was wearing an orange parka. Police were frustrated and began to lose hope, until they spoke to Nancy Holder, an ex-classmate of Chase's from ten years earlier. Bumping into him on the same day he had broken into the Edwardses' home, she had mistaken him for a homeless man. Years of substance abuse had changed his appearance dramatically. Looking agitated, he had approached her and asked her, 'Were you on the motorcycle when Kurt was killed?' Shocked that an apparent stranger had known her high school boyfriend had died in an accident, she undoubtedly showed it in her expression. It was then that he revealed, 'It's me, Rick Chase.'

At the time of the incident, Nancy had felt unnerved; Chase had followed her to her car and begged for a lift. She had refused and quickly driven away and, although she had been frightened by this unkempt and threatening looking former schoolmate, she could never have imagined the terrifying fate she avoided in refusing his plea.

After hearing a description of the murder suspect, Nancy contacted police, telling them she believed Chase was their man. On checking his background, they soon discovered that a .22 calibre pistol was registered in his name: the same type of weapon used in the murders. They immediately went to Chase's apartment to arrest him, but he refused to answer the door, pretending not to be home. Acting like they were leaving, officers walked away from his apartment and apprehended him when he tried to leave, believing the coast to be clear.

Seeing Chase in the flesh undoubtedly confirmed to the

officers waiting to pounce that they had their man. He was wearing an orange parka and was in possession of Dan Meredith's wallet, which, along with a box he was carrying full of bloodstained cloth, was stained in blood. Chase also matched the FBI profile perfectly.

After obtaining a warrant, police searched Chase's apartment and the evidence they found was incriminating beyond measure. They had undoubtedly found the Vampire's lair, and it really was a house of horrors. The grotesque and blood-curdling list of evidence must have haunted those who discovered it. His walls and floor were covered in dried blood, his kitchen utensils were similarly stained, and the fridge contained both animal and human body parts, including human brains. These were later discovered to belong to David Ferreira, Evelyn Miroth and Teresa Wallin. They also discovered a blender coated in coagulated blood and decaying matter as well as the .22 calibre pistol used in the murders. They had their monster and, just five days after the heinous massacre at Evelyn Miroth's home, he was charged with six counts of first-degree murder.

When his trial began, on 2 January 1979, the demon was escorted into the room by five police officers; they were taking no chances. More than one hundred witnesses would testify against him, and the prosecution was fuelled with a desperate desire for the ultimate punishment: the death sentence.

Rumours and reports hinted at neurological abnormalities lurking within the recesses of Chase's brain. If true, these invisible puppeteers could have manipulated his behaviour, stoked the flames of aggression and propelled him further down the twisted path of depravity. It was perhaps this unseen hand that sculpted a disturbed individual into a true harbinger of death. Therefore, his defence team argued that he was not guilty by reason of insanity and that he was guilty of second-degree murder only. This would allow Chase to face a lesser charge and to live out the rest of his life in prison. The judge was determined he would face trial, however, and ultimately declared him legally sane. The horrors of the crimes committed on victims as young as David and Teresa's unborn baby meant it would be intolerable for his victims' survivors to be denied true justice.

So, on 8 May 1979, following a four-month trial, the jury took just one hour to find Chase guilty of all six counts of first-degree murder. After deliberating for a further four hours, they decided his heinous crimes did deserve the ultimate punishment and he was sentenced to death by gas chamber.

Even after he was transferred to San Quentin State Prison, Chase's delusions continued. Here, in a series of interviews with FBI agent Robert Ressler, Chase continued to speak of Nazi UFOs that had telepathically told him to commit his atrocities and requested a radar gun to help him apprehend them. On another occasion, he produced a handful of macaroni cheese and handed it to the agent, asking him to check it because he believed the prison guards were trying to poison him. Also, when quizzed about his need for blood, Chase continued to assert that, without it, he would die and he told Ressler that 'if the door was locked, that means you're not welcome', confirming that he believed if a door was unlocked, he was invited to a blood fest.

In prison, Chase's notoriety preceded him. Because of the brutal and horrific nature of his murders, many inmates feared him and wanted him dead, but were too scared to commit the act because of Chase's unpredictability. Instead, they constantly encouraged him to kill himself. On 26 December 1980, this strategy proved successful and prison staff found his lifeless form lying on his bed. After storing his medication for months, he had taken a fatal overdose, and his reign of terror was ended by his own hands.

At the time of his heinous crimes, Chase was suffering from psychosis, schizophrenia and extreme paranoia and believed that, without consuming the blood of others, he would die. He was certainly aided and abetted by a failed system and an ineffectual and wilfully blind mother. Undeniably, though, he was a terrifying and dangerous individual who had been damaged by an abusive childhood, untreated mental illness and a serious drug and alcohol addiction. He was a damaged and dangerous man who turned into a serial killer in the space of a month. Without his apprehension and incarceration, his murderous rampage would undoubtedly have continued. Catching a killer whose crimes were opportunistic and random, and whose victims spanned in age from twenty-two months to fifty-one years, was difficult. His lack of modus operandi certainly made it impossible for authorities to predict his next move and without the intervention of Nancy Holder, more victims would have fallen prey to this deranged and very sick individual.

The story of Richard Trenton Chase is a chilling journey through the shadows of the human mind. It serves as a stark reminder of the intricate, multifaceted tapestry that can be woven to form a killer. In the twisted corridors of his psyche, a storm of psychological, biological and environmental factors converged, crafting the monstrous figure that emerged to cast a long, dark shadow over the pages of true-crime history.

These demons are often formed behind closed doors, after years of abuse and neglect, hidden from their communities and only emerging to wreak havoc when it is far too late to help them or their victims. If there is one lesson we can learn from this terrifying case, it is to not make yourself vulnerable, to always lock your doors and to never allow a vampire into your home.

5

Robert Hansen: A deadly game

On 13 June 1983, at approximately 5 a.m., a trucker driving along Fifth Avenue in Anchorage, Alaska, got the shock of his life. He witnessed seventeen-year-old Cindy Paulson, an exotic dancer and sex worker, running for her life, half naked, bloody and handcuffed. This good Samaritan stopped to help her and drive her to the nearest motel, where she contacted her boyfriend and called the police. What Cindy would later divulge to them is the stuff of horror movies.

Once law enforcement arrived, Cindy was able to recount her terrifying ordeal. Still wearing the handcuffs he had imprisoned her in, and bloody and shaking, she explained how the man, who had introduced himself as 'Don', but would later turn out to be Robert Hansen, had approached her and offered her two hundred dollars for oral sex. She had entered his car, where he had immediately cuffed one wrist. Although she had desperately struggled to free herself, the threat of his gun and his assertion that he would kill her unless she cooperated, forced her to allow him to cuff her other wrist. He subsequently drove her to his home, where he took her money and jewellery, then raped and tortured her.

Although Hansen initially placed a rope around Cindy's neck, he reassured her that, if she complied, she would survive her ordeal. During the several hours she endured at his home, however, he boasted about his many hunting trophies, showing her them as he gloated. Seeing his real name on these trophies, Cindy came to a chilling realisation; Hansen had no intention of letting her escape with her life.

Leaving Cindy chained to a post in his basement, Hansen slept for a few hours before forcing her into his car, lying her on the back seat and covering her in a blanket. Helplessly lying there, Cindy's life must have flashed before her eyes. She had no idea where the monster was taking her, but she felt a cold and clawing certainty that this journey was to be her last. Shockingly, Cindy found herself at Merrill Field airport, where his small blue and white bush plane waited for them. Although Hansen assured her that he was taking her to his cabin and would bring her back, Cindy instantly saw through this lie. She knew this would be her last journey, unless she could somehow save herself.

As Hansen loaded his plane with supplies, Cindy took her chance. Although still handcuffed, she ran for the nearest road and, with Hansen in pursuit and threatening to shoot her, she made it onto Fifth Avenue, where the trucker stopped and rescued her.

While Cindy waited for law enforcement to arrive, another call was being made to the police. A security guard at Merrill Field had observed Hansen's odd behaviour and felt uneasy. Fortunately, he had the foresight to make a note of the suspect's car registration plate and, together with Cindy's statement, would eventually help bring to justice perhaps the most terrifying serial killer Alaska has ever faced.

Cindy proved an astute victim when interviewed, describing her abductor and his home in vivid detail. The disturbing description of his barred windows and the bullet holes in his floor, as well as his weapons and hunting trophies, made chilling listening. Cindy was also able to describe the plane he planned to use, even remembering its tail number. In fact, en route to hospital, Cindy showed officers the airfield and the spot where his plane remained parked. While there, the vigilant security guard shared his concerns and gave police the details of his suspect's vehicle.

Thanks to Cindy's and the security guard's statements, authorities were easily able to trace the owner of the plane, Hansen, and confirm that he was also the owner of the vehicle seen by the security guard at the airfield. Cindy was then able to identify him using police photographs. The evidence was damning.

Horrifyingly, however, although police visited Hansen's home and questioned him, he denied abducting and raping Cindy. In fact, he claimed he was *her* victim, asserting that she demanded a huge and unreasonable amount of money for her services. He was even able to provide an alibi, as two of his friends vouched for his whereabouts at the time in question. His humble appearance and his position in the community as a respected family man and baker made police doubt Cindy's account. In fact, despite her accurate description of his home, the evidence of her severe sexual assault and her being found in handcuffs, police discounted her indisputable evidence. They failed in their duty to take any evidence from the alleged crime scene and allowed this heinous predator, who would go down in the annals of crime history as the 'Butcher Baker', to continue his rampage for another four months.

Born to Danish immigrants Christian and Edna in 1939, Hansen grew up in Estherville, Iowa. The elder of two sons, he had a difficult relationship with his father, who was a strict disciplinarian. Hansen's father was a domineering figure who had very strict expectations of his son. It has been reported that he would frequently belittle and berate young Hansen, further damaging his already fragile self-esteem. Such relentless criticism from a primary caregiver can engender feelings of worthlessness, inadequacy and an overwhelming desire to regain power and control.

Combined with this, Hansen suffered from a pronounced stutter as a child, and was left-handed, which made school life more difficult for him as these issues were less accepted during his formative years than they are today. He also suffered from severe acne, which left him both physically and emotionally scarred. Children can be cruel, and Hansen's peers were reportedly no exception. He was a frequent target of ridicule and bullying, experiences that often lead to feelings of deep-seated anger, humiliation and resentment in many individuals.

Hansen's social skills were further inhibited as a child because of the family business – a bakery – which meant that when not at school, he had to work long hours for virtually no pay. Even if Hansen had been a naturally gregarious child, his strict upbringing would have prevented him from being outgoing. As it was, however, he lacked friendships and was socially awkward among his peers. Even the hobbies he pursued were solitary and included fishing and hunting, an early indication of his predatory behaviour. As a young teenager, he enjoyed killing animals of any description: birds, stray cats and dogs. He relished the stalking as much as the kill, and this aberrant behaviour foreshadowed the dark paths he would later take.

After leaving school in 1957, Hansen signed up as a US Army reservist. Still working full-time in the family bakery, he served one weekend a month. Here he found success for perhaps the first time in his life, proving himself an accomplished marksman and undoubtedly benefiting from his considerable prior hunting experience. He was also known to volunteer as an assistant drill sergeant at the police academy in Pocahontas, Iowa. Although he found success in this field, it was around this time that Hansen began using sex workers and, probably as a result of his deviancy, was discharged after only a year of service.

Despite Hansen's difficulty in forming relationships, he married a local girl in 1960 when he was just twenty-one years old, but this relationship was short lived as, in December of that same year, he and a friend set fire to a local school bus garage, allegedly as an act of revenge for his unhappy experiences at school. After his friend confessed their crime to authorities, he was arrested and sentenced to three years in prison.

While serving time, Hansen was diagnosed with manic depression and periodic schizophrenic episodes. It was also suggested that a diagnosis of 'infantile personality' (now known as immature personality disorder) might be appropriate. This condition manifests itself in a lack of emotional development and low tolerance to stressful and anxiety-inducing situations. Medical opinion was that he was obsessed with getting revenge on people whom he believed had wronged him. This would certainly explain the arson attack.

It was not long before he began to exact his revenge against the female sex for its rejection of him. These feelings would have been exacerbated when his wife divorced him while he was in prison, where he ultimately served twenty months before being released on parole.

In 1963, at the age of twenty-four, Hansen married again. This time, he and his second wife, Darla, had two children. Sadly, however, having a family did not curb his criminal behaviour and he earned various convictions for petty theft.

In 1968, Hansen moved to Anchorage with Darla. He was well-liked and respected among his community and he became a successful businessman. With its vast, rugged wilderness, Alaska provided the perfect backdrop for his escalating criminality. It was also here that his love of hunting flourished; his weapons of choice being either rifles or bows and arrows. Being an adept marksman, he broke several local records and some of his kills were featured in hunting publications. But beneath this veneer of respectability, his sinister proclivities were festering.

It was not long after Hansen's move to Anchorage that young women began disappearing in the local area. Tragically, it would take authorities years to connect the dots, leaving a serial killer free to take the lives of many innocent young women.

In December 1971, eighteen-year-old Celia 'Beth' van Zanten disappeared. She was kidnapped while hitch-hiking to a local convenience store. Although she managed to escape her abductor, she froze to death in the wilderness after falling down a ravine. The gruesome discovery of her body was made three days later, on Christmas Day, by hikers. Naked from the waist down, her bra and chest had been slashed with a knife, her hands had been bound behind her back with speaker wire and she had been gagged.

Around the same time as the discovery of Beth's body, Hansen's offending behaviour began to escalate, and he became known to authorities. Although his subsequent crimes would bear ominous similarities to Beth's abduction, police would miss the connection and many more innocent women would suffer as a result. Arrested for the attempted kidnapping at gunpoint of a real-estate secretary and the abduction and rape of an eighteen-year-old sex worker, Sandra Patterson, the police failed to see the true extent of this chameleon's cruel capabilities, and missed the clear similarities to other crimes. Sandra's abductor had told her he wanted to slash her bra with a knife, he took her to an area similar to where Beth's body was found and stripped her to prevent her escaping. Both women were in their late teens. Staggeringly, despite the serious nature of these offences, he was sentenced to only five years in prison and, even more horrifyingly, served just six months. After this, he was released on work release.

In July 1973, another innocent young woman disappeared in Seward, Alaska. A quiet girl who enjoyed fishing and hunting on the Yukon river with her family, Megan Emerick was studying at Seward Skill Centre when she disappeared. Friends saw her walking out of a dormitory room before vanishing and spent three days searching for her before finally reporting her as missing to the authorities. Like so many victims of these terrifying monsters, her body has never been found.

In 1977 Hansen's name would come to the attention of authorities again after he stole a chainsaw. Because of his previous record, he was sentenced to five years in prison, where he was diagnosed as bipolar and ordered to undergo psychiatric treatment. Shockingly, his sentence would be reduced by the Alaska Supreme Court, and he was released after only a year. Although he was prescribed lithium, authorities failed to monitor his activities on release to ensure he was taking his medication. It is clear that he refused to heed their advice.

Once he was released from prison, rather than counting himself lucky to have got off so lightly, Hansen continued down the path of criminality, filing a false insurance claim asserting that his home had been burgled. Many of the belongings he claimed were stolen, including a number of hunting trophies, would later be discovered in his possession, and he would say he had retrieved them from a backyard sale and forgotten to report it.

The money from the pay-out allowed him to follow in his family's tradition, and he opened a bakery. In 1982, he bought himself a Piper Super Cub bush plane, even though he had been denied a licence because of the medication he was supposed to be taking. It seems, despite his previous aberrant behaviour, authorities left him free to plan and pursue his darkest desires completely unchecked. He was, undoubtedly, the perfect example of a chameleon, able to live two completely incompatible existences. His neighbours respected him as a local businessman and father, and even the police, who knew about his previous crimes, failed to see his true depravity and gave him the nickname 'Bad Bob the Baker'.

By the early 1980s, however, some of Hansen's murder victims were finally being discovered by the authorities. In July 1980, the skeletal remains of a young woman were unearthed by construction workers in a shallow grave near Eklutna Lake. The body was discovered several months after her murder, so it was badly decomposed and had been ravaged by wild animals. Investigators put this victim's age at death at between sixteen and twenty-five. She had been killed by a single stab wound to the back. Because she was never identified, she became known as 'Eklutna Annie'.

Later that same year, the badly decomposed body of twenty-four-year-old Joanna Messina was discovered in a gravel pit near Seward. A trained nurse, she had left her husband in New York to travel to Alaska, without ever saying goodbye to her family. Devastatingly, she would never see or speak to them again.

In 1982, hunters near the Knik river made the horrifying discovery of another young woman's body. This time the victim would turn out to be twenty-three-year-old Sherry Morrow, who had worked as a topless dancer. She had been shot three times in the back. Cartridges from a .223 Roger Mini-14 hunting rifle would also be discovered near her body. Bizarrely, no bullet holes were discovered in her clothing, suggesting she had been naked when she was killed, and dressed post-mortem.

In September that year, the body of Paula Goulding was found in a shallow grave along the Knik river. She had been reported missing five months earlier and, like Sherry, had been a topless dancer. Like Sherry also, she had been stripped naked, shot in the back and re-dressed.

Eventually, and far too late, Alaskan state troopers

conceded that they had a serial killer on their hands, and that this serial killer had a 'type'. The missing and discovered victims were all in their twenties, between five foot four and five foot seven and weighed between 120 and 125 pounds. They were all slim and usually busty. There was also an undeniable link between these victims and survivor Cindy Paulson.

Alaskan police decided to seek the help of the FBI and an offender profile was compiled. Based on the three murder victims, it was concluded that the killer would be an experienced hunter with low self-esteem and a history of being rejected by women, would possibly have a stutter and would have committed acts of arson and theft during their lifetime. It was also suggested that he would likely be a well-respected member of the community who would keep souvenirs of his victims.

Using this profile, detectives searched lists of suspects. Time was about to run out for Robert Hansen who, although initially dismissed, now seemed to fit the FBI profile perfectly. He also owned a plane, which enabled easy access to the remote locations of the crime scenes. With Cindy Paulson's statement about her alleged attacker added to this, authorities now had a prime suspect. They obtained a search warrant for both Hansen's property and plane.

In October 1983, police searched Hansen's home and found a raft of incriminating evidence, including jewellery that belonged to the missing women. They also discovered a large stash of weapons in a secret compartment in his attic, including a Remington Model 552 rifle, a Thompson contender 7 mm single shot pistol, a Winchester twelve-gauge shotgun and, most significantly, a .223 calibre Mini-14 rifle. This was the weapon used to murder both Sherry Morrow and Paula

Goulding. Police also discovered more jewellery, newspaper clippings and a number of ID cards, some of which belonged to the missing women.

Hansen was arrested. Now the friends who had previously given him an alibi in the Cindy Paulson abduction case realised their horrendous mistake and retracted it, admitting they had lied. Even in the wake of all this insurmountable evidence, though, Hansen initially refused to admit his crimes. Eventually, however, even he realised it was pointless, and he confessed to multiple murders. Rather than accepting responsibility for his heinous acts, the despicable monster blamed the victims. As far as he was concerned, sex workers deserved everything they got; his long-standing hatred of women was aimed at them and he felt justified in his killings, believing sex workers to be lowest of the low and unworthy of life.

At the time Hansen had begun offending, Anchorage was booming because of the construction of the trans-Alaska pipeline, and hordes of construction workers had been attracted to work on this project due to good pay. In turn, this attracted those who wished to make money out of them, including sex workers and exotic dancers. This had provided an ideal hunting ground for Hansen, who knew that strippers and sex workers were harder to track and less likely to be missed. Fortunately for him, sudden disappearances were also common in the area as people came and went overnight.

His modus operandi was truly terrifying: he would solicit a sex worker, abduct them and take them to his home, rape and torture them, then take them to his plane and fly them into the Alaskan wilderness. He would then release them, stripped naked, and they would be forced to run for their lives as he hunted them like animals with his rifles and bows and arrows. It is horrifying to imagine the physical and psychological anguish victims must have experienced at the hands of this cold-blooded killer.

Hansen soon admitted that he had begun killing in the 1970s, and it became clear to police that he was likely responsible for many more murders than the four women they had discovered. Despite this, they offered him a plea deal: he would be charged with just four murders and Cindy's abduction and rape, and serve his time in a federal facility, rather than a maximum-security prison. In return, he would have to divulge the true extent of his criminality and give details of his other victims. Knowing this was his best chance of living a reasonable life, he reluctantly agreed.

In February 1984, Robert Hansen pleaded guilty to four counts of first-degree murder for the killings of Paula Goulding, Joanna Messina, Sherry Morrow and the unidentified 'Eklutna Annie'. He was sentenced to four hundred and sixty-one years without the possibility of parole.

Although this was justice of sorts, real justice was never truly achieved as, in accordance with his plea deal, he finally confessed to a horrifying seventeen murders and thirty rapes over a twelve-year period but was never tried for the majority of these. It transpired that 'Eklutna Annie' was actually his first victim. Having picked her up in a bar, he had offered her a lift home. He coldly recounted her tragic fate, telling authorities that she had become afraid and asked to be let out of his car but that he had told her that he would not harm her if she cooperated. She must have seen through his lie though because, at one point, he claimed his car got stuck in the mud, and she had made a desperate bid to escape. Tragically, he caught her and, although she pulled a knife from her purse and desperately fought for her life, she was quickly overpowered and ultimately murdered by the depraved monster.

Justice may not have prevailed for the majority of Hansen's innocent young victims, but each and every one of them deserves remembrance. They were Cecilia Beth van Zanten, Megan Siobhan Emerick, Mary Kathleen Thill, 'Eklutna Annie', Joanna Messina, Roxanne Easland, Lisa Futrell, Sherry Morrow, Andrea Altiery, Sue Luna, Robin Pelkey, DeLynn Frey, Paula Goulding, Cindy Paulson, Malai Larsen, Teresa Watson, Angela Feddern and Tamera Pederson. Each of these young women lost their lives and futures at the hands of an unscrupulous monster and each of them deserved justice.

Although Hansen led authorities to grave sites, only twelve of his victims' bodies were ever recovered, eleven of which have been identified. Sadly, the identity of 'Eklutna Annie' is still a mystery today, although revised facial reconstruction of this victim has been released by the National Center for Missing & Exploited Children. Advances in DNA profiling will hopefully establish her true identity in the future.

Police believe Hansen was responsible for many more murders than those he confessed to, but he refused to admit to them, probably because the victims were neither sex workers nor exotic dancers. It appears that his first killings simply stemmed from his intense misogyny and that he selected women who caught his eye. He only adapted his MO later to specifically target sex workers, because he believed he was more likely to get away with these murders. Perhaps even a monster like him could not justify his earlier murders when questioned by interrogators. During a search of his home, investigators found macabre flight maps marked with hand-drawn crosses which matched the locations where many of his victims' remains were found. Horrifyingly, there were thirty-seven crosses in total, not seventeen. This is likely to be a true reflection of the extent of his massacre.

In 2021, thirty-seven years after her murder, one of his victims, who had become known as 'Horseshoe Harriet' because her body was discovered at Horseshoe Lake, was finally identified as missing nineteen-year-old Robin Pelkey. She had been living on the streets when she was killed and had never been reported missing.

The scale of Hansen's degeneracy will never be fully known. He was exceptionally good at what he did, a sadist who enjoyed the planning of his murders as much as the actual kill. He was an organised offender who enjoyed torturing his victims before murdering them. He was also able to hide his victims' bodies in remote locations, where they would be desecrated by wildlife. Authorities' inadequacy also aided him in his crimes, as they did not even realise they were hunting a serial killer for over a decade after his killings began, allowing him to kill at least seventeen innocent women. Even more frighteningly, if Cindy Paulson had not escaped, Hansen may not have been caught when he was, and many more women could have lost their lives at the hands of this monster.

Hansen lived until the age of seventy-five, dying of natural causes after serving thirty years in prison. When he died, he cruelly took the truth of his murderous rampage to his grave. Indisputably, his name has become synonymous with some of the most heinous crimes in Alaskan history and, while his crimes are undeniably monstrous, a closer examination of

Hansen's psychology and life reveals a tangled web of early experiences and pathological developments that may have played a role in shaping the monster he became.

What makes a young boy who loves hunting and fishing choose such a deviant path? What makes a man who seems to have achieved the social acceptance he always craved throw it all away? Hansen's childhood was undoubtedly marked by several experiences and conditions that could have laid the groundwork for his later psychopathology. Childhood experiences, particularly negative ones, play a significant role in shaping an individual's psyche. For Hansen, the constant ridicule and bullying due to his stutter and acne scarred him deeply. Humans have an innate desire to be accepted, and consistent rejection can lead to feelings of worthlessness and rage, and a deep-seated need to reclaim power. His oppressive relationship with his father might have further entrenched feelings of powerlessness and inadequacy. This could have sparked an obsessive need for control in his later life, especially over women who represented those who had mocked and rejected him in his youth.

Plagued by feelings of inferiority and social isolation, young Hansen sought solace in fantasies. He would daydream about exacting revenge on those who had wronged him. These fantasies became increasingly violent as he grew older and were played out in the crimes he came to commit.

In adolescence and early adulthood, there were already signs of Hansen's devolving moral compass and emerging violent tendencies, such as when he burned down the school bus garage – an act that was seemingly motivated by revenge against society. Over the years, he racked up several other arrests for theft. As his depravity grew, his crimes began to take on a sexual nature and he was convicted of assaulting a young woman, leading to a stint in prison. This propensity to combine violence with sexual activity would become a defining characteristic of his most heinous crimes.

Hansen was also able to dehumanise the women he killed; his choice of victims, often sex workers or other marginalised people, could be seen as a continuation of his need to exert power over those he deemed weaker or less valuable. It is horrifying to contemplate, but Hansen's passion for hunting seemingly overlapped with his predation of women. By releasing them into the wilderness and then hunting them down, he was literally treating them as game and dehumanising them to the level of animals. This act can be seen as the ultimate exertion of power and control: the very things he felt deprived of in his earlier life.

In the absence of healthy coping mechanisms or therapeutic intervention, Hansen's violent fantasies became his refuge. Over time, the line between fantasy and reality blurred, culminating in a murderous rampage that lasted over a decade. Robert Hansen's story is a chilling testament to how unchecked psychological trauma and pathology can escalate into extreme violence. While nothing can excuse his heinous crimes, understanding the roots of his behaviour can offer insights into the dark recesses of the human mind. It also underscores the importance of early intervention in the lives of those showing signs of psychopathy, and the profound and lasting impact of negative childhood experiences.

6

Israel Keyes: The predator's blueprint

On the crisp dawn of 7 January 1978, in the rustic beauty of Cove, Utah, Israel Keyes was born into the fold of a large Mormon family. Poverty was his earliest companion; the scarcity that defined his childhood manifested itself in the frugal way of life practised by his household. As the second of ten children, self-reliance epitomised his early, difficult years.

Educated at home, far from bustling school corridors and lively playgrounds, the Keyes children were brought up under the watchful eyes of their parents, Heidi and John. Their upbringing was unique, a testament to their parents' staunch distrust of government, and their scepticism towards modern medicine. Their home was a place where the doctrines of self-sufficiency reigned supreme, and reliance on others was seen as weakness.

When Keyes was just five, however, his family underwent a seismic shift in faith. They rejected their Mormon beliefs and sought solace in the bosom of the wilderness, moving to dense, untamed woods near Colville, Washington, where they exchanged modern amenities for the austerity of a one-room cabin without electricity, heating or running water. Here they began a life off-grid, in a world dictated by the rules of nature. This isolated upbringing cast Keyes in the mould of a socially awkward child.

While enduring their frugal existence, the Keyes family found comfort in the arms of fundamentalist Christianity, joining 'The Ark', a sect espousing the harsh rhetoric of white supremacist Christian Identity ideology. As their faith blossomed, so did the antisemitic views that underpinned their church. Coincidentally, their transition was reflected in their neighbours, the Kehoes, a family as fiercely anti-government as themselves, who shared their vehement belief in white supremacy. Keyes found companionship with the Kehoe brothers, Chevie and Cheyne, and their bond flourished over time, even though Chevie would gain notoriety in 1996, following his conviction in a triple murder case. Perhaps these boys had recognised their like-minded warped tendencies at a young age.

As the 1990s waned, the Keyes family once again felt the call of the road. They moved to Maupin, Oregon, a stopover before they finally settled near an Amish community in Maine. The quiet and peaceful surroundings were a stark contrast to the violence that had begun to bloom in young Keyes' heart, as he began displaying elements of the MacDonald triad, a tell-tale sign of potential violent behaviour. His cruel treatment of animals was a chilling indicator of his emerging psychopathy and, as time went on, those around Keyes couldn't help but notice his disturbing idiosyncrasies;

a woman who knew him as a teenager would later recount how she felt a lingering sense of danger in his presence, triggered by a horrifying incident where Keyes mercilessly gutted a live deer. The deer wasn't his only victim, however, as he began to break into neighbours' homes – an insidious pastime that would prove to be a rehearsal for his future crimes. Reflecting on his aberrant behaviours, Keyes once remarked, 'I've known since I was fourteen that ... there were things that I thought were normal and that were OK that nobody else seemed to think were normal and OK.'

Adolescence saw Keyes turn his back on Christianity. His father, unable to reconcile with his son's apostasy, disowned him, but he found comfort in his mother's unwavering love. Declaring himself an atheist, though, he descended into a dark fascination with Satanism.

At twenty, Keyes exchanged his civilian life for a military uniform. He served in the US Army from 1998 to 2001, stationed in Fort Lewis, Washington; Fort Hood, Texas; and the deserts of Egypt. Despite his psychopathic leanings, Keyes shone as a model soldier; his conduct was so exemplary that he was honourably discharged. His fellow soldiers remembered him as a quiet, introspective man who obliterated his weekends with excessive drinking.

In the seemingly quiet years between 2001 and 2007, Keyes created a home and appeared to find peace with his partner and daughter in the Makah Reservation community of Neah Bay, Washington and the traditions of its legendary whale hunters.

The peace he found in Washington was short-lived and ended in 2007, when he left his partner and embarked on a new journey to Alaska. In those freezing expanses, he built his future, establishing Keyes Construction and making a name for himself as a reliable travelling handyman. Choosing a quaint residential neighbourhood in Anchorage, he began his new life with his girlfriend and his ten-year-old daughter, whom he was given custody of; he was able to hide his true nature in the guise of being a doting father. This move would not only mark a new chapter in his life, but also trigger a series of horrific crimes that would shock the country.

Immersed in a grim world of his own creation, Keyes conducted thorough research into the modi operandi of other notorious serial killers, as if attempting to decode a dark and mysterious craft. His objectives were not geared towards mimicry, however, and, insisting upon originality, even in this perverse domain, Keyes took pride in devising his own methods and strategies for his unique and horrific exploits. His gruesome curriculum comprised films and documentaries that focused on serial killers, with Ted Bundy, one of the most infamous killers of all, holding a particular fascination for Keyes. Both men shared the disconcerting trait of being highly organised with an unnerving desire to 'possess' their victims. But the men differed in their choice of victims and their motivations for travel: Bundy focused his murderous attention on attractive young women, while Keyes, with a more indiscriminate approach, did not limit his activities to a specific victim type. Bundy's travels were always work-related, whereas Keyes travelled extensively with the sole purpose of committing his heinous crimes, always ensuring he covered his tracks to evade detection.

Despite Keyes' exemplary military career, his horrific journey seems to have begun before he enlisted. Later he confessed to a horrifying incident that occurred between 1996 and 1998, when he was between eighteen and twenty years old. He assaulted a young girl, aged between fourteen and eighteen, near the Deschutes river in Maupin, Oregon. Intending to kill her, Keyes managed to isolate her from her friends. After assaulting her, he unexpectedly spared her life. This event did not come to light until a decade later, when the FBI, as part of their investigation, attempted to locate her. Unfortunately, her assault was never reported, leaving a key piece of the puzzle lost in time. Reflecting on the event, Keyes' comments to investigators sent shivers down their spines: 'It was weird ... She was scared ... but also just talking, just like, about random stuff. I don't know. It was weird ... I was just convinced that I had screwed up that time in Oregon because you know, I ... I let her go.' His disturbing reflections were accompanied by a grim determination: he would not spare his future victims.

During questioning, Keyes maintained that he committed his first murder in 1998, took a break for three years while he completed his military service, then resumed his gruesome campaign in 2001. Interestingly, this contradicts the widely held belief that serial killers cannot control their compulsions to kill and sheds a chilling new light on his capacity for self-control. Contrary to his version of events, suspicions have arisen that connect Keyes to the disturbing case of Julie Harris, a twelve-year-old double-amputee who went missing from Colville, Washington, in March 1996. Harris, a Special Olympics athlete, was awaiting a ride to church when she vanished. A month later, her prosthetic feet were found on the banks of the Colville river, and her skeletal remains were discovered a year after her disappearance. Her murder remains unsolved and, although Keyes lived in the area at the time, he has always denied any involvement.

In time, the chilling landscapes of Alaska would become the epicentre of this killer's criminal activities. As a travelling handyman, Keyes traversed the country, perhaps leaving victims in as many as ten different states. He funded his murderous escapades through robberies and burglaries, and reportedly burgled twenty to thirty homes across the United States and engaged in several bank robberies between 2001 and 2012. It appears his crime spree knew no bounds, yet the full extent of his criminal activities remains uncertain.

The key to Keyes being such a formidable adversary for law enforcement was the apparent randomness of his actions, which deviated significantly from patterns typical of most serial killers, many of whom have a specific victim type: a pattern that often helps authorities in building their profiles and ultimately apprehending them. By selecting victims without any discernible pattern or preference, Keyes defied this norm, thereby confounding authorities. His chilling reply when queried on how he chose his victims, 'I didn't. It was just random', will haunt victims' families for the rest of their lives.

The randomness of his choices did not affect his meticulous approach to murder, though, and he ensured his activities were hard to trace; he avoided killing in his hometown and never targeted the same area twice, reducing the likelihood of being tracked down geographically. His ability to evade modern forensic detection was almost uncanny. He would keep his mobile phone turned off during his killings, thereby leaving no digital footprint and, to avoid any financial trails, he preferred cash transactions. All these practices allowed him to remain a phantom, an elusive predator, leaving very little evidence in his wake.

Keyes' modus operandi was undoubtedly terrifying in its

precision. He would fly to a location within the US, rent a vehicle and drive hundreds if not thousands of miles in search of his next victim. His preferred hunting grounds were secluded and remote places, like parks, campgrounds, walking trails or cemeteries. When he set his sights on a home, he had specific criteria: an attached garage, an empty driveway and no visible evidence of children or dogs. In the proximity of his chosen killing grounds, Keyes buried murder kits – a macabre collection of tools including shovels, cable ties, plastic bags, money, weapons, ammunition and bottles of Drano, a drain cleaner which he used to hasten decomposition. He buried these in secret locations across the country, waiting to be unearthed when required. Two of these kits were later discovered in Eagle River, Alaska and near the Blake Falls Reservoir in New York. Keyes admitted to leaving others in Wyoming, Texas and potentially Arizona.

After carrying out his murderous act, Keyes ensured the body was disposed of miles away, often in another state. This practice of separating abduction and disposal sites added an additional level of difficulty for investigators, and his meticulously strategic approach to murder marks him as one of the world's most organised killers. Strangulation was his preferred method of execution; he took perverse pleasure from the intimate, agonising struggle of his victims as they lost consciousness.

In April 2009, Debra Feldman, a forty-eight-year-old woman, went missing in New Jersey. Estranged from her family and suspected to have been a drug-addicted drifter, she might have also resorted to prostitution to finance her addiction. Keyes was known to have frequented sex workers and, when shown her photo by investigators, he visibly reacted, leading them to speculate on his involvement in her disappearance. It is conjectured that he may have buried her near Tupper Lake, New York, reflecting his consistent pattern of separating the locations of abduction and disposal of bodies. Sadly, the full circumstances of Debra Feldman's disappearance are still shrouded in mystery.

Keyes' operational precision and attention to detail were chillingly displayed in the murders of Bill and Lorraine Currier in June 2011. After travelling from Chicago to Essex, Vermont, a distance of nearly a thousand miles, he found the Curriers' home during a night-time stroll. He deduced the household's demographic based on the external features of the home: a pool and barbecue signified an older couple, while the absence of toys in the garden suggested no young children resided there.

His entry into their home was swift and clinical. Dressed entirely in black, with an unlit headlamp around his forehead, Keyes cut the phone line and entered through a window in the kitchen. His intrusion was quick – it took merely six seconds – a tactic he referred to as a 'blitz attack'. The Curriers awoke to the horrifying reality of a masked man in their bedroom, a stranger who swiftly asserted control. They were made to roll over on their bed and their wrists were bound with cable ties, while Keyes demanded information about any money, safes or PIN codes. Personal belongings were hastily packed into two suitcases and, fifteen minutes after his arrival, Keyes informed them they were leaving the house.

The Curriers' harrowing ordeal was just beginning as Keyes forced the terrified couple into their own car, threatening them with Lorraine's own handgun. Then he drove them to an abandoned farmhouse that he had scoped out earlier, a place forgotten by time and so desolate and lonely that even the most blood-curdling of screams wouldn't be heard. They were bound, helpless and entirely at the mercy of a man who had invaded their peaceful home. Despite their terrifying predicament, they attempted to appeal to their captor's humanity. They stressed Bill's need for medication and their lack of wealth, hoping these factors would encourage Keyes to spare them. They even offered him their vehicle as a desperate bargaining chip. However, Keyes, with his calculated agenda, was not swayed by their pleas. Instead, he reassured them with a fabricated narrative, claiming that the ordeal was a mere kidnapping for ransom. He insisted they would remain unharmed, a lie that must have given the couple a glimmer of false hope.

Arriving at the abandoned farmhouse around the eerie quiet of 4 a.m., Keyes had to deal with his captives. He tied Bill to a stool in the dark, grim basement of the farmhouse, then turned his attention back to Lorraine, who had taken advantage of his focus on her husband to attempt an escape from the car. But her desperate bid for freedom was short-lived. Keyes caught up with her before she could reach the main road, physically restraining her before dragging her back to the farmhouse. She was taken to an upstairs bedroom, where her arms and legs were bound to the bed with duct tape. A rope tied around her neck, tethered under the mattress, rendered her utterly helpless, despite her spirited struggle.

Meanwhile, Bill was showing a similar resistance in the basement. He managed to break the stool to which he had been tied and began to loosen his restraints. This act of defiance, this slight loss of control, irked Keyes, a man for whom the satisfaction of his gruesome crimes came from the power he exerted over his victims. His annoyance led him to abandon his alleged original plan of sexually assaulting Bill. In his rage, he attacked Bill with a shovel before shooting him multiple times.

With Bill no longer a source of resistance, Keyes turned his attention back to the terrified Lorraine; he boiled water on a portable propane stove he'd brought along, never revealing the purpose to the investigators and leaving them to imagine the worst possible scenarios. He cut away her clothes and assaulted her, adding another layer of horror to an already nightmarish situation. Lorraine was then taken downstairs to the basement, where she came face-to-face with the grim sight of her husband's lifeless, blood-soaked body. It was in this horrific setting that Lorraine's life was ended, strangled with a rope at the merciless hands of Keyes. He then meticulously cleaned the aftermath of this horrific crime scene: dousing the bodies in Drano and packing them into bin bags. They were then concealed under a pile of wood and refuse in a corner of the basement: a final, cruel indignity. The farmhouse was demolished soon after and the debris, probably including the hidden remains of the Curriers, taken to a landfill site. Despite an intense three-month search, the authorities never managed to recover the bodies. In fact, were it not for Keyes' eventual confession, their disappearance would remain a mystery.

Even the most successful serial killers run out of luck and, for Keyes, this change in fortune began on 1 February 2012, when he found his monstrous compulsions too overwhelming to control. On this cold evening he laid eyes, and eventually hands, on Samantha Koenig, a young woman at the very beginning of her adult life – a life full of potential. Loved by her family, her friends and acquaintances would describe her as a beacon of kindness with a caring personality that made her well-liked and cherished within her community. Yet, on this fateful evening, Samantha's life took a tragic turn as she ended her shift at Common Grounds coffee stand on Tudor Road in Anchorage, Alaska. Unknown to the unsuspecting young woman, Israel Keyes was watching nearby in his vehicle. Armed and with malice in his heart, he approached her. The last images of Samantha alive are chilling, captured on a surveillance video, showing her being coerced by an armed man, Keyes, and led away. He had a white pickup truck parked across the street that became her vehicle of abduction, a chilling beginning to her horrendous ordeal.

The gruesome events that followed the abduction saw Keyes taking Samantha to his home where, sipping wine in a chilling display of cold-heartedness, he calmly divulged the horrific fate that awaited her. He stole her debit card from her car and forced her to tell him the PIN. He then chained her up in his shed and, robbing her of any remaining dignity, sexually assaulted her. Keyes' calculated savagery didn't end there. He used his preferred method of murder, strangulation, to kill Samantha the next day. Then, showing an unnerving ability to compartmentalise his heinous act, Keyes stowed Samantha's body in his shed and left for a two-week cruise in the Gulf of Mexico.

His meticulous planning extended to efforts to conceal Samantha's abduction. He used her mobile phone to send text messages to her boyfriend, who had grown worried when he went to pick Samantha up from work, only to find her missing. Several hours later, a text from Samantha's phone arrived stating she was tired and going on vacation. However, this abrupt and uncharacteristic message rang alarm bells, leading her boyfriend to contact the police.

Investigators, eager to piece together the events, scrutinised footage from the security camera at Samantha's coffee booth. Initially, nothing seemed concerning. Samantha was seen wrapping up her tasks before her shift ended. But then the appearance of a masked man at the window signalled the beginning of the crime. The exchange looked like a typical robbery, with Samantha backing away, her hands slightly raised; an indication that Keyes probably had a gun. Following Keyes' instructions, Samantha turned off the lights, after which he jumped in through the window and began the horrific abduction.

News of Samantha's kidnapping spread fast, leading to weeks of intensive searching by local authorities and heartbroken friends and family. Her disappearance was headline news, triggering an outpouring of shock and fear within the local community. The exhaustive search by police, friends and family was in stark contrast to the chilling serenity of Keyes' vacation. Samantha's father, James Koenig, made an emotional public appeal, his voice shaking with despair, painting a picture of a family racked with unimaginable pain. When Keyes returned to Alaska, more than three weeks after Samantha's abduction and murder, he removed her body from his shed, where it had been preserved in the cold. He then began a macabre grooming process. He applied make-up to her face, brushed her hair, and – unnervingly – sewed her eyes open with fishing line. The intent was to create the illusion of life where there was none. He took a photograph of the body with a four-day-old issue of the *Anchorage Daily News*, to give the impression that Samantha was still alive.

This cruelly culminated with Keyes sending text messages from Samantha's mobile phone to her boyfriend, directing him to a park where he'd left a ransom note, cruelly offering Samantha's loved ones a glimmer of hope. They couldn't have known that the photograph accompanying the note was of Samantha's posed and lifeless body. It's unbearable to think of the anguish her loved ones must have felt when they discovered the horrific truth. Keyes' master manipulation showed the depths of his psychopathy, underscoring the monstrous nature of his crimes.

While the community was gripped by the search for Samantha, Keyes was conducting his grisly cover-up operations. He dismembered Samantha's body and, over the course of three separate trips, disposed of the parts in the icy waters of Matanuska Lake, located thirty-five miles north of Anchorage. In a chillingly casual and grotesque act, Keyes drilled a hole in the ice and discarded the body parts while pretending to ice fish, later allegedly consuming the fish he caught.

As a response to the ransom demand, Samantha's father, torn between hope and despair, deposited an initial five thousand dollars into the account associated with Samantha's stolen debit card. The police stood ready to track the card's activity, hopeful that it would lead them to Samantha. But when the card was first used several hours later in Alaska, law enforcement was just minutes too late in reaching the ATM. The CCTV footage showed a man wearing dark glasses, a hood and a face mask.

A week later, the stolen debit card was used again, this

time at an ATM in Wilcox, Arizona, nearly four thousand miles away. Additional withdrawals followed in Lordsburg, New Mexico; Humble, Texas; and Shepherd, Texas. It was clear that whoever was using Samantha's card was heading east. Fortunately, the perpetrator made a crucial mistake at the Arizona ATM. Despite being heavily disguised, the ATM camera managed to capture the background image of his white Ford Focus rental car. So, when officers of the Texas Highway Patrol and Texas Rangers spotted a vehicle matching the description in a parking lot in Lufkin, Texas on 13 March 2012, they tailed him and pulled him over. While Keyes' name meant nothing to the officers initially, a search of his vehicle quickly linked him to Samantha. They found her ID, debit card and mobile phone in the car, along with a gun. Keyes was arrested and extradited to Alaska two weeks later, initially on credit card fraud charges.

Until this moment, Keyes had managed to stay off law enforcement radar. In fact, Frank Russo, the Assistant US Attorney in Anchorage, would later state that one of his colleagues had used Keyes' services as a handyman. This speaks volumes about the dual life that he was leading and the ease with which he managed to blend in to normal society.

On 2 April 2012, after two months of meticulous searching, a forensic dive team found Samantha's remains in Matanuska Lake. It took them a painstaking ten hours to locate all the body parts. On 18 April Keyes was indicted on charges of Samantha's kidnap and murder, along with charges of attempting to extort ransom payments from Samantha's family, even though he knew she was already dead. His trial was set to begin in March 2013, where the threat of the death penalty loomed over him. By now, the full extent of Keyes' atrocities had come to light, painting a chilling portrait of a psychopathic killer who had hidden in plain sight.

The bleak atmosphere of the FBI's field office in Anchorage was intensified by the presence of Keyes, who calmly requested an Americano coffee from Starbucks, a Snickers bar and a very particular brand of cigar. Only once these demands were met did he begin to recount a sinister narrative spanning over a decade. His audacious demeanour, which was in equal parts disturbing and intriguing, sent a chilling undercurrent through the room as he recounted his life of crime, starting with his admission to a series of bank robberies in New York and Texas: acts that in themselves would have been significant. But Keyes didn't stop there; he confessed to setting a Texas home on fire after breaking in, showing a complete disregard for property and life. Subsequently, the FBI corroborated his story, confirming his involvement in this and a robbery at the Community Bank branch in Tupper Lake, New York, in April 2009.

The true horror, however, lay not in these initial revelations but in the more significant admission that followed. He confessed to the murder of Samantha Koenig, providing a chilling account that confirmed the investigation team's worst fears. His confession, at once dispassionate and precise, painted a vivid picture of the night of the murder: his choice of a .22 calibre pistol, his deliberate selection of a coffee booth due to its late operational hours and Samantha's desperate attempt to escape – each detail was narrated with a disturbing level of detachment. The cruel lie he told Samantha, assuring her safety if she cooperated, underlined the predatory nature of his mind. Later, an FBI agent claimed Keyes described Samantha's killing 'as someone else would discuss what they had for lunch'.

After his arrest, Keyes participated in twenty-four interviews over the span of seven months, during which he admitted to a further seven murders. He divulged these with the same cold detachment, offering tantalising bits of information but carefully withholding any detailed evidence, including the identities of his victims. This led authorities to believe he had been living a meticulously crafted double life for at least fourteen years – the same length of time they suspected him to have been an active serial killer.

Keyes seemed to derive some form of perverse enjoyment from his exchanges with the investigators. Feeding them just enough information to keep them hooked, he agreed to lay bare all the horrific details of his crimes if they assured him of a death sentence within a year. His claimed his primary concern was to protect his young daughter from unwanted publicity, but it was hard for the investigators to disentangle any genuine sentiment from his complex web of manipulations. So, in an attempt to draw more information from Keyes, the investigators resorted to psychological manipulation, promising him a swift execution if he confessed more. This tactic bore fruit when Keyes shed light on an unsolved double homicide in Vermont. A quick Google search led the investigators to the Curriers, and Keyes confirmed their hunch. His confirmation that he had murdered them was chilling, not least because he had not known them prior to their deaths.

As he recounted the events, Keyes' reaction disturbed the detectives interviewing him. One, a Detective Bell, commented, 'It was chilling to listen to him. He was clearly reliving it to a degree, and I think he enjoyed talking about it . . . A couple of times, he would kind of chuckle, tell us how weird it was to be talking about this.' His evident physical excitement – an indication of deriving sexual gratification from the recollection of his crimes – added an extra layer of horror to the investigation.

In addition to these admissions, Keyes confessed to murdering four more people across three separate incidents in Washington state, with one of the bodies disposed of in the depths of Lake Crescent. These confessions revealed the extent of his ability to cover his tracks, disposing of victims in remote areas where they were unlikely to be found. Keyes' remorseless journey through life, leaving a trail of victims in his wake, marked him as a unique and disquieting figure in the annals of criminal history.

The chilling crimes of Keyes were not confined to populated regions; they extended into the wilderness that formed the backdrop of his upbringing. His time living in Washington with his partner and child saw him acquire a boat, a tool that would become an integral part of his macabre undertakings. Authorities became increasingly interested in Lake Crescent, a body of water notable for its intimidating depth that plunges to seven hundred feet. This suspicion was rooted in their belief that Keyes may have used the lake as a grim disposal ground. Their suspicions were confirmed when Keyes admitted to discarding a victim's remains into its obscure depths. This body has remained elusive to discovery, swallowed by the lake, underscoring the chilling effectiveness of his disposal method.

Keyes audaciously confessed to ending the lives of two individuals between 2005 and 2006 and taking the lives of a couple he had abducted. He confessed to another macabre incident, where he executed a murder in one state and transported the victim's body to another, New York, for burial. Given that Keyes owned a dilapidated cabin and a vast expanse of ten acres in the small town of Constable in Franklin County, New York, authorities believed his spine-chilling revelations.

Once captured, Keyes still proved a determined adversary: on 23 May 2012, during a court hearing, in an audacious bid to escape, he broke the restraints of his leg irons and attempted to leap over the courtroom railing. His attempt was thwarted when he was subdued by a swift taser discharge and immediately restrained so that his grim tale could reach a fitting end at the Anchorage Correctional Complex.

Here, under suspicion of having committed Samantha's murder, he concealed a razor blade, which he later used to slash his wrists as well as strangling himself with a twisted bed sheet. A blood-stained, four-page suicide note was found hidden beneath his lifeless body. The note, written on a yellow legal pad, was so obscured by his blood that it required sophisticated FBI lab techniques to be deciphered. This 'Ode to Murder', as one investigator aptly labelled it, consisted of a series of macabre poems. His writing, while devoid of any new evidence or clues about his heinous crimes, unveiled a disturbing insight into his psyche, suggesting a perverted take on Stockholm syndrome and a deeply embedded disdain for humanity:

With Your Brain Died Also Your Soul
Soon, now, you'll join those ranks of dead
or your ashes the wind will soon blow.
Family and friends will shed a few tears,
pretend it's off to heaven you go. But the

reality is you were just bones and meat,
and with your brain died also your soul.

In 'Your Petals I'll Crush', he writes:

Violent metamorphosis, emerge my dark moth
princess, I would come often and worship
on the altar of your flesh. You shudder
with revulsion and try to shrink far from
me. I'll have you tied down and begging to
become my Stockholm sweetie. Okay, talk is
over, words are placid and weak. Back it
with action or it all comes off cheap. Watch
close while I work now, feel the electric
shock of my touch, open your trembling
flower, or your petals I'll crush.

His poetry is a harrowing peek into a mind devoid of empathy and brimming with cruelty.

Keyes seems to dismiss the comforting ideas of the afterlife or a soul's existence beyond death. His assertion 'soon, now, you'll join those ranks of dead' shows his belief that death is imminent and inevitable for all. He further dehumanises his victims by reducing them to 'just bones and meat', suggesting a complete lack of empathy and remorse. His poetry suggests denial of spiritual belief and the concept of an afterlife. For Keyes, death is the end, nothing more than a physical breakdown. The poems offer a chilling perspective into his nihilistic outlook and make us understand he believes there will be no retribution for him in the afterlife, as it simply does not exist.

Years after his suicide, in 2020, the FBI released the macabre drawings they found concealed under Keyes' jail-cell bed. The eleven skulls and a single pentagram drawn in Keyes' own blood were haunting silent reminders of his horrific crimes. Of particular note was the phrase 'WE ARE ONE' inscribed at the bottom of one of the drawings. The FBI believes this grisly collection is a morose tally of his victims, a haunting testament to the horrific scale of Keyes' cruelty.

The full magnitude of Keyes' monstrous crimes is shrouded in uncertainty. Investigators estimate that he could have been responsible for the murders of up to twelve people, perhaps even more. Some of these speculated victims may not have been confined to the United States. His cold-blooded response when probed about potential victims in Canada was, 'Canadians don't count', epitomising his grotesque disregard for human life. To piece together the puzzle of unsolved crimes that overlapped with Keyes' timeline, and possibly bring closure to cold cases, the FBI publicised a comprehensive list of thirty-five trips that Keyes made across the country between 2004 and 2012.

In the annals of criminal history, Israel Keyes looms large: a serial killer whose brutal practices were meticulously planned and chaotically random in equal measure. From the methodical process of selecting his victims to the intricate execution of his heinous acts, Keyes epitomises the profile of an organised and calculating predator. His predilections place him firmly within the profile of a 'lust killer', one who derives pleasure from the act of killing and its associated feelings of power and control. He was a man who revelled in the fear of his victims, their loss of consciousness serving as a perverse satisfaction to his twisted desires. His victims were objects to be dominated, their innocence violated before their lives were cruelly snuffed out. It was as if he viewed the act of murder as a grand production, the stage being set across disparate geographical locales for the denouement of his grim tableau. Keyes was a psychopath in the purest sense, a man who exercised predatory control without an ounce of remorse.

Bizarrely, despite his heinous crimes, Keyes adhered to a self-imposed code of ethics, refusing to harm children or parents. This was likely influenced by his own status as a father. The psychological paradox here is fascinating – a brutal serial killer, displaying what appears to be a protective instinct towards children; a soulless monster somehow capable of exhibiting a tiny fragment of humanity.

His undoing lay in the breaking of his own rules. In the case of Samantha Koenig, he allowed himself to become sloppy, killing at home and using her debit card. Whether this was a result of overconfidence or a sign of his unravelling mental state, we may never know.

Sadly, Keyes' suicide in custody denied justice to his victims and their families. He also took with him the truth about the extent of his crimes, forever obscuring the full scale of his atrocities. Despite this, the legacy of his reign of terror serves as a stark reminder of the capacity for evil that can reside in the human heart. In the words of a family friend of one of his victims, 'He should have been executed ... But the world's better off he's gone.'

Living next door to Israel Keyes would have been like residing next to an enigma, a seeming paradox wrapped in the everyday disguise of a neighbour. Keyes, as we know from his chilling legacy, was a man who moved through life with the precision of a chess master, each move calculated, each decision weighed against the backdrop of his horrific objectives. But if you were his neighbour, would you have been able to see past the facade and recognise the monster that lurked beneath? It's highly likely that you would have been none the wiser. Keyes was, in many respects, a master of deception. He led what appeared to be a normal life, maintaining an illusion of ordinariness that effectively hid his true nature. He held a job, had a girlfriend and raised a child. In the context of his surrounding community, Keyes was just another face in the crowd, an unremarkable man leading an apparently unremarkable life.

Perhaps, upon deeper inspection, there might have been minor cracks in his veneer, faint whispers of the darkness that lay within. Maybe it was in the way he always seemed to be on the move, restlessly journeying across the country for reasons he kept to himself. Or perhaps it was the unusual interest he took in the news, always eager to catch up on the latest reports of bank robberies and unsolved murders. Could these quirks have been seen as early warnings of his sinister double life? Perhaps. Yet it's also equally plausible that Keyes' peculiarities could have been mistaken for mere idiosyncrasies, quirks of a private man who kept to himself. Monsters like Keyes are often frighteningly adept at hiding in plain sight, their insidious actions camouflaged by the mundane routines of daily life.

In the end, it's clear that the unassuming man who might have waved hello as you fetched your morning paper, or the friendly face you might have seen at the local store, concealed a horrific secret. Israel Keyes was a chameleon, able to blend seamlessly into the fabric of society while leaving a trail of devastation in his wake. And perhaps that is the most terrifying realisation of all, that such evil can reside so close, yet remain undetected.

7

Robert Maudsley: The shadow behind the glass

Although this book has focused on American serial killers so far, there have been many heinous killers in the UK too. Robert Maudsley is certainly an enigma worthy of discussion and acts as the perfect prelude to a discussion of our home-grown serial killers.

Serial killers usually earn their infamous reputations while at liberty. Born evil or socialised to become heinous predators and often hiding in plain sight, they stalk and kill their prey to satisfy their deviant urges until they are apprehended and incarcerated. Usually, early behaviours foreshadow the horrors that are to come, and prison becomes the place where these are contained or, even better, rehabilitated. This is not always the case, however, and in some horrifying instances, prison becomes a breeding ground for heinous and aberrant behaviour.

Prison's purpose should be to reform criminals into

productive and law-abiding members of society. This should not be an aim, but a requirement. After all, what is the point of incarceration and release if the prisoner's behaviour deteriorates during their sentence? What is the point of spending over six billion pounds on the prison system every year if it fails those it should rehabilitate? Worryingly, a systematic review of criminal reoffending rates in 2019 proved we are falling short of these ideals. It found that over forty per cent of prisoners reoffend within the first twelve months after release, and a staggering seventy-eight per cent after nine years.

A personification of the failure of the UK prison system is Robert John Maudsley, or 'Hannibal the Cannibal' as he became known in the media. He looms as an ominous figure in the annals of British crime. With the blood of fellow inmates on his hands, his name sends shivers down the spine, drawing a visage of a man far removed from societal norms. His crimes are undeniably heinous, yet the whispered tales of his upbringing and the eventual, seemingly draconian, imprisonment beg the question: is the monster made, or born?

Born in Speke, Liverpool, in 1953, Maudsley's early years were defined by neglect. At the tender age of six months old, he was taken into care, along with his siblings, Kevin, Paul and Brenda. The children's parents, George and Jean, struggled with their role but, after losing their first four children to Nazareth House in Crosby, they went on to have eight more.

Maudsley and his three siblings spent nine years in this Roman Catholic establishment, run by nuns who appeared to epitomise kindness and compassion to the outside world. However, for the children handed over to the 'Sisters of Nazareth' in the many homes they ran across the United Kingdom, the reality was horrifyingly different. Former residents tell tales of systematic abuse suffered under a cruel and ruthless regime, which was both physical and sexual. It appears these 'sisters of Christ' were devoid of love and sadistically enjoyed tormenting the innocent young children placed in their 'care'. Instruments of punishment included canes, sticks and leather belts and the children unlucky enough to be placed there suffered constant deprivation and pain. Although authorities were allegedly told about the true horrors of Nazareth House, they did nothing to stop the nuns' reign of terror, and undoubtedly failed every child forced to endure this inhumane existence.

Ironically, there was never any evidence to suggest that the Maudsley parents were abusive before giving up their first four children; they simply struggled with the demands of parenthood. In spite of the poor conditions at Nazareth House, though, Maudsley bonded with his brothers while there, and they lived like a family of sorts. Although his parents would visit on occasion, they were strangers to him, having lost him at such a young age.

Just as life was about to improve for one of Maudsley's brothers, as a couple had formally begun the adoption process, George and Jean decided to claim their children back, perhaps spurred by the knowledge that they were about to lose a child permanently. In spite of years having passed, and the possibility of a positive new start for one of the siblings, they were successful and had their four first-born children returned to them, supposedly on a trial basis, under the watchful eye of the council.

From the outside, the Maudsley household might have seemed normal, but once again this begs the question – how well do you know what's happening next door? Because life became even worse for the Maudsley children on their return home, as the siblings began to suffer a life of abuse at the hands of their cruel and authoritarian father, who seemed to enjoy using violence and was aided and abetted by a mother who enjoyed seeing her children punished for what she considered to be poor or unruly behaviour. The siblings now suffered under a different but equally harsh and cruel regime, being regularly beaten, locked in their rooms and forced to sleep on the cold, hard floor. Their callous father also forced Robert and his brothers to steal lead from rooftops, beating them even harder if they were caught.

Because Robert was too young to remember his parents and had not bonded with them before his removal from the family, it seems he was singled out by a sadistic father who enjoyed inflicting violence and abuse on him. Maudsley would later recount that as well as the beatings, his father would regularly rape him. His memories of that time are poignantly brutal, and it is unsurprising that they scarred his fragile psyche permanently: 'All I remember of my childhood is the beatings. Once I was locked in a room for six months and my father only opened the door to come in to beat me, four or six times a day. He used to hit me with sticks or rods and once he bust a .22 air rifle over my back.'

After a year of this suffering and torment, Robert was finally rescued by social services and placed in foster homes. But this meant he was ripped from the brothers he had come to love; his cruel parents would tell his siblings he had died. Robert's unstable life was already creating the character he would become, and his young experience had taught him, if nothing else, that adults could not be trusted and that he was on his own in a world that was full of cruelty and deprivation. In the space of a few short years, he had been abandoned by his parents, placed in the care of sadistic nuns, returned to even more sadistic parents, then removed to be placed in a series of foster homes. Unsurprisingly, after such a tumultuous start in life, Maudsley began exhibiting criminal behaviour and was arrested for theft and burglary as an adolescent.

In 1969, Robert was able to escape the foster care system. At just sixteen years old, he existed by doing odd jobs while travelling around the country. It seems anything was better than the torment he had suffered at the hands of those who should have protected him. Tragically for him, however, the scars of his life of abuse ran deep and it is not surprising that young Robert turned to drugs. In fact, his mental health was so poor that he would go on to attempt suicide, by overdose, on two occasions.

In order to fund his drug habit, young Maudsley began working as a rent boy. Used to a life of abuse, being sexually abused by older men in this role did not faze him. Growing up without self-respect or a feeling of self-worth, this mal-treatment was an expectation born out of experience. He would later chillingly allege that this is where his deep-seated hatred of paedophiles began to evolve and that these execrable experiences would prove catalytic for his future crimes. As his mental health deteriorated, he found himself in psychiatric care on a number of occasions, where he would divulge to staff that he could hear voices instructing him to kill his parents. Although never officially diagnosed, it is probable he was suffering from some kind of schizoaffective disorder. Let down again, however, he was abandoned to his own devices, and this would have catastrophic consequences.

By now Maudsley was twenty-one years old and regularly undertaking sex work. Broken and damaged by the experiences life had thrown at him, it was at this still young age that he committed his first murder. The victim was a thirty-year-old alleged paedophile, John Farrell. It transpired that Maudsley had been stalking the streets, looking for prey, any prey. Initially, he had gone to London's West End, armed with a knife and determined to make an apparently motiveless kill. Initially failing in his mission, he walked to Playland Arcade, a venue frequented by gay men, with murderous intent. On leaving there, he bumped into Farrell, who was known to him as a previous client. Although Farrell had been with another young man at the time, he made the fateful mistake of leaving with Maudsley and did not live to tell the tale. He took Maudsley back to his home, and while Farrell was making them tea, Maudsley stashed a pocketknife beneath the bed. He explained to police: 'After we had the tea and talked, we went to bed. Johnnie got into the bed and went to the side nearest the wall, and I got in the open side to be near the knife. We started to kiss and masturbate each other, and I thought then of killing him, but I went on masturbating him thinking that the feeling might go and that I might not feel like killing him in the morning. After we finished kissing and masturbating, we both tried to sleep but we were both restless and started to whisper to each other. Then we went to sleep but I still had the feeling I wanted to hurt him. When we woke up, I made a cup of tea. That was about 8.10 a.m. or sometime about then. I still had the same feeling.'

By the time the pair had eaten breakfast, Maudsley had transferred the knife into his coat and claimed that it was at this point that Farrell began showing him pictures of young men he'd had sex with. He did not, however, claim that any of them had been underage. He stated: 'All of a sudden, the feeling came on. I took the knife from my pocket in my right hand, I rushed across the room and stabbed him in the chest, he fell back on the bed and got up and said something like "I've got to get out". The blood spurted out as soon as I stabbed him. He made a mad rush for the door and fell over a chair; it was the big armchair I had been sitting in. His head must have hit the door, his head was down by the door, and I stabbed him in the back or side quite a few times. I told him that I was sorry, but I had to do it. When I said this, I could see his face ... I could have robbed the house but all I wanted to do was kill someone. I put the knife in the sheath and went upstairs to the bathroom to wash myself. All I remember about John is seeing his face and saying I am sorry.'

After the brutal murder of Farrell, Maudsley divulged that he had contemplated a second murder, but had managed to contain the urge by calming himself down with a coffee. Then he handed himself in to the police. It was later discovered that Maudsley had taken money he found at Farrell's home, probably with the intention of buying drugs. Any honourable reason for this brutal murder seems unlikely and was, perhaps, a poor attempt at justification of this heinous crime.

Maudsley was declared mentally unfit to stand trial and was, instead, sent to Broadmoor; a high security hospital for the criminally insane that has housed many notorious killers including Peter Sutcliffe, Ronnie Kray and Charles Bronson. Here his alleged disdain and hatred for paedophiles flourished as he attempted to mould himself as a vigilante on the side of righteousness – though he had a skewed sense of morality.

It was in 1976, a full three years after his incarceration, that his seething hatred for paedophiles became impossible for him to control. Aided and abetted by another patient, David Francis, the aberrant pair held another patient hostage for several hours, threatening to gouge out his eyes. Although the victim survived unscathed, Maudsley's next choice of target was not so lucky. His prey on the second occasion would be his former accomplice, who was being held in Broadmoor as a convicted paedophile. This time he joined forces with David Cheeseman, a brutal rapist who had raped and sexually assaulted a sixteen-year-old girl. They dragged Francis into a cell, barricaded the door and sadistically tortured him for over nine hours. Unable to intervene, staff could only listen to his blood-curdling screams.

By the time staff eventually managed to break into the cell, what they witnessed would turn the strongest of stomachs. Francis' body had been partially skinned, he had been garrotted and his skull had been cracked open like an egg. There was a spoon sticking out of it and Maudsley would later claim that he had used it to eat some of his victim's brain matter, a boast that would gain him the nickname of 'The Brain Eater' among his prisoner peers, and the equally disturbing 'Hannibal the Cannibal' from the press. Even though this would prove a fabrication after Francis' autopsy, as the brain, although badly damaged, was found to be fully intact, the moniker would stick. The spoon he had allegedly eaten from was plastic and had been fashioned into a crude, pointed weapon, which had penetrated his victim's brain when he rammed it into his ear.

After this heinous and sadistic murder, Maudsley was deemed fit enough to stand trial and was convicted of manslaughter and sentenced to life in prison. Rather than being returned to Broadmoor, however, it was decided that he would be incarcerated in Wakefield Prison – known as 'Monster Mansion' due to the high number of murderers and sex offenders housed there. Inmates have included Ian Huntley, Harold Shipman and former Lostprophets frontman and convicted paedophile Ian Watkins. Maudsley was incensed and demanded, unsuccessfully, to be returned to Broadmoor.

Just weeks into his sentence at Wakefield, in July 1978, Maudsley decided his campaign of terror would begin. Filled with a determination to kill sex offenders and paedophiles inside the prison, he planned to kill seven in a single day. He began by luring forty-six-year-old Salney Darwood, a lifer convicted of killing his wife, into his cell, where he garrotted him and repeatedly smashed his head into the cell wall, before hiding the body under his bed.

Leaving his cell, Maudsley went on the hunt for his second victim, attempting to lure others to his brutal lair. Many would later recount that they had refused because they had seen the madness in his eyes. Fifty-five-year-old Bill Roberts, a paedophile serving a seven-year sentence for the sexual assault of a seven-year-old girl, was not so lucky. Stabbing him as he lay on his bunk, Maudsley then hacked at his skull with a home-made serrated knife and smashed his head into the wall. Roberts did not stand a chance and was dead within minutes.

After the brutal killings, he entered the guards' room, placed his weapon on the table and coldly asserted that they would be 'two down' at the next roll call, confessing that he adored the sight of blood. Maudsley went to trial at Leeds

Crown Court in 1979, where he claimed: 'When I kill, I think I have my parents in mind. If I had killed my parents in 1970, none of these people need have died. If I had killed them, then I would be walking around as a free man without a care in the world.'

Although Maudsley's defence team argued that his heinous behaviour and violence was a result of the pent-up aggression and trauma caused by his abusive and unnatural childhood, he was ultimately found guilty of two counts of murder and returned to the very prison where he had wreaked havoc. The then home secretary, Michael Howard, later ordered that he must never be released.

Authorities now faced a quandary: how do you deal with a lifer who is a very real threat to the prison population they are placed within? The extreme solution was to hold him in solitary confinement until a suitable alternative could be created. In 1983, in the basement of Wakefield Prison, this 'suitable alternative' was constructed. Known as 'the cage', six-foot-two Maudsley's final home is an eighteen-by-fourteen-foot cage that can only be reached after passing through seventeen locked steel doors. The cage itself is encased in transparent bulletproof plastic, so he can be continually observed like an exhibit in a freak show. A small slot was cut into the bottom, where food would be placed.

The glass cage that confines him, reminiscent of Hannibal Lecter's cinematic prison, ignites debates on human rights and evokes haunting queries. Is his treatment a mirror reflecting society's own inhumanity? Would death be more merciful than the cold, isolating glass walls?

The whole cell was designed to protect Maudsley from hurting himself, while giving him every reason to want to end his suffering. His bed is a concrete slab, his toilet and sink are bolted to the ground, his table and chairs are made from pressed cardboard, and he eats from plastic plates, using a plastic spoon. Even the pen he is given is a biro, as a ball-point is considered too dangerous. His only glimpse of the outside world is through a one-centimetre ventilation hole, and during the one hour a day when he is allowed to exercise. Even then, he is taken to a small yard surrounded by high walls and escorted by four prison guards.

Maudsley's reputation has negatively impacted his already unbearable existence. It is alleged that he went twelve years without a haircut because no prison barber was willing to take the risk. He also suffers from a speech impediment due to the decades he has spent without human contact. Particularly cruelly, he has even been denied photographs or correspondence with his family. He stated: 'I am left to stagnate; vegetate; and to regress; left to confront my solitary head-on, with people who have eyes but don't see, and who have ears but don't hear, who have mouths but don't speak; consequently, I too am left with no voice, nowhere to turn to but inward.'

Maudsley is unquestionably a very dangerous and dam-aged individual, but he still claims today that the only threat he poses is to rapists, paedophiles and sex offenders. Whether this is true, or whether he is simply a psychopath with irresist-ible urges to kill is debatable.

In the mid-1990s, Maudsley appeared to have a chance of salvation when psychologist Dr Robert Johnson became the first person to take an interest in him since he had been placed in solitary confinement. Johnson believed 'it was [his] duty as a doctor to discover why he had become a serial killer'. Sitting near the door of Maudsley's cell, he was undeniably aware of the risk he faced and warned him, 'If you frighten me, I can't help you.' Finally, and perhaps for the first time in his life, Maudsley felt understood and heard and maybe even dared to allow himself a glimmer of hope.

Johnson spent two and a half years analysing why his patient had taken such a deviant path. Tragically, however, just as Maudsley began opening up to and trusting him, authorities stopped the meetings, leaving him to fester alone in his cell again. One can only imagine the impact the loss of the only human contact he'd had in decades had on his already damaged mind. To be teased with the gift of human interaction and have it cruelly ripped away must have been a devastating blow. Although Johnson was never given a reason for this cessation, and the letters he subsequently wrote went unanswered, he finally received a poignant three-word message that simply and devastatingly summed up Maudsley's unendurable existence: 'All alone now.'

Indisputably, solitary confinement is a harsh and inhumane punishment. Seventy-year-old Maudsley has now spent a shocking forty-five years in his cage. He is not being rehabilitated; instead he is enduring an intolerable existence that must torture his already damaged mind every single day. He has been forgotten and abandoned once again and his own words emphasise the horror of his existence: 'The prison authorities see me as a problem, and their solution has been to put me into solitary confinement and throw away the key, to bury me alive in a concrete coffin. It does not matter to them whether I am mad or bad. They do not know the answer and they do not care just so long as I am kept out of sight and out of mind.'

In 2000, Maudsley petitioned for his solitary confinement to be relaxed, but this was denied. He then pleaded for a budgie, claiming, 'Why can't I have a budgie instead of flies, cockroaches and spiders which I currently have? I promise to love it and not eat it.' Even this was refused, as was his request for a cyanide capsule to end his suffering.

Maudsley has been subjected to a level of solitary confinement never seen before in this country and, in December 2021, he was given the sobering news that he would never be released from solitary confinement and will remain in his underground prison until he dies. The reality is that authorities fear the impact of him having been alone for so long and they now realise that, given his history, they can never take the risk of allowing him to mix with the general prison population. Their treatment of him has undoubtedly exacerbated the problem that is Robert Maudsley.

Some believe that the glass prison used to house Dr Hannibal Lecter in the novel *The Silence of the Lambs* was partly inspired by his incarceration. Whether this is true or not, it does not seem likely that Maudsley will ever escape the claustrophobic walls he has found himself imprisoned within. Instead, what is far more likely is that his mental decline and depression will continue until his physical health fails him and he finally dies. Similar to Lecter, though, Maudsley is said to have a genius-level IQ and a love of classical music, poetry and art. He was apparently keen to take an Open University course in music theory, a privilege that has been given to many prisoners throughout the years but denied him. One can only imagine the torture an intelligent and inquisitive mind must suffer when trapped in a glass cage and denied any form of human contact or conversation.

Although it has taken decades, it appears Maudsley has been allowed some comforts to make his existence more bearable in recent years: he is now allowed to watch television, listen to music and play on a PlayStation 2. In fact, it is claimed that he feels he is treated more like a man than a monster today. Unsurprisingly after so long, he seems to have accepted his reputation as a monster too, as it is alleged that he has told authorities that, if he were ever released, he would kill again. This assertion is the ultimate evidence of the complete failure of a system that should have felt a responsibility to treat and reform him during over four decades of incarceration. In fact, the ultimate evidence, perhaps, of just how beyond reform he is, is that he now considers his solitary and cruel prison to be his 'safe place'. This is a damning indictment of a system that boasts humanity by banning the death penalty while inflicting decades of suffering and torment on an incarcerated prisoner that it does not know what to do with.

The corridors of Wakefield Prison echo with stories of Maudsley's solitude. Sequestered for twenty-three hours a day, the man behind the myths is shrouded in a silence that amplifies his internal cacophony. The solitude, intended as a shield for others, becomes a sword piercing through the remnants of Maudsley's sanity. Each tick of the clock in his glass cell is a stark reminder of society's paradoxical treatment of criminals. The facade of rehabilitation shatters, unveiling a system where punishment eclipses reform, where the shadows behind the glass are forgotten, left to grapple with their demons alone.

The whispers in the prison's dark corners pose a grim hypothesis – would Maudsley be better off dead than living in the purgatory fashioned by the hands of justice?

Yet to advocate for the death of Maudsley is to traverse a slippery slope. It would be an admission that some souls are beyond redemption, a capitulation to the darkness that dwells within the human psyche. In the quest for justice, the line between retribution and vengeance blurs, casting shadows on the very values that distinguish society from the individuals it condemns.

Maudsley is certainly a unique and difficult case, but his cruel and inhumane incarceration has to raise important ethical issues. Is it acceptable to simply punish an offender without offering any prospect of treatment or reform? Is that genuinely the desired outcome of our prison system? Maudsley is certainly not alone in committing horrific crimes, yet no other prisoner in the UK prison system has been subjected to the same prolonged psychological torture of solitary confinement. Its endless monotony and persistent denial of human contact is a guaranteed way to destroy someone's mental health and send them spiralling into madness.

As the debate rages on, the figure behind the glass remains an enigma, a reflection of society's struggle with its own shadows. Maudsley's fate, whether shackled by chains or by the eternal silence of death, serves as a haunting reminder – humanity, in its pursuit of justice, must not lose its own.

8

Gary Allen: Blood and water

Some criminals are so dangerous, so duplicitous that the police will go to incredible lengths to bring them to justice. Gary Allen is one such criminal: a man with a core as cold as ice, he had to be stopped, no matter what the personal sacrifice for the officers involved in his capture.

Allen was born on 27 September 1973, and raised in the English city of Kingston upon Hull. From a very early age, it was clear he was a monster in the making, exhibiting uncontrollable temper tantrums and cruel and aggressive behaviour towards his siblings. At the tender age of eight, he was referred to a psychiatrist but sadly, this did little to temper his deviant tendencies, and he even gained a reputation for starting fires: one of the traits identified in the MacDonald triad as an early warning sign of things to come.

As a result of his aberrant behaviour, he spent two terms, between January 1982 and July 1983, at Baynard House in Hull, a child psychiatric unit. Here staff would note his unnerving ability to lurch from pleasant and placid to intense rage in a single moment and record a number of unprovoked attacks on other residents.

Allen's deviant behaviour would define his teenage years and reached a crescendo when he viciously attacked his helpless mother with a metal clothes prop while she was bedridden and recovering from surgery. In another horrific incident, at the age of fourteen, he grabbed a girl by the throat and brutally slammed her head on the ground. Unsurprisingly, he went on to spend time in care and, while there, attempted to strangle the fifteen-year-old son of his foster carer. These acts of violence were the forerunners of even more heinous crimes to come.

Allen would go on to join the British armed forces where his violent tendencies continued to affect his behaviour, resulting in him being reprimanded for attempted theft and criminal damage, and causing him to throw a TV through a window when the UK entry did not win the Eurovision Song Contest. At twenty-one he threatened a housemate with a diver's knife and, two years later, he confided to a friend that he had tracked down an individual who had damaged his vehicle and, in an act of mindless violence, had smashed their fingers. In Allen's sick mind, every single act against him was a personal affront that needed punishing.

As an adult, Allen became a loner, casually walking among the unsuspecting people of Hull while quietly cultivating a misogynistic hatred of women, especially sex workers, whom he considered to be 'the lowest of the low'. In time, his twisted mindset would unravel in a dark, disturbing pattern as he targeted this specific group of vulnerable women. His disdain for them was not arbitrary but had roots in his early experiences, prejudices and a warped understanding of control and power dynamics. It was not until 1997, however, that he would come to the attention of the police during their investigation into the murder of Samantha Class. Samantha was only twenty-nine when she was brutally killed. The gruesome discovery of her partially submerged body was made by three unfortunate schoolgirls on the foreshore of the Humber Estuary on 26 October. Various items of her clothing were missing, and a shoe, her underwear and a pair of tights would be found upstream a few days. Traces of her blood were also discovered at this secondary location.

Samantha had been a single mother of three children: Sophia, Aiden and Lewis. She had been undertaking sex work to support her young family and she was last seen alive on the evening of 25 October, when she left her children with carers. As Samantha kissed her children good night, she could not have imagined she would never see them again; in a tragic stroke of misfortune, she encountered twenty-four-year-old Allen at around midnight as he was driving around the city, looking for a sex worker to sleep with. Samantha stepped into his vehicle and she would not be heard from again. The depraved monster would take her from her children and change their lives irreparably in a callous act of lust and violence.

Her brutally murdered body would be discovered the following grim morning; she had suffered thirty-three harrowing injuries, including cluster injuries to her head and body, multiple broken ribs and considerable internal bleeding caused by injuries to her heart, spleen, liver, adrenal glands and kidneys. Only a demon could have caused such devastating injuries to this innocent young mother. The autopsy later went on to reveal that she had been viciously beaten, stamped on and strangled to death with a ligature before her lifeless body was driven over by a car as she lay face down in the mud. As a final indignity, she was flung into the Humber.

In Allen's damaged perception, sex workers represented the epitome of his scorn for the feminine. They were figures he could manipulate and exert dominance over without fear of reprisal. They were also individuals on the margins of society, often overlooked, which allowed him to conduct his nefarious activities unnoticed. From his jaded perspective, sex workers were women who had made choices that left them devalued and less worthy of life. The power dynamics at play, the act of 'purchasing' someone's time, fed into his need for control, amplifying his sense of superiority and entitlement. He saw himself not as an ordinary client but as an arbiter of their fate. It is a chilling revelation of how his twisted thought process worked as he turned a human interaction into a stage for his gruesome acts.

Although the police forensic team discovered semen on Samantha's body, they were unable to find a DNA match. This changed, however, in 1998, when, in a stroke of fortune, Allen was stopped by police while driving erratically under the influence of alcohol. A DNA sample was taken from him and matched the semen sample taken from Samantha's body. Allen was immediately arrested, but feigned innocence, claiming that although he had driven to the red-light district of Hull on the night of 25 October 1997, and met Samantha, he simply had sex with her and paid her thirty pounds for her service. Unfortunately, his car was not available for forensic examination as Allen had disposed of this vital piece of evidence at a scrapyard shortly after her murder.

When the case went to trial in 2000, the prosecution was

confident in its strength; a guilty verdict was surely a foregone conclusion. Yet arrogant Allen was determined to walk away a free man and pleaded not guilty to Samantha's murder; he only admitted to having sex with her and claiming he left her safe and well, having refused to drop her back at home, as he wanted to leave the scene. He falsely claimed that he had felt ashamed of using a sex worker and that he had never used one before that night. When challenged that scrapping his car suggested guilt, he argued that it was because he owed his flatmate money, as he was living in his front room, and he had no other means of finding the funds.

To the shock of almost everyone in court, the jury believed Allen's cunningly fabricated story and found him not guilty. Even the defence barrister was astounded. No one else was ever tried for Samantha's murder because the police knew they had their man; they were not looking for other suspects because they knew they did not exist. To them it was simple; Allen had got away with a heinous murder. On the day he walked free from court, he was given some money, dropped off at Sheffield train station and told to 'get as far away from Yorkshire as possible'.

You might expect a man who had just got away with murder to keep a low profile. Not Allen. In fact, soon after the trial, he was on the police radar again. Rather than filling Allen with a sense of relief that he had literally got away with murder, the acquittal seemed to spur on his thirst for violence and he was arrested for an attack on a sex worker in Plymouth (where he had relocated after the trial) in March 2000. He had taken the woman to a dark, secluded place before choking and attempting to sexually assault her. He violently pushed her to the ground, hit her face and stuck his fingers down her throat, while attempting to rip off her clothes, before being disturbed after a lorry driver called the police. Although fate stepped in and saved his potential victim on this occasion, not all of the women lured into this heinous predator's trap would live to tell the story.

Allen was charged with attempted assault occasioning actual bodily harm and indecent assault. This time he was found guilty in court, and, in December 2000, he was sentenced to five and a half years in prison. Allen's ruthless nature is clear from the fact that he actually ended up serving an extended sentence of almost ten years due to extra time being added for various breaches, including an incident in 2004, when he'd been released early on licence and removed his electronic tagging device.

When Allen was eventually released in 2010, a condition was that he had to attend regular meetings with probation officers. It was in one of these meetings that arrogant Allen disclosed the full extent of his detestation of sex workers, revealing his warped and dark nature. One of his probation officers later reported, 'he described prostitutes as being "scum" and "the lowest of the low"'. He also chillingly asserted, 'the pleasure of hurting builds from the planning stage'. He claimed 'prostitutes are easy targets ... they go with anybody. I just want to hurt people, can't tell you how far ... I enjoy thinking about it ... I just really enjoy different types of violence'. To another he confessed his darkest fantasies of restraining a sex worker and telling her, 'I'm going to kill you and hurt you. No one is ever going to see you again.' It is clear that, contrary to what he had told jurors in the Samantha Class case, Allen was an organised offender who planned his attacks and enjoyed contemplating and fantasising about the act of violence before perpetrating it. He enjoyed inflicting cruelty, asserting, 'I like to frighten them. I like to cause pain. I like to make them cry. I like blood. I like to hurt them ... it makes me feel good.'

The more time passed, the more the police realised that Allen was a dangerous sexual predator and killer. By now he had been convicted for breach of a sexual offences order, had two convictions for battery and an offence of possession of an offensive weapon. In fact, in 2010, police were so worried about the safety of local women that they launched an undercover operation called 'Operation Misty'. Allen had now moved to a flat in Rotherham, no doubt chosen because of its close proximity to the red-light district. 'Operation Misty' would cleverly create a whole social world around him to encourage him to reveal his secrets, specifically his involvement in Samantha's murder.

In an incredible move, undercover officers, complete with fake girlfriends, wives and children, would befriend Allen and create a fabricated world around him to lull him into a false sense of security. In an operation that would last two years, seven officers – five men and two women – would pose as Allen's friends to build relationships with him. During that time, more than four hundred hours of secret recordings would be obtained.

The officers involved in the operation would play characters with similar deviant tendencies to Allen – characters who liked to inflict violence upon women; they would strike up friendships with him that would encourage him to boast about his crimes. One officer who would be known as *Scott* was the first to befriend him. Moving into a nearby flat and claiming to have convictions for sexual violence, he was the perfect 'friend' for Allen. Unfortunately, this strategy did not work at first, as Allen saw *Scott* as a 'meal ticket' and was not keen to confide in him. It was then decided that the character *Ian* would be created, and it would be he who would more effectively gain Allen's trust, as *Scott's* 'nutcase cousin'. Theatrics of the highest standard were used from the very beginning, as selfless officers dedicated themselves to this cause. Before taking on the role, the officer playing *Ian* analysed Allen's psychological reports, ensuring he would have the best chance of success. He even spent weeks with his arm in plaster, to maintain the facade.

Once everything was in place, and before meeting Allen, *Ian* took a ferry to Holland, where he covered items of clothing in pig's blood from a local butcher. *Scott* and Allen would then meet him at the port, and he would be introduced as an apparently similarly violent individual. The undercover officers hoped that meeting *Ian* would trigger something inside Allen and to a degree it did, as he immediately volunteered to burn *Ian's* clothes, which he believed were evidence of murder.

Over the next few months, *Ian* wove his way into Allen's confidence, making him truly believe that he, too, was a deviant criminal, and that he needed Allen's help planning a murder. The undercover officer asserts today that this was because Allen wanted violence in his life, and he believed *Ian* to be the epitome of brutality. In spite of this, though, Allen shied away from talking about women or sex workers at first. One night, however, things changed dramatically. During a pub lock-in, misogynistic Allen was rude to a barmaid. She retaliated, calling him a 'silly little man' and, for the rest of the evening, he completely shut himself off, becoming so quiet and seething with so much rage that he could hardly function. Feeling humiliated that a mere woman had dared to speak to him in that way, Allen could not let it rest. On leaving the pub, he chillingly told *Ian*, 'Just so you know, I'm going to go back and kill her.' His misogyny could not allow a woman to get the better of him, and his underlying psychopathy made vengeance a desideratum.

Obviously, the undercover officer's acting skills were really put to the test at this point and, having made sure police officers had warned the barmaid that her life might be at risk, he managed to talk Allen out of his vengeful plot. He told him he would not be able to carry out a murder they were currently planning, if he got into trouble with the police. In fact, Allen was so invested in this fake murder plot that he had already bought paper suits and applied for a passport, bragging to *Ian*, 'I've done it before.' Unfortunately, though, because Allen had been drinking, and the evidence would have to be given under caution so that it would be admissible in court, *Ian* had to stop the conversation. Even more frustratingly, five days later, on 6 December, Allen backtracked, claiming he had never actually killed anyone, but he still assured *Ian* that 'using violence was not a problem'.

On another horrifying occasion, Allen told *Ian* that the landlord of a local pub was going to allow him to run a brothel upstairs. Feeling a sense of nervousness and dread creeping through his bones, the undercover officer became certain Allen would kill a sex worker that night. Taking matters into his own hands and determined that another innocent victim would not satiate this depraved monster's appetite, he rang his boss and arranged surveillance. Sure enough, Allen hired a sex worker later that evening, feigned discomfort when she took him to a house where there were other people and persuaded her to go down a back alley. There he began strangling her and, were it not for the surveillance team intercepting him and stopping him in the act, he would undoubtedly have killed her. The undercover officer later described that moment as 'one of the proudest of [his] career' as he knew he had saved a life that would have been callously snuffed out by this evil predator. Allen was clearly a criminal of the worst kind; he had to be stopped, but it was not going to be easy.

On 16 February 2011, officers finally got their breakthrough when Allen confided in *Ian*, admitting to killing Samantha Class. He told the undercover officer that he had approached Samantha for sex, which had taken place in his car. He alleged that she had then accused him of rape and demanded all his money when the condom he was using had burst. He claimed that this had caused him to 'flip' and strangle her with a bit of string he had in his car. The undercover officers had finally got their man, but were appalled and astounded when they were told by the Director of Public Prosecutions that the confession was not enough. For officers who desperately wanted justice for Samantha's family, this was a devastating blow. In fact, the officer acting as *Ian* asserted that it was 'a major let-down in [his] career' that they had to sit on the confession for 'a good few years'. As a result of this failure to bring Allen to justice, another innocent victim would tragically lose her life at the hands of this nefarious perpetrator.

The sad reality was that trying Allen again for Samantha's murder, whatever evidence was gathered, was not going to be straightforward. This is because, before 2003, the double jeopardy rule applied to crimes in the UK, meaning that if you were tried and acquitted of an offence, you could not be retried at a later date, regardless of new evidence being found to prove a suspect's guilt. This was in place to protect individuals, ensuring they could not be repeatedly tried for the same offence, and ensured closure for those found innocent at trial. Frustratingly, though, this also meant that many guilty people escaped justice. A prime example of this was William Dunlop, who confessed that he had killed twenty-two-year-old Julie Hogg ten years earlier. Sadly, because he had previously been tried and acquitted of her murder, he could only be charged with perjury for lying at that trial. It was a recommendation of the 1999 Macpherson report into the Stephen Lawrence case that the double jeopardy rule should be removed to allow further prosecution if new evidence emerged.

Exceptions to the double jeopardy rule were finally introduced by the Criminal Justice Act 2003 where, in very limited circumstances, a person acquitted of a crime could be investigated and retried. One very important reason for this was the advances in DNA evidence, because the ability to match traces at crime scenes to specific individuals had a huge impact on criminal cases. So, for the double jeopardy rule to be set aside, new compelling evidence of a person's guilt has to come to light; it only applies to the most serious offences, like murder or rape, and it has to be determined by the director of public prosecutions that a retrial would be in the public's interest. They would then make an application to the Court of Appeal, who has the power to quash the previous conviction and order a retrial. This was exactly what the police investigating Allen were hoping for. Allen's confession to the undercover officer was the first piece of 'new and compelling evidence' in the jigsaw and, in the years that followed, they continued to keep a close eye on him.

By 2018, Allen was forty-five and had been living in Rotherham for six years. It was here that thirty-eight-year-old Alena Grlakova had the misfortune of meeting him while he was waiting at a bus stop on his way to work. Alena had moved from her native Slovakia to South Yorkshire ten years earlier, with her husband and four children but, by the time she met Allen, her life had taken a downward turn, and she was planning on returning to Slovakia. She had previously separated from her husband in 2013, after becoming addicted to drugs and alcohol occasionally using sex work to fund this habit, but desperately wanted to be reunited with her children.

Becoming a 'friend' of Allen's, rather than simply another sex worker, Alena represented a deviation from his usual pattern. This shift might indicate a significant development in his murderous psyche, where his sadistic desires were evolving, becoming more dangerous and unpredictable. This change not only heightened the threat Allen posed but also deepened the mystery surrounding his motivations. Perhaps Alena, in some unperceived way, was a reflection of the figures from Allen's past who had deeply wounded him. Perhaps she bore some resemblance, some echo of his emotionally distant mother or some other female figure who had failed him, thereby becoming the perfect representation of what he despised and feared.

Undoubtedly, Alena was a vulnerable woman and therefore made the perfect victim for a predator like Allen. Developing a friendship with him, Alena began visiting Allen's flat at 13A Bradbury's Close, Rawmarsh, where he would often ply her with drink. On 26 December 2018, however, Alena had gone to Allen's flat uninvited. He had been furious and thrown her out, recording the whole ordeal while chillingly threatening that he was going to 'beat the fucking living shit out of [her]'.

Alena was last seen alive that same Boxing Day evening, having left Allen's home to go to a nearby pub. It is believed she was brutally murdered by Allen later that night, or in the early hours of 27 December, having returned to his flat. Alena's husband subsequently reported her missing, but her body was not found until over three months later, on 8 April 2019, when, similar to Samantha, she was found partially buried in a stream by a police officer who could smell decomposing flesh. Stones had been placed on her body in an attempt to conceal it, but it was clear she had suffered serious injury to her neck, as her head was in an unnaturally extended position. She was also naked from the waist down. A pathologist would later confirm that Alena, like Samantha, had been strangled to death.

From a psychological perspective, it can be inferred that Allen's choice to kill Alena was driven by a subconscious desire to confront his past and reclaim control. By exerting the ultimate power, the power of life and death over her, he was symbolically overpowering the women who had, in his perception, dominated and scarred him in the past. Or perhaps Alena's status as a seemingly unattainable figure, someone who saw him as a friend, rather than a client, could have served to heighten the thrill and satisfaction Allen derived from his actions. As he descended further into his murderous spiral, it's possible that his urges had escalated to the point where he needed to take greater risks to achieve the same sense of control and domination.

Whatever the reason, the cold, brutal murder of Alena marked a frightening evolution in Gary Allen's bloody reign. The selection of his victims was no longer merely predicated upon convenience or their marginalised status; instead, he had begun to reflect a deeper, more complex web of psychological motivations. The unfortunate Alena had found herself caught in this web, a pawn in a deadly game orchestrated by a disturbed mind. The echoes of her tragedy serve as a chilling reminder of the unpredictability and profound depths of Allen's malevolent psyche.

Unfortunately, due to the length of time Alena had been left in the water, her body was in an advanced state of decomposition when it was discovered. Allen had methodically planned the concealment of her body, buying hand trowels, a shovel and gloves. He had chosen a place he believed she would not be found and was no doubt aware of the damage the water would cause forensically. His arrogance made him believe that, as with Samantha before her, he had got away with murder.

Satisfyingly, however, the police investigation was able to identify a significant series of telephone calls between Allen and Alena before she disappeared. This, along with the purchases he had recently made, led to his arrest later that same month and, during the investigation, his mobile phone was seized. On it were a number of harrowing images of deceased and bloodied naked and semi-naked women. Some of these were sex workers who had been strangled to death with ligatures. It was also discovered that Allen had made disturbing internet searches including 'ways to commit the perfect murder', clearly indicating not only his warped and misogynistic attitude towards women, but also the absolute arrogance he felt in his ability to get away with murder.

In a stroke of luck, police managed to obtain footage from Allen's neighbours which showed Alena entering and exiting his flat. At around the same time, drains had become blocked near his property; on investigation, a football-sized ball of wet wipes was discovered to be the cause. It was clear that Allen had been wiping everything down with these but had not been clever enough to predict the blockage. Finally, police had the evidence they needed to charge him again.

It was now clear that the police had a solid case against Allen in relation to Alena's death; he was the last to see her alive, there were recordings in which he was threatening her, he had purchased tools to help conceal her body and he had made various visits to the murder location. They also now had the 'new, compelling evidence' they needed to retry him for the murder of Samantha Class in 1997. So, in 2019, the director of public prosecutions, Max Hill QC, made an application to the Court of Appeal to have Allen's acquittal for Samantha's murder overturned. He personally presented the new evidence to them; outlining Allen's pattern of offending, specifically targeting sex workers and killing them by strangulation, his abhorrent comments to probation officers that had been previously documented, and the recordings made by undercover officers, which included his confession to *Ian*. Allen's acquittal was immediately quashed and a retrial for Samantha's murder was granted by the court.

By now the undercover officer who had played the role of *Ian* had retired, but he was determined to attend court and help achieve justice for Samantha and her family, as well as ensure Allen was kept off the streets, so that no other families would have to feel the devastation of his victims' loved ones. During his trial at Sheffield Crown Court, Allen faced two counts of murder for Samantha's and Alena's deaths. He continued to behave arrogantly, though, perhaps believing he could get away with murder yet again. To this end, he complained vehemently that he had 'been fitted up in a conspiracy' and that probation officers had lied about what he had said. In relation to the damning recorded confession, he protested that he had simply told *Ian* what he thought he wanted to hear and that he had wanted to pass himself off as 'criminally minded'. In fact, he claimed that he was guilty of nothing more than wanting to 'big himself up'.

Allen's trial lasted seven weeks and his arrogance and duplicity were on show throughout as he listened impassively to the allegations against him. At one point, during cross-examination by the prosecution, he even pompously demanded, 'Stop with the commentary and just ask me the questions.' Eventually, however, on 17 June 2021, after two days of deliberation, the jury unanimously found Allen guilty of two counts of murder. This meant that, after more than two decades, justice would finally be served for the murder of Samantha Class and some semblance of peace would be brought to her grieving family.

At Allen's sentencing hearing, the judge, Mr Justice Goose considered a number of factors before determining his jail time: the significant degree of pre-medication in the way he had targeted his victims, choosing sex workers because of his hatred of them; the particularly horrific nature of Samantha's murder, causing her significant suffering before she died; his attempt to conceal the bodies of his victims; and his previous convictions.

Ultimately, Allen was sentenced to a minimum term of thirty-seven years' imprisonment and Justice Goose praised the tireless work of the committed police officers, particularly those who had selflessly worked undercover, for helping bring this aberrant criminal to justice. The memory of Samantha's daughter Sophia's personal thanks to those officers who achieved justice for her mother still affects *Ian* today.

After the hearing, Sophia stated: 'Gary Allen may have his sentence, but my family and I have and will continue to suffer the bigger sentence. I can never have my mother back. I have got to live with that and there will always be a break in my heart.'

This was the first case in UK history involving both a double murder and the double jeopardy rule and, although his murders were more than twenty years apart, Allen was ultimately brought to justice for both. The tragic reality is, however, that authorities fear this depraved criminal may have committed many more murders; his evil mindset and his ability to target the most vulnerable and readily available victims certainly supports this theory. Following his conviction, police all over the UK were asked to re-look at unsolved violent crimes and the National Crime Agency is still looking at unsolved attacks on sex workers for possible links to Allen today.

Sadly, meticulously organised offenders like Allen are notoriously difficult to apprehend, and it is very likely that he is a serial killer with many more heinous murders to his name. *Ian* recounted arriving at his home one day to find Allen removing all of his hair. He acknowledges that he was very forensically aware, making it possible he had many other victims.

Allen's deeply entrenched hatred of women in general, and sex workers in particular, while sickening and inhuman, provides a disturbing insight into his psyche. It reinforces the notion that his murderous rage was not the result of random impulses but a manifestation of deep-seated psychological damage, an echo of his internal turmoil painted in the blood of the innocent. A man as arrogant and cold-hearted as Allen is unlikely to ever confess the full extent of his crimes to give other victims' families a sense of closure. That would require both a level of empathy and a semblance of humanity that a man like Allen is incapable of exhibiting. The undercover officer still contends that 'the only reason Allen would ever talk is if he were to get something out of it'. For a psychopath spending the rest of his life in prison, it is unlikely that the prize will ever be worth the confession.

9

David Smith: Decades of deceit

As September dawned in 1991, a grim discovery was made in west London: the sadistically mutilated body of an escort worker found in her flat, after being declared missing by her boyfriend. The hunt for the perpetrator, nicknamed 'The Ripper' in the press, saw a convicted sex offender charged with her murder but later acquitted. The victim's devastated and angry mother prophetically warned he would kill again and, eight years later, he proved her right, in a virtually identical crime. Catching this heinous killer would not be easy, however, and it would take the 2003 change in the double jeopardy law to finally bring him to justice for a murder committed three decades earlier. This is what happens when a dangerous sexual predator is given the opportunity to fulfil his sadistic desires and remain at loose; the case of David 'The Ripper' Smith, a man who believed in his own omnipotence and literally got away with murder so that he could kill again, is one that will horrify the hardiest of minds.

In 1991, thirty-four-year-old David Smith was living with his mother in Hampton, south-west London. Working as a lorry driver, his colleagues could not begin to imagine the monstrous double life he led, and that he was a chameleon of the most terrifying kind. They called him 'Honey Monster' and 'Lurch' because of his six-foot-three height, size fourteen feet and large, eighteen-stone build; but they saw him as a harmless oddball, and were oblivious to how far from the truth this was.

Polite and softly spoken, although this conscientious employee had a reputation of being a loner, he was not disliked by his colleagues. Yet this pleasant facade hid a much darker and terrifying secret; he was a sexual sadist who enjoyed inflicting pain and suffering upon any prey unfortunate enough to fall into his callous and cruel clutches. His aberrant desires, combined with his sheer size and the fact that he was a martial arts expert, made him a very real and present danger to women. This monster would remain at large far longer than he should have and would walk among the people of London in plain sight, hunting for potential prey to satisfy his very deviant desires.

Although there are no stories of abuse or any indication that Smith had a cruel or unnatural childhood, his perverted behaviour began early, and his teenage years were consumed with his obsessive misogynistic fantasies about women. This developed into serious criminal behaviour with a string of sex offences as he reached adulthood. In 1976, aged just eighteen, he raped a woman at knifepoint in her home in front of her young children. Having spotted her fixing curtains in her living room, he had brashly knocked on her door and forced entry by threatening her with a seven-inch blade.

A similar instrument would mutilate future victims, who would not live to accuse him of his foul crimes. Undeterred by the presence of her children and probably getting a sick thrill from their terrified screams, he brutally assaulted her, scarring their fragile minds for ever. Their mother, feeling an overwhelming urge to protect those most precious to her, had no choice but to comply as he acted out his warped and twisted fantasies. He was subsequently given an appallingly inadequate sentence of just four years in prison. One cannot but wonder how this injustice came to pass, and the lenient sentence would certainly have exacerbated his feelings of power and arrogance.

Almost a decade later, in 1987, Smith found himself working as an unlicensed cab driver, the perfect role for a pernicious predator. During a ride home, he locked a thirty-year-old female customer in his car, only releasing her after she screamed, fought and attempted to kick his car window through: an act of defiance and desperation that certainly saved her life. Although he was charged and convicted of false imprisonment for this, and had a previous record for rape, his lenient punishment of a two-year suspended sentence must have further played into this sadist's sense of power and, yet again, it is staggering to contemplate how this was deemed retributive by a court of law. Reflecting his sense of invincibility, despite being a convicted rapist, he even ran his own escort agency at one point, hiring girls out for £250 a time for sex and taking a cut of their takings. His motivation for this was undoubtedly to satisfy his desires for power and domination.

Surprisingly, and perhaps evidence of this predator's ability to hide his true nature in plain sight, Smith managed to find himself a wife in 1982. According to him, his brief marriage was a wholly negative experience. He would later claim that his wife had been controlling and domineering. Within months, she had allegedly had an affair with their lodger and then, he claimed, she fractured his relationship with his father by stealing money. No doubt these events would contribute to Smith's misogyny, as well as engender feelings of emasculation within him. He would later claim this experience set him on a course of violence towards women. Blaming his ex-wife for his foul deeds shows the extent of his feelings of entitlement, as well as his inability to accept responsibility for his deviancy. After all, his horrific rape of an innocent mother occurred long before their marriage.

After Smith's marriage failed, he returned to live with his mother in Markhole Close, Hampton. Suddenly responsibility free, and flush with cash, he began frequently using the services of sex workers and it was around this time that he developed an unhealthy obsession with a number of different women. In October 1989, he visited a naturist club in Kent called the 'Eureka Club'. Here he would fatefully meet a woman named Janet and the relationship that ensued would exacerbate his sick fantasies and play out in his future murders. Initially he approached her and her husband and was invited back to their camper van with others for sex. He continued to have sex with Janet on a number of occasions, including at her home, and would later confide that she had had breast implants and a hysterectomy and had allowed him to study the scars on her chest and stomach. Titillated by Janet's scars, his deviant mind became infatuated with them, but Janet soon called an end to their relationship. Smith would later callously recreate Janet's scars on his victims, to resemble the object of his desires who, ultimately, had pushed him away. Janet didn't only represent Smith's lustful desires; she was also a symbol of abandonment and rejection.

By August 1991, Smith was on an escalating spiral of violence and depravity, and he was charged with the attempted rape of another woman, an escort he took to the Retreat Hotel in Ashford. According to her, she went to the bathroom and, when she returned, the door to their room had been locked. She discovered Smith waiting for her, minus his trousers, wearing plastic surgical gloves and holding a Stanley knife. Like his taxi passenger before her, this potential victim's refusal to comply saved her. Desperately determined to fight for her life, she somehow managed to escape and flag down a passing police car. Smith was arrested again.

Devastatingly, he was later acquitted of attempted rape at trial, when his victim, a sex worker who possibly felt intimidated at the prospect of court, failed to turn up and give evidence. The predator was at liberty again, and his insatiable desires, combined with multiple rejections from women, were about to have deadly consequences. The fate of another innocent woman would be sealed by this tragic turn of events.

Thirty-three-year-old Sarah Crump was a much-loved sister, daughter and aunt who had plans of a future filled with love and family. Described by those who loved her as a bubbly, popular and trusting person with an amazing smile, she was in a relationship with her long-term boyfriend, Mohammed Younis, when her life was brutally cut short. Although she had previously worked as a psychiatric nurse, at the time of her murder she was working as a secretary in the chiropody department at Wimbledon Hospital. She was considered an

excellent employee and had been offered a permanent position. Things were looking good for this young couple.

What neither her boyfriend nor family knew was that
Sarah was living a double life.

Some evenings, she was doing escort work under the name
of 'Angie'. Desperate to have a baby, but unable to conceive,
she was saving for fertility treatment. It is believed she had
started doing the escort work to fund her IVF, as her desperate desire for a baby consumed her. Tragically, this wish for
a family would cost her her life, as it was through her escort
work that her path fatally crossed with the depraved Smith
when, using the name Duncan, he arranged to go to her flat
for sex in return for £150.

Leaving work at 2 p.m. on the afternoon of 28 August 1991,
Sarah returned to her one-bedroom flat at 4 Joyner Court,
Lady Margaret Road, in Southall, west London. She could
have had no idea of the fate that awaited her when, that same
evening, just ten days after Smith had attempted to rape his
previous escort, the monster arrived at her door.

With his feelings of rage and entitlement escalating, Smith
had meticulously planned her murder before meeting her
and, during their earlier conversations, he had told her he
had once been attacked by another man at an escort's house.
Sarah had naively and innocently assured him this would not
be a risk at her home, as there would be no one else present.
Her reassurances sealed her own fate. Smith had, of course,
lied. He simply needed to establish that Sarah would be
alone, so that he would be able to act out his sadistic desires
undisturbed. He employed another tactic to ensure this was
definitely the case, once he had arrived, telling Sarah that he
had planned to pay for her services by cheque, but did not

have his guarantee card with him. He knew she would not accept a cheque without it and told her he would have to go to a local cashpoint first, to get the money. Later, records obtained from the cashpoint would confirm that he had indeed withdrawn £150 for her services.

In truth, this was all a ruse concocted by Smith to ensure he was able to carry out his heinous crime undetected. If someone else had been at the property with her, it gave him an opportunity to leave and not return, while if she was indeed alone, he would return with the cash and carry out his violent and brutal fantasies at his leisure.

Exactly what transpired at the property may never be known. Sarah undoubtedly expected it to be just another escort job, a consensual sexual encounter in return for cash, but Smith had other ideas; he had gone to her flat armed with a knife, intending to play out his darkest fantasies. What is certain is that, at 2 a.m., Sarah called her escort agency, as was the standard safety protocol to confirm that the client had left: a protocol Smith was aware of. Making that call must have offered her a glimmer of hope, as she made deliberate mistakes that should have alerted her boss to the danger she was in. In fact, when spoken to by police, agency boss Lisa Pegg confirmed Sarah's client had left her flat, but she would later recall that Sarah had sounded strange on the call, that she had not given her escort name or real name, and that the call had been very brief and abrupt.

Tragically, Lisa did not pick up on the danger Sarah was evidently in and missed a very real opportunity to save this desperate young woman. True to his usual MO, it is believed Smith was threatening her with his knife and had forced her to make that call, holding it to her throat as he had done with other victims. Sarah was then cruelly forced into her bedroom, where the monster made her lie naked on her bed and brutally and sadistically murdered her.

After Sarah's murder, a practised Smith coldly and painstakingly got rid of any evidence that could identify him from the scene. He removed his fingerprints from anything he had touched and washed blood from himself in her bathroom sink, arrogantly taking his time, as he was in no rush. After all, it was the early hours of the morning, and no one had any reason to suspect that Sarah was in danger. The sick monster could relish every moment of his post-murder high.

When Sarah failed to turn up for work the next day and her boyfriend was unable to contact her, he became worried and finally managed to get some keys to access her flat on 1 September 1991. Only briefly going inside and calling her name, he did not check her bedroom and presumed she wasn't home. Concerned about her, and undoubtedly filled with a nagging sense of dread, he reported her missing that same day. It was unlike Sarah to disappear without informing her loved ones of her whereabouts.

When officers entered her flat, a scene of cruel carnage met their eyes, and it certainly spared Mohammed and her family that they were not the ones to discover her mutilated body. Walking towards her bedroom, they noticed blood in the bathroom and realised that a truly dreadful sight awaited them. Sure enough, as they entered her bedroom, they noticed her blood-smeared dressing table and, on her blood-soaked bed, they discovered her brutally butchered body.

Whether she was sexually assaulted before or after her death was never fully determined. Based on the harrowing story Smith would later recount to a fellow inmate, however, it is likely she was assaulted before as well as after death. It was also impossible to establish whether she was tortured before being killed, or whether the extensive mutilation had occurred post-mortem. Fatal wounds had been inflicted on her neck, severing her carotid artery, and to her chest. She had been viciously stabbed in her heart, aorta and left lung. Smith had then proceeded to cut off both her breasts, before opening up her torso and removing a piece of her small bowel. These were placed next to her on her bed. Her heinous murder would later be compared to Jack the Ripper's savage killings in the press.

It was soon discovered that Smith, a known sex offender, was the last person to have been in Sarah's flat. He was arrested immediately and charged with her murder. Determined to get away with this brutal killing, he pleaded not guilty and was held on remand for eighteen months, awaiting trial. He falsely claimed he had gone to Sarah's flat for a massage and nothing more. and had left her unharmed. However, a massage would have cost around £25 at that time, not the £150 he had withdrawn from the cash machine, which was the going rate for sex.

Smith's trial took place at the Old Bailey in July 1993, during which the defence accused police of incompetence and withholding evidence. It also argued that fingerprints found on the bedroom door handle and on a drawer under Sarah's bed had been left by the real, unidentified killer. Staggeringly, and at great risk to society, Smith was acquitted by the jury. This mistake would mean another woman would lose her life.

Sarah's family were devastated by this inconceivable injustice. Her mother, Pat Rhodes, firmly believed Smith had escaped justice and warned he would kill again. She would be proved right. Meanwhile, police closed the file on her case because they knew they had their killer; they were not looking for anyone else in connection with poor Sarah's murder because they knew Smith was responsible.

Smith next came to the attention of police again in April 1999. He had visited a brothel in Ilford, Essex for a night described as 'for broad-minded adults' where, it transpired, an S and M orgy was taking place. It featured a 'love dungeon' filled with instruments of sexual torture: a veritable Aladdin's cave for a man like Smith. While in the club, he became fixated on a cross which patrons could be tied to and subjected to S and M torture. Filled with barely containable lust, he had asked if one of the women working there could be tied to it so that he could inflict pain on her, but he had been refused; this was for customers only. He left the club feeling both angry and sexually frustrated. As midnight approached, his unsatisfied lust reached a crescendo, overwhelming him completely. He needed a body to satisfy his sadistic desires and sought out a sex worker in Paddington.

The unfortunate individual he approached that night was twenty-one-year-old Amanda Walker, a young mother with a two-year-old son, who was new to sex work. Coming from a respectable family in Swarcliffe, Leeds, she had been arrested in Paddington earlier that night for solicitation but, in a stroke of bad luck, had been released at around midnight. Making her way back to Paddington, she was approached by Smith and fell into his despicable trap. After getting into his car, she was driven to a secluded wooded area in Wisley, Surrey, near to the Royal Horticultural Society's estate. Sex workers and their clients frequented the area, but it was also a place Smith knew well because it was a popular dogging site, and he had enjoyed many evenings there, spying on couples having sex. Poor Amanda was not seen alive again.

Her desecrated and brutalised body was not found until almost five weeks after her disappearance, on 27 May 1999, to the heartbreak of her family. She was discovered following complaints about a pungent smell from members of the public. She had been buried in a shallow grave and covered with leaves. Because of decomposition, it was difficult to establish a cause of death; however, it was very clear that she had been brutally and sadistically murdered; her genitalia had been badly mutilated. Again, media outlets would compare the killing to the murders of Jack the Ripper.

The killer had dumped Amanda's blood-stained clothing on a local footpath and police searched their database of known sex offenders in the area close to where her clothes had been found. Smith was quickly identified as a potential suspect as his home was just a mile away. His DNA subsequently proved an exact match to the blood found on Amanda's clothing; witnesses had also seen a man matching his description picking her up on the night she was last seen alive. He was quickly arrested.

True to form, Smith pleaded not guilty to Amanda's murder at trial. Instead, he claimed he had engaged in consensual sex with her on the night she had been murdered but had left her unharmed. It was the same story he had given authorities following Sarah's killing eight years earlier; he claimed his blood had got on Amanda's clothes as, before meeting her, he had fallen and hit his face on the pavement after leaving the sex party. He even had the arrogance to insist that she had tended to his cut lip, and that he had bled on her during these ministrations.

Fortunately, no one believed his fabrication and Smith was convicted of Amanda's murder in December 1999. He was initially sentenced to life with no minimum term, although this was later set at eighteen years. During his time at Wakefield Prison, he would regularly play cards with serial killer and disgraced GP Harold Shipman. They seemed to discover an affinity with each other, which made them friends of sorts.

It was also inside these walls that Smith finally admitted to killing Amanda to a prison psychologist. According to Smith, something inside him had 'snapped'; he had grabbed hold of Amanda and refused to let go. He then claimed that, during the struggle, she had screamed and bitten his finger hard, causing him to bleed on her. He had then forced her to undress and accidentally suffocated her by placing his hand over her mouth during sex, before burying her body in a shallow grave.

Of course, this description of Amanda's killing was only Smith's account of what had transpired, and his version missed out some very important details; namely the lustful and depraved satisfaction he had enjoyed while mutilating her genitals. There was a reason Smith did not mention this: he did not want to be connected to the murder of Sarah Crump, eight years earlier, which had also involved mutilation and for which he had been acquitted.

Like many killers, however, Smith was full of bravado and enjoyed the thrill that ruminating on his crimes gave him. Like many offenders, as time passed, he found it impossible to resist talking about his murders. In fact, while being held on remand at Highdown Prison for Amanda's murder, he made a gruesome confession to fellow inmate Steven Williams – a confession that would have profound repercussions in Sarah's unsolved murder case.

Williams and Smith saw each other regularly in prison and Smith would boast about the S and M clubs he used to visit in London, recounting how he had relished seeing girls tied up and in pain.

As time passed, he opened up more to Williams until finally he described in detail not just Amanda's killing, but also Sarah's. He even had the audacity to describe how he had mutilated her body by cutting her breasts off and claimed that killing her had been 'sexy'. He went on to boast about how he had managed to 'get away with it' as police had no evidence against him.

He then described Amanda's horrifying murder, claiming that he'd bound her wrists and wrapped her in polythene, then cut her 'downstairs' before and after having sex with her. He told Williams he liked to see girls' flesh cut and enjoyed watching and feeling the blood flow from them when he was raping them.

Smith had clearly misjudged the man he had chosen to boast to and confide in. Even though he was a sex offender himself, Williams was appalled by what he had been told and notified authorities immediately. Despite more than a decade having passed since Sarah's murder, Metropolitan Police had kept her case under review. They were convinced they had caught the right man originally but, according to the double jeopardy rule, like Gary Allen, Smith could not be tried again for an offence for which he had already been acquitted. Thankfully, when this changed with the Criminal Justice Act of 2003, there was a prospect of retrying Smith for Sarah's murder.

The new evidence authorities needed to retry Smith came in compelling and multiple forms. There was Smith's prison confession to Williams, along with the striking similarities between Sarah's and Amanda's murders. Both women had been sex workers and both were mutilated after death. There was also Smith's pattern of increasing violent behaviour towards women, and finally, there was new fingerprint evidence. Unidentified fingerprints found at Sarah's crime scene, which the defence had claimed were from the real killer, turned out to belong to the previous owner of the flat.

In 2022, the Court of Appeal approved an application for a retrial of Smith to finally achieve justice for Sarah Crump, quashing his earlier acquittal. At the time, Smith had already served his minimum term for Amanda's murder and was – frighteningly – on the cusp of being released on licence. Once again, he pleaded not guilty to Sarah's murder.

But on 26 May 2023, twenty-four years into his sentence for Amanda's murder, and more than thirty years after Sarah was killed and her body mutilated, sixty-seven-year-old Smith was found guilty of Sarah Crump's murder at Inner London Crown Court and sentenced to life with a minimum term of twenty-seven years. The monster showed no emotion when sentence was passed. Mr Justice Bryan stated: 'I have no doubt your pre-meditated and planned intention that night was to kill and sexually mutilate an escort to satisfy your perverted and sadistic sexual desires.'

He also acknowledged that no sentence could ever compensate Sarah's family for their loss or suffering. Thankfully, it is more than likely that Smith will die in prison and, even if he does manage to survive his minimum term, he would be in his nineties if and when released. He has never expressed any remorse for his crimes or for the suffering of his victims and their families. In a stroke of real injustice, Sarah's parents both died before having the opportunity to see their daughter's killer finally convicted. Their sentence really was a life sentence, and the knowledge that their daughter's heinous killer had literally got away with murder must have caused them unimaginable pain and heartbreak. After his sentencing in 2023, Sarah's family's statement described what they had lost and what kind of callous creature Smith really was: 'Thirty years may have passed but we still miss Sarah – she was a shining light in a murky world who wished for the best but found the worst of humanity.' They also poignantly said, 'If only Mum and Dad were here with us today to share this momentous occasion.'

Sarah's sisters described the pain of having to listen to the details of his vicious murder as 'excruciating'.

It is suspected that Smith is responsible for many other unsolved sex offences and murders. It is highly unlikely that a vicious predator like him only committed the offences he was apprehended for, especially considering his job as a lorry driver, travelling all over the country. He certainly had the means, desire and aberrant potential to be a prolific serial killer. In fact, after his conviction, in 1999, forces across the country re-examined unsolved murders of sex workers to see if they could link him to those crimes too. Moulds of his size-fourteen feet were taken because he was specifically suspected of the murders of Linda Donaldson and Maria Requena, in 1988 and 1991, which bore similarities to Sarah's and Amanda's murders and police believed were linked.

Smith is an unrepentant sexual sadist and predator of women, who was willing to use whatever force necessary to satisfy himself and his deviant desires. His targets were almost exclusively sex workers: ideal victims, whom he could get alone at a location of his choice, having come armed with a knife that he was determined to use. Smith killed purely to satiate his perverted sexual fantasies. It is highly likely that we will hear the name of this brutal murderer again. A man who killed so sadistically and who managed to walk among us in plain sight is unlikely to have allowed decades to pass between his ruthless murders. One can only hope that, if this is the case, every one of his victims will be named and known and granted the justice they deserve.

10

David Fuller: Grave secrets and the twisted double life of a killer

David Fuller was a 'family man', a father of three who, for much of his adult life, cunningly managed to stay under the police radar. Although he was described as an 'oddball' by some, the apparently innocuous pensioner was hiding a horrific secret beneath his veneer of respectability; he was guilty of some of the most shocking crimes ever dealt with by the English criminal justice system, spanning three decades.

Born on 4 September 1954, his criminal life began early: at school he got into trouble for stealing bikes and damaging properties in fires – one of the MacDonald triad's tell-tale signs of things to come. By the 1970s, however, his criminal activity had escalated, and he was convicted of a number of 'creeper type' domestic burglaries: insidious crimes that would make his victims feel frightened and vulnerable. He would often break into properties through rear windows. These crimes clearly set the scene and proved catalytic for his later perverse activities, the prologue to the murders he would commit a decade later.

Although Fuller found himself in court, in 1973 and 1977, and pleaded guilty to three domestic burglaries and a string of other offences, he was never actually jailed or convicted of a violent crime. Perhaps the facade of 'pleasant man' fooled the judge, as it would fool so many others in the years to come – a chilling reminder that evil personified walks with us every day in ordinary towns and unmemorable places. Fuller would use his pleasant persona to successfully evade the law for four decades.

In 1987, twenty-five-year-old Wendy Knell had her whole life ahead of her. As the manager of SupaSnaps on Camden Road, Wendy was a happy, independent young woman, who was described by her family as, 'funny, hard-working and longing for children'. She was in a successful relationship with her long-term boyfriend, Ian Plass, who was intending to propose to her on a planned trip to Paris. Her future looked bright, and she was excited about what it held.

Little did Wendy realise, as she went about her everyday business, politely chatting to people in the shop where she worked, that evil was lurking in plain sight. At the start of summer, a season filled with so much hope, life and promise, how was Wendy to know she would never see another, and that her well-made plans of marriage and a future filled with love and children would be savagely snuffed out?

On 22 June 1987, Ian dropped Wendy off at her bedsit in Guilford Road, Tunbridge Wells, where she had moved after the breakdown of her previous marriage. It was the last time he would see her alive. Unbeknown to Wendy, David Fuller had been secretly stalking her for many months, having identified her as an ideal victim because she was vulnerable: she was young, she lived alone and she had a ground-floor studio flat.

Wendy never stood a chance. That evening, Fuller entered her property, possibly through an unlocked window, and carried out a brutal and horrific attack on her; he viciously beat her around the head with a blunt object, then strangled her to death. Although she lived in a flat and the walls were thin, neighbours did not hear her scream, and this, along with the orderly nature of her home and the lack of any defence wounds, suggests she was taken completely by surprise by a killer who would turn out to be even more monstrous than anyone had the capacity to imagine.

Tragically, Ian discovered the body of his innocent and beautiful girlfriend. Having been alerted by Wendy's mother that she hadn't arrived at work on the morning of 23 June 1987, he went to her flat, already filled with a sense of foreboding. When the front door went unanswered, he gained entry through an unsecured window and discovered the horrific scene that would change his life irrevocably. What he witnessed would later be described as 'the stuff of nightmares'. Filled with adrenaline and concern for Wendy, Ian spotted her on the bed. Desperate for her to be OK, he urged her to wake up, before taking in the grim reality of the scene before him: although Wendy's head was visible, her body was covered by her duvet. Ian pulled the duvet off her shoulders, lifted her right arm up and attempted to open one of her eyelids. It was then he realised life as he knew it had come to an end. Devastated, he left the flat to alert the police.

A post-mortem later revealed that Wendy had been sexually assaulted: semen was found in her mouth, vagina and on her duvet. There was also evidence of anal penetration. Authorities believed that this heinous sexual assault could have taken place after death: blood-pattern analysis suggested her body had been moved into different positions while she was bleeding profusely from head wounds, allowing her monstrous attacker to sexually assault her in a variety of ways. Frustratingly for police, the only clue was a distinctive bloody footmark on the cuff of Wendy's blouse and a fingerprint on a plastic bag.

Wendy's heinous murder sent shock waves through her local community, which was devastated by such a violent crime and the loss of such a promising young woman. Worse was to come, however, as, later that same year, another innocent young woman would lose her life in similarly horrific circumstances.

Like Wendy, twenty-year-old Caroline Pierce had her whole life ahead of her. Living just a quarter of a mile away from where Wendy had worked, she was eminently aware of her vulnerability, and had recently arranged for window locks to be repaired at her flat. Like Wendy, she had a good job, as manager at Buster Browns, an American restaurant on Camden Road, and was a happy, lively young woman.

Caroline spent 24 November 1987 with friends. Saying goodbye to them and taking a taxi home on that cold and dreary evening, she could never have imagined the horror that awaited her. Although neighbours would later report hearing a number of high-pitched screams that night, tragically no one went to investigate. It is unclear if she ever actually made it into her property, because Caroline vanished that night and would not be found until 15 December, when a farm worker discovered her naked body almost forty miles from her flat, in a water-filled dyke on Romney Marsh. Caroline's body had been carefully hidden. In fact, were it not for the elevated position of the tractor's cab, she would probably have remained undiscovered for much longer.

Caroline's body was naked, apart from a pair of tights and, like Wendy, it was determined that she had been beaten around the head with a blunt object and strangled. Unfortunately, due to decomposition and the fact that her body had been left in water for so long, the full extent of her ordeal was never fully established. But it was clear that she had been sexually assaulted, as semen was found on her tights.

The brutal killings of these two young women soon became known as 'The Bedsit Murders', due to the fact that both victims had lived alone in flats. The police were certain that the cases were linked and the public, unsurprisingly, was on high alert. As a result of the climate of fear, and the belief that a deranged serial killer was on the loose – a killer with warped sexual desires who spent time desecrating their victims' bodies after death – there was a significant police presence in the area. Knowing they were looking for a highly organised, dangerous, methodical killer, who had selected his victims coldly and after observing them for some time, the police desperately tried to find clues to lead them to this pernicious perpetrator. Sadly, though, forensic science was in its infancy in 1987, and the National DNA Database wouldn't be created for another eight years, so both Wendy's and Caroline's murders would remain unsolved for decades, while a dangerous and evil predator would be free to continue his vile campaign at his leisure.

In 2008, Kent Police formed a cold case unit to review

unsolved murders and, by 2019, following massive advances in DNA science, the team decided to review the cases of Wendy and Caroline. Thirty-two years had now passed since their murders, which had been a life sentence in itself for their grieving loved ones, as there could be no form of closure while the callous killer was still at large.

Using the latest scientific techniques, new samples were collected from the evidence saved from Caroline's crime scene; they were found to match those taken from Wendy's. This was pivotal in reinvestigating the cases because it was the first time a scientific link had been made between the murders. Police now knew they were looking for the same evil perpetrator; they even had a full DNA profile of their man. Unfortunately, though, that individual was not on the National DNA Database. Investigators were determined they would catch their killer, though, so they turned to plan B, searching the database for a potential relative using the familial DNA process. The National Crime Agency was able to identify a list of one thousand potential relatives, which was quickly short-listed to just ninety. It looked like they were closing in on the killer.

A massive national effort ensued, involving more than twenty other police forces across the country. All ninety individuals needed to be interviewed and give voluntary samples until, finally, one man was identified as very closely matching the DNA found at the crime scenes. That person had a relative that perfectly fitted the profile of the man they were looking for; he was in the correct age range and lived close to Tunbridge Wells. That man was no other than David Fuller himself. His brother's DNA had been matched to him, and the chances of the crime scene DNA belonging to someone else were a billion to one. This was exactly the breakthrough officers needed.

In the early hours of 3 December 2020, police attended Fuller's home in Heathfield, where he lived an apparently ordinary life with his wife and teenage son. He was immediately arrested, and a sample of his DNA was taken. Within thirty-six hours, police had a positive crime-scene DNA match and, after over three decades, it seemed that they finally had their killer. Of course, nothing is ever that easy and it is rare that a brutal murderer accepts their fate without a fight. Fuller was no exception to this rule. Instantly, he denied any involvement in the murders and even went as far as claiming he didn't know Tunbridge Wells (a town that was a mere twenty-five minutes from his home). Police would later discover Fuller's invoices for electrical work he had carried out in the town, as he had trained as an electrician while working in the navy shipyards of Portsmouth as a younger man.

The exemplary work of the scenes of crime officers and scientists that worked on the original case back in 1987 proved invaluable over thirty years later. They had carefully preserved samples and, as the investigation continued, the net around Fuller began to tighten: a bloody fingerprint on a plastic Millets bag found behind Wendy's bed matched Fuller's left forefinger. The police then worked hard to determine whether he also matched the bloody footprint found on Wendy's blouse. Working with Clarks footwear archivists to identify the shoe, it turned out it was their distinctive 'Sportstrek' trainer and police managed to find photos, from the 1970s and '80s, of Fuller wearing them. Police also managed to establish that Fuller had often visited Romney Marsh in Kent, where Caroline's body was found. It transpired that he was a keen cyclist and often visited the marsh with his cycling club, or when birdwatching. One of his fellow cyclists would later describe him as friendly and helpful, emphasising how this cunning chameleon could lead two such disparate existences.

Fuller lived a double life, able to blend seamlessly into an apparently normal existence, while simultaneously committing heinous crimes. Like many before him, he lived comfortably in two very different worlds. He had married for a third time in 1987 (the year the two murders took place) and his new wife, a special educational needs teacher at Broomhill Bank in Tunbridge Wells, had lived in a staff house located just a couple of miles from both Wendy's and Caroline's flats. It was discovered that, around this time, there had been a number of complaints from young women of a prowler spying through windows and entering their properties when they were out. One of those properties had been Caroline's flat. Also, contrary to his claim that he didn't know Tunbridge Wells, it transpired that Fuller had once lived just one hundred yards from the street where Wendy lived.

Finally, the pieces of the jigsaw were coming together for the police, and they knew that, after all these years, they had their man. They even had his meticulously kept diary entries to collaborate their evidence; he documented visiting Buster Browns, where Caroline worked, and still owned photos in SupaSnaps sleeves which suggested he'd visited Wendy at her workplace too. Yet, during questioning, he still stubbornly refused to admit he'd been to either location.

The full extent of the monstrous man's depths of depravity was yet to be discovered, however, and would only begin to surface after the police searched his home. Police learned that Fuller had worked in hospitals for many years. In fact, he had secured a job in the maintenance department of Kent and Sussex Hospital in 1988, just one year after the double murder. Working as an electrical maintenance contractor, he managed to dodge any criminal record checks, as it was the employee's responsibility to disclose any past crimes at that time. Unsurprisingly, Fuller kept quiet about his previous record. In fact, by the time he left, in May 2011, he had been promoted to maintenance supervisor. He was then employed as an estate supervisor at Pembury Hospital in Tunbridge Wells.

The nature of Fuller's job meant he had access to areas of the hospital that would ordinarily be out of bounds – like mortuaries, where there was no CCTV to preserve the dignity of patients. For a man as cold-blooded and sadistic as Fuller, this was a dream come true. He would wait until mortuary staff had left (they usually worked from 8 a.m. to 4 p.m., whereas his shift would be from 11 a.m. to 7 p.m.). Then he would enter the mortuary, carrying maintenance equipment in case he was challenged. Although there were cameras on the corridors leading to the mortuary and swipe-card system logs, no checks were ever made to establish if any staff members were making an unusual number of visits to the mortuary.

This failure in the system played directly into Fuller's foul hands; investigators would later analyse over one hundred and fifty thousand hours of footage and swipe card data to track his movements and discover that he had entered the mortuary thousands of times. What Fuller did while alone in that mortuary is the stuff of horror movies. A search of his home would later reveal a huge catalogue of explicit material which proved he had been abusing the corpses of women and girls. Later, investigators would establish that Fuller had abused the cadavers of at least 102 females between 2008 and 2009; the youngest being just nine years old and the oldest one hundred. In order to abuse the innocent nine-year-old, the callous monster would have had to remove clothes, toys and a letter from her grieving mother. She would later describe her daughter as 'the kindest and bravest person she had ever met, who laughed like no one else and was truly grateful for her life'. When she finally faced Fuller in court, she told him, 'You raped my baby ... she could not say no to the dirty sixty-six-year-old man who was abusing her body. It really does break my heart.'

In total, of his identified victims, three were under the age of eighteen. Two of his victims, Mary and Helen Akande, who were sixteen and twenty-two years old, had been sisters who had died in a car crash alongside their father. Their mother had been the only survivor of the crash, and Fuller's reprehensible actions caused her fresh agony and torment.

Another victim, twenty-four-year-old Azra Kemal, who died falling from a bridge in July 2020, was abused by Fuller prior to, and only hours after her mother visited her to say goodbye. After discovering Fuller's actions, she stated, 'I had spent two hours in the mortuary sleeping with her. And that gave me some sort of comfort. Little did I know that my daughter had been violated prior to that day and the evening of that day. So, whilst I'm stroking my daughter's hair ... a man had crawled all over her skin.' In fact, she was so traumatised by Fuller's abuse of her daughter that she decided to take the law into her own hands; she went to the police station where he was being held, armed with a kitchen knife and a determination to kill him. Police officers managed to prevent her from attacking him, handcuffing her and keeping her in a cell for her own protection. She bravely maintained afterwards, 'If I'd found him, I'm 99.9 per cent sure I'd have put that knife straight through his heart because he put a knife through mine.'

Police soon established that Fuller had not only taken photos of his foul crimes, but also video footage. He transferred these to four portable hard drives, which he hid in a box screwed to the rear of a chest of drawers in his wardrobe. One hard drive alone contained more than 800,000 images and 504 videos. Another contained hundreds of images of raped and murdered women and girls downloaded from the internet. Police also found a number of printed images of the malevolent monster committing acts of abuse: sickening images of him with his penis in the mouths, anuses and vaginas of corpses, and images of him penetrating their bodies with his fingers and tongue. He would regularly abuse the same corpse over and again, some both before and after post-mortems.

The forensic team soon realised that, although Fuller's original victims, Wendy and Caroline, had been living and therefore murdered by him, he followed a particular MO with all his victims, dead or alive. He identified his living victims, stalked them mercilessly, and learned their movements; with his deceased ones, he found out as much information as he could, using social media to stalk them. He often removed corpses from fridges and abused them on the floor in various positions, as he did with his live victims. His meticulous attention to detail and organisation was another similarity; he obsessively recorded images of abuse, cataloguing and indexing his collections, even using a black notebook to record his crimes. This arrogant trait would prove invaluable to the police and authorities when his case came to court.

The extent of Fuller's depravity knew no bounds, and police quickly discovered he had paedophilic tendencies; as well as abusing the dead bodies of young girls, police found explicit images of children, many being classed as category A, which showed penetration of children by adults. One showed a child around the age of three being orally raped and a video showed a child of about six years old being vaginally raped. Others were category B – one showed a girl lying on a bed while a man masturbated over her – and category C, showing a girl exposing her genitalia. Fuller's grotesque stash of sexual abuse images was the biggest ever discovered by police. It totalled around four million images and around one million videos.

Police even found a pen camera in in one of Fuller's jackets, which he had used to film his wife's friend when she had come to visit; he had filmed her undressing, showering and using the toilet, and had even photoshopped her head onto corpses he had abused. It seemed there was no sanctuary safe from his grotesquely warped and deviant mind.

So, when questioned by police, Fuller could not deny his abuse of corpses. After nine officers spent five months working through the evidence found on hard drives, CDs, floppy discs, mobile phones and photo prints and rolls of film, the evidence was indisputable. Of the 102 victims sexually abused by Fuller, around eighty were identified, many through the arm bands they were wearing. The operation to trace and notify families was huge and devastating and involved 166 family liaison officers, 27 police forces and 320 staff a day over five days.

Although it was clear that Fuller's abuse of dead bodies was evidence of his involvement in the murders of Wendy and Caroline, especially through his abuse of them post-mortem, he still refused to admit to their murders. In fact, the evil monster showed absolutely no remorse, only self-pity. It would, therefore, be left to a judge and jury to determine his fate.

Fuller was finally brought to trial at Maidstone Crown Court on 1 November 2021. Despite the overwhelming evidence against him, he still denied the two counts of murder, admitting only to the sexual offences relating to his abuse of dead bodies. The prosecution highlighted Fuller's depraved sexual predilections, his desire for sexual gratification by observing vulnerable women, gaining control of them, killing them and sexually assaulting them after their deaths.

In a shocking turn of events, on the fourth day of his trial, Fuller clearly realised he was bang to rights and changed his plea to guilty. Mrs Justice Chema-Grubb faced a difficult task determining the sentence for this monstrous offender. He faced a total of fifty-three charges, many historical, and was given a twelve-year sentence for the abuse of corpses at hospitals and the possession of prohibited images and videos. For Caroline's and Wendy's murders, the judge imposed a full life term without the possibility of parole. This recognised the planning and pre-meditation of the murders and the sexual and sadistic nature of the killings.

Fuller is unquestionably one of the most cruel and sadistic criminals to pass through the English criminal justice system; he is a remorseless sadomasochist, a murderer, a necrophile and a paedophile who was able to hide in the shadows, avoiding detection for over thirty years. Police believe that Fuller could have committed further crimes between 1987 and 2008 which are yet to be accounted for. A monster with such a voracious appetite for depravity could not have lived an ordinary life for over two decades.

Fuller's horrific crimes undoubtedly left devastation in their wake, not just for the victims, but also for his own families: those women and children who had been duped into believing their father and husband was a mild-mannered man. Following Fuller's conviction, his ex-wife and children were devastated, disgusted and in shock, acknowledging that they 'didn't know' the monster who had carried out these crimes. His shell-shocked current wife filed for divorce and sold their house. None of them recognised the monster who had been hiding in plain sight.

The women Fuller abused were not the only victims of his depravity; their families' lives were destroyed too. The judge acknowledged that those whose relatives had been desecrated by Fuller had had their world shaken and lost their ability to trust hospitals. Wendy's and Caroline's families' lives were blighted for thirty-four years, their nightmarish ordeal beginning the day they had to identify their daughters' bodies. Wendy's father was determined that justice would prevail, asserting, 'One day someone's going to ring that door and say, "we've caught him" and there will be a celebration, by God there will be, especially if he goes down for a very, very long time.' He was right, but tragically the wheels of justice turn slowly and, when that great day finally arrived, he had already died.

Fuller was indisputably a monster, who showed no regard for his victims or their families. Understanding the psychology of his actions is difficult and complex: like many violent criminals, there's often a motivation rooted in a need for power and control. Abusing bodies, especially in such a hidden and taboo manner, could have given him a sense of dominance or control that he felt was lacking in other areas of his life; one of the primary attractions for a necrophile is the desire for an unresisting, non-rejecting partner. His desecration of Wendy's and Caroline's bodies, post-mortem, clearly demonstrates this deviant desire in Fuller.

Fuller also successfully managed to hide his aberrant behaviour for years, which suggests an ability to compartmentalise his life; a psychological defence mechanism where someone suppresses their thoughts and emotions, effectively 'splitting' their life into separate parts to avoid the cognitive dissonance of confronting their actions. This was evident when, even after he was caught and shown irrefutable evidence, Fuller continued to deny his guilt.

Perversely, Fuller's job may have been the reason why he did not kill any other women after Wendy and Caroline. Finding himself in a position where corpses were readily available to him, in the hospitals where he worked, removed the need for him to stalk and murder vulnerable young women. This reduced the risk of him being caught, while allowing his deviant tendencies free reign. Undoubtedly, the flaws in the hospital systems where he worked, combined with his innate ability to compartmentalise his two very incompatible lives, provided him the opportunity to live a seemingly ordinary existence while committing heinous crimes over a period of more than three decades. A chameleon of the worst kind, the world is a safer place with him behind bars. It is a cruel travesty, however, that it took so long for justice to prevail.

11

Dorothea Puente: Evil wearing a benevolent mask

Although this book has focused on male serial killers thus far, and female serial killers are rare by comparison, there are certainly exceptions to that rule. The final five cases demonstrate that women are just as capable of murder as men ...

Dorothea Helen Gray was born on 29 January 1929 in Redlands, California. She was the sixth of seven children, and her parents, Jesse James Grey and Trudy Mae Gray, were both alcoholics. Her life with her parents was unstable; her father would often threaten to kill himself in front of Dorothea and her siblings, and he died of tuberculosis in 1937, when she was just eight years old. Less than a year later, her mother was killed in a motorcycle accident, leaving their seven children orphans. This tragic start in life certainly set the stage for her turbulent journey.

Dorothea's childhood was a tapestry of sorrow, marred by the early loss of her parents. Thrust into the tumultuous waters of foster care, and split from the security of her siblings, Dorothea navigated a labyrinth of homes, each chapter of her early life tainted by abuse and neglect. These formative years were dominated by experiences that would cast long, ominous shadows over her actions.

Imagine a young Dorothea, a child orphaned and tossed about in the turbulent sea of the foster care system. Each home, each encounter with neglect or abuse chiselled away at her young psyche, shaping something twisted in the shadows of her being. These early scars were an ominous prologue to the horrors she would later unleash. In these formative years, one could argue, the seeds of a sociopath were sown – a being capable of monstrous deeds, devoid of the empathy and compassion that tether most to the realm of humanity.

In 1945, she finally left the care system and made a bid for independence at the tender age of sixteen, where she found herself in Olympia, Washington and began to scrape a living as a sex worker. Later that same year she met and married Fred McFaul, a soldier who had returned from the Second World War. From its offset, their marriage matched her earlier life experiences, being plagued with violence and instability. Although they had two daughters together between 1946 and 1948, both were given up. One was sent to live with family, while the other was adopted. Unsurprisingly, they divorced in 1948 and, left shipwrecked on turbulent seas, Dorothea returned to California.

In the spring of 1948, she was arrested for buying clothes using forged cheques in Riverside, California. After pleading guilty she was sentenced to four months in jail, then three years on probation but, rather than serving her probation in Riverside, she skipped town and moved to San Francisco to begin a new life that would shock even the most hardened of people.

Here she met her second husband, merchant seaman Axel Bren Johansson. By now the seeds of deceit were well and truly planted and Dorothea was living under the false name of *Teya Singoalla Neyaarda* and passing herself off as a Muslim woman of Israeli and Egyptian descent. This marriage was no better than her first and the couple's relationship was volatile at best, as by now she had developed drinking and gambling habits, and Axel struggled to deal with her aberrant and unreasonable behaviour. In fact, whenever her husband was at sea, she would invite men to their home and gamble away his hard-earned money.

In 1960, when she was thirty-one years old, Dorothea was arrested for owning and operating a brothel, under the guise of a bookkeeping firm, in Sacramento. Found guilty, she was sentenced to ninety days in the county jail. By now her actions were becoming impossible to live with and, after her drinking, dishonesty and a range of criminal behaviour culminated in her offering to perform a sex act on an undercover police officer at a brothel, Axel had her committed to DeWitte State Hospital. Here she was diagnosed as a pathological liar with an unstable personality.

The couple divorced in 1966, when she was thirty-seven years old, after which she assumed the new identity of *Sharon Johansson*. In this guise, she managed to hide her true nature from those around her and cunningly passed herself off as a devout and philanthropic Christian, providing sanctuary for women who were victims of abuse for free in her home.

By 1968, Dorothea was married again, this time to Roberto Jose Puente. Mirroring previous relationships, the marriage was short-lived, and the couple separated after sixteen months, with Dorothea citing domestic abuse in her divorce papers. Although their divorce was finalised in 1973, they continued a tumultuous relationship until 1975, when she finally filed a restraining order against Roberto. She would continue to use his name, however for more than two decades, and it is that name that would become infamous in the annals of criminal history.

As the pages of her life turned after her divorce, Dorothea emerged as a seemingly benevolent figure in Sacramento. She became the proprietor of a boarding house, a residence for the elderly and disabled. The house, located at 1426 F Street, was owned by Ricardo Ordorica, whom she called her nephew because she had managed to engender such a close relationship with him. His building had two storeys and the Ordoricas lived on the ground floor, while Dorothea rented the upstairs flat. It is here that she began establishing herself as a community-minded good Samaritan, helping the neediest and those on the fringes of society. To the outside world, and particularly to her unsuspecting neighbours and tenants, she embodied the archetype of a charitable soul, a matron of kindness tending to the needs of the less fortunate: aiding people suffering from mental illness by hosting meetings, helping people sign up to receive Social Security benefits and even baking them cakes.

Here she also cunningly established herself as a well-respected member of Sacramento's Hispanic community, funding charities and scholarships. She cleverly changed her appearance to make herself look older, like a grandmotherly figure people would trust. She even found the time to marry again, this time to Pedro Angel Montalvo, although this marriage was even less successful than the previous ones, lasting only a week.

On 21 December 1978, when Dorothea was forty-nine years old, however, her carefully constructed facade began to unravel when she was convicted of illegally cashing thirty-four state and federal Social Security cheques that belonged to the tenants in her boarding house. Astonishingly, despite being given five years' probation and being ordered to pay four thousand dollars in restitution, she was able to re-integrate herself into the community she had betrayed and continue running her boarding house.

In the autumn of 1981, she met Ruth Munroe, a retired clerk. At that time, Ruth was in an unhappy marriage to Harold Munroe, whom she had met after retiring. Although she was healthy and otherwise happy, Ruth suffered from pain and had been prescribed Tylenol and codeine by her doctor. Her husband introduced his wife to Dorothea shortly before he was diagnosed with terminal cancer.

In March 1982 Harold became hospitalised and left Ruth at the mercy of Dorothea. The women soon became best friends and then partners, serving breakfast and lunches in a Sacramento bar. Their friendship flourished so well that Ruth's family became close to her too, and she even encouraged Ruth's son, William, to call her Grandma, even though she was younger than his mother. Her carefully constructed facade certainly fooled those around her, and the benign grandmother persona undoubtedly lulled those she knew into a false sense of security.

In fact, Ruth was so enamoured with her new best friend, and so fooled by her kind and caring facade, that she moved into Dorothea's flat in April 1982 from where she filed for divorce from Harold because his medical bills were escalating. At that time, Ruth was a healthy mother and grandmother, having five children of her own and eighteen grandchildren, most of whom would visit her at Dorothea's property. It seems they were as trusting of Dorothea as their mother and grandmother.

Towards the end of April, Ruth began feeling ill, chillingly telling a friend at a beauty parlour one day that she felt so poorly that she thought she was going to die. That same evening, her son William visited her at the flat she shared with Dorothea and noticed that she looked very unwell. She was drinking a green liquid that appeared to contain alcohol, which was unusual for Ruth as she rarely drank, and her son was surprised. His mother reassured him that the concoction was something Dorothea had made to help calm her. Satisfied that she was in good hands, he left her in the care of her apparently loyal and attentive friend. Over the next two days, however, her condition worsened and on 27 April, Dorothea tried to prevent William seeing his mother, claiming the doctor had just visited and given her a shot to sedate her. Her daughter Rosemary also attempted to see her that evening but was similarly unsuccessful.

At 5.30 the following morning, Dorothea rang Rosemary and told her that something was terribly wrong with her mother. Unbeknown to Ruth's trusting family, she was already dead at that time. When they questioned her about the 'shot' the doctor had given their mother, Dorothea claimed it was a misunderstanding and that it had been a shot of alcohol that she had prepared for her friend. She also told police that Ruth had a heart condition and that she had been alive at 4 a.m. but unresponsive at 5.45. It would later transpire that Ruth had not been treated by a doctor at any point in April 1982.

Subsequently, a toxicology report would reveal high levels of Tylenol and codeine in Ruth Munroe's system and her cause of death would be ruled as respiratory depression from a codeine overdose. Although no alcohol was found in her bloodstream, her stomach contained five ounces of a dark green fluid. It was estimated that she had died at around midnight the previous evening: she had not been alive at 4 a.m. as Dorothea had claimed. Police officially ruled her death as suicide, dismissing her children's assertion that she was not depressed, although the cause of death was officially marked 'undetermined' by the coroner.

While she was living a seemingly benign and respectable existence with Ruth, Dorothea's criminal tendencies were quietly continuing. In fact, on 16 January 1982, she picked up seventy-four-year-old Malcolm McKenzie from a bar and took him back to her apartment. There she spiked his drink and robbed him of money and jewellery, which included a diamond ring that had belonged to his mother. In May of that same year – after Ruth's death – another friend, Dorothy Osborne, discovered cheques, credit cards and other personal belongings missing hours after Dorothea had visited her home for drinks.

Finally, her criminal activity began to catch up with her and, in July 1982, she was convicted of three grand theft charges, one of which related to Malcolm McKenzie, and was sentenced to five years' imprisonment. While incarcerated, she began writing to a seventy-seven-year-old retiree from Oregon: Everson Theodore Gillmouth. On 9 September 1985, Dorothea was released after serving only half of her sentence, even though she had been diagnosed as schizophrenic and was incapable of showing remorse or regret. It was advised that she should be closely monitored. On leaving the prison, she was picked up by Everson and Ricardo Ordorica and returned to her flat. Her relationship with Everson developed quickly and she soon persuaded him to open a joint bank account with her.

It was not long before Dorothea reopened her boarding house, where she accommodated homeless people without friends or family who were suffering from mental illness: tough cases that social services struggled to deal with. That October, just one month after leaving prison, she wrote to Everson's sister telling her they were going to marry on 2 November.

Ominously, during the same month she had claimed she would marry Everson, Dorothea hired handyman Ismael Florez to install wood panelling in her home. Once completed, she paid him an eight-hundred-dollar bonus, sold him a red 1980 Ford pickup truck – the same make and model that Everson owned – and asked him to build her a six foot by three foot wooden box so she could store items safely. Florez returned to Dorothea's home later and discovered the box nailed shut. Even though the box now weighed around three hundred pounds, he was persuaded that it simply contained junk and helped her dump it in a river in Sutter County.

On 1 January 1986, the box was discovered by fishermen. On opening it, police found the decomposed remains of an unknown elderly man. Tragically, he would not be identified as Everson Gillmouth for three more years, leaving Dorothea free to continue her secret campaign of terror virtually unchecked. In fact, she regularly collected his pension and forged letters to his family so that he appeared to be alive and well.

Dorothea was still running her boarding house, living among her community and fooling those around her into believing in her philanthropic intentions. Wearing chiffon dresses, thick-rimmed glasses and allowing her hair to grey, she became the archetypal grandmother figure once more. What appeared as benevolent and selfless from the outside proved very different from within, however. While living in her care, residents had their mail read and their Social Security cheques and money taken from them. Although she would pay them a monthly sum, she took the rest to cover her so-called expenses. Alarmingly, although she had been ordered to stay away from elderly and vulnerable people because of her previous crimes, parole agents did not stop her while they had the chance, despite making frequent visits to her establishment. They too were possibly taken in by her benign facade.

Even when one of her tenants, fifty-eight-year-old Eugene Gamel, was found dead in her care in July 1987, she was able to successfully pass it off as a suicide, as he had overdosed on amitriptyline and ethanol. She calmly informed law enforcement he had a history of suicide attempts, and they took the word of this apparently benevolent and caring old lady.

Things changed in 1988, however, when Dorothea Puente was fifty-nine. An outreach counsellor with Volunteers of America named Judy Moise realised a man placed in Puente's care had disappeared. Fifty-two-year-old Alvaro Montoya had been homeless and had struggled with his mental health for years before being placed with Puente. After he missed an appointment with her on 29 August, Judy contacted her to ask where he was. Although Puente claimed he had gone to Mexico with his brother, the social worker grew suspicious as she knew Alvaro had been ostracised by his family.

Concerned for her patient's safety, Judy spoke to another of Puente's tenants, who told her that he believed something was wrong; Puente had been digging a lot of holes in her back yard and a man had been seen clearing out Alvaro's clothes. There had also been a foul smell reported in the boarding house. Alarmingly, it transpired that Puente had been designated as Alvaro's benefits payee since March of that year.

Determined to cover her tracks and throw Judy off the scent, manipulative Puente persuaded Donald Anthony, a former convict she had met when he undertook some work in her garden, to contact Alvaro's social worker claiming to be his brother. Agreeing to do her dirty work, he rang Judy and told her he had picked Alvaro up from Puente's boarding house and taken him to Utah. Still suspicious, however, vigilant Judy called the police.

When police questioned Puente, she stubbornly retold the same story: Alvaro was on holiday with his brother. Another tenant, John Sharp, initially appeared to back her claim, asserting that he had seen Alvaro only days earlier. Clearly living in fear of this apparently benign old woman, however, he managed to surreptitiously hand police a piece of paper on which he had written, 'she's making me lie for her'.

Finally, on 11 November 1988, police returned to Puente's property and began to dig up her garden. It soon transpired that the life of Dorothea Puente was a meticulously crafted illusion: a mask that concealed a macabre reality. The discovery of multiple bodies buried within the confines of her property unveiled a series of heinous murders. The grandmotherly figure, once revered for her kindness, had been methodically drugging her vulnerable tenants, orchestrating their untimely demises and cashing their Social Security cheques for her own financial gain.

The first body unearthed was that of seventy-eight-year-old Leona Carpenter. Two years earlier, on 21 October 1986, Puente had summoned a notary to Leona's hospital bedside after she had suffered a flurazepam overdose, to give Puente power of attorney. Just ten days later, the supposedly neighbourly good Samaritan had begun cashing her Social Security cheques. After being released from hospital, Leona had returned to live with Puente before being re-admitted in February 1987, then disappearing altogether.

Although Puente was questioned by police about Leona's body, she remained calm and completely unruffled, denying any knowledge of it. The following day police began digging up other areas of her garden and Puente cleverly claimed she felt unnerved and panicky and asked permission to visit her nephew. They naively agreed; surely a frail elderly woman could not be guilty of such a heinous crime! Unsurprisingly, Puente did not return to her boarding house, and, on 13 November 1988, an all-points bulletin was issued for her arrest.

On 15 November 1988, Charles Willgues of CBS met Puente in a bar in Los Angeles. Although she was using the alias *Donna Johansen*, he remembered having seen her on a morning newscast and got in touch with another CBS reporter, Gene Silver. The following day they alerted police to her whereabouts, and she was arrested.

On 17 November 1988, Puente was flown from Los Angeles to Sacramento where she was formally charged with the murder of Montoya, in spite of insisting on her innocence and her good reputation. The discovery of poor Leona's body was only the beginning of the horror story, however, and the truth was literally about to be unearthed.

Five more bodies would be discovered in this apparently kindly old woman's garden. Seventy-eight-year-old Betty Mae Palmer had arrived at Puente's boarding house in 1986 and her partially dismembered body was discovered in Puente's front garden. Her head, hands and lower legs were never found. Toxicology reports revealed she had doxylamine, haloperidol and flurazepam in her system. Puente had cashed almost seven thousand dollars' worth of benefit cheques belonging to Betty.

Sixty-two-year-old James Gallop moved into Puente's accommodation in February 1987. After a malignant tumour was discovered in his colon, he had agreed to further tests but had failed to turn up for his appointment. In fact, Puente had contacted his doctor telling him James had gone to LA. His body was discovered under her gazebo. Toxicological testing showed he had amitriptyline, nortriptyline, phenytoin and flurazepam in his system.

Vera Faye Martin was sixty-one when she moved in with Puente on 2 October 1987. On 19 October, she failed to wish her daughter a happy birthday, which was out of character and a cause for concern. Her body was found under Puente's shed. The toxicology report showed she had flurazepam in her system and, again, Puente had cashed over seven thousand dollars' worth of Vera's Social Security cheques.

Sixty-five-year-old Dorothy Miller moved into an upstairs flat in Puente's home on 21 October 1987. Just weeks later, she had disappeared, yet Puente had continued forging cheques in her name to the value of over eleven thousand dollars. Dorothy's remains were discovered under a slab of concrete near some rose bushes. Tissue samples from her brain revealed the presence of carbamazepine and flurazepam.

Benjamin Fink was sent to live with Puente on 9 March 1988, and, although his brother regularly visited him, by the end of April he had disappeared. Another tenant had reportedly complained of a foul smell coming from his room, which Puente had blamed on a faulty sewer. His body was discovered in a hole near her shed that had been filled with concrete. His toxicology report revealed the presence of amitriptyline, loxapine and flurazepam in his system.

On 31 March 1989, Dorothea Puente was charged with nine counts of murder. Most of her victims had been drugged until they overdosed, and she had then dragged them to open graves in her garden where they were buried. Although she pleaded not guilty, by the end of her trial 156 witnesses had testified and more than 22,000 pages of transcript were recorded.

On 26 August 1993, when Puente was sixty-four years old, she was found guilty of killing three of the people found buried in her garden. A jury found her guilty of the first-degree murder of Benjamin Fink and Dorothy Miller and the second-degree murder of Leona Carpenter. As the jury was unable to reach verdicts on the other victims, a mistrial was declared on those counts. Spared the death penalty, because the jurors found themselves deadlocked again, she was sentenced to life imprisonment without parole at Central California Women's Facility in Chowchilla, on 10 December 1993.

The psychological landscape of Dorothea Puente's mind was a labyrinth of horror. Her tumultuous childhood, replete with instability and emotional turmoil, may have sown the seeds of her later malevolence. These early scars could have twisted her perception of control and empathy, warping her into a figure capable of such cold-blooded acts. Her adeptness at maintaining a facade of normalcy and kindness points to a deeply manipulative and deceptive psyche, a persona that could skilfully navigate the societal norms while harbouring sinister intentions.

To the outside world, Puente was a paragon of community spirit, a caretaker for the forgotten. Yet beneath this carefully curated facade lurked a mind governed by sociopathy's cold, calculating tenets. She was a master manipulator, her charm and seeming kindness mere tools in her arsenal, deftly wielded to deceive and exploit. Her story points towards the enigmatic and often unfathomable aspects of the human psyche, probing the question of how an individual, so ordinary in appearance, could harbour such extraordinary and horrific secrets.

Her choice of victims – the vulnerable and marginalised – spoke volumes of her need for control, a twisted echo of the powerlessness she once endured in her youth. Here was a woman who, in her quest for dominance, had turned her boarding house into a macabre stage where she played both caretaker and reaper, all while the unsuspecting world applauded her community spirit.

At the core of Puente's dark saga was an insatiable greed, a materialistic hunger that saw human lives as mere stepping stones to financial gain. Her actions were not just the machinations of a sociopath, but of a predator driven by avarice. Each cheque she cashed from her deceased victims was a testament to her utter disregard for human life, a grim trophy of her manipulation and deceit.

Even as the true horror behind her grandmotherly facade was exposed, Puente remained an enigma, her mask of normalcy never fully slipping. She faced trial and judgement with the same eerie calm and detachment that had enabled her to commit her crimes. In her lack of remorse and her apparent inability to grasp the gravity of her actions, the full extent of her detachment from human emotion was laid bare. It is therefore particularly unjust that she managed to live to the age of eighty-two, dying of natural causes in prison. Her grandson, William Harder, still claims today that the grandmother he knew 'wasn't all bad' and that he always saw her as human, despite her crimes.

Dorothea Puente's story is a chilling reminder of the depths of human depravity. Her life, a tapestry of manipulation, greed and murder, challenges our understanding of human nature. It forces us to confront the unsettling reality that sometimes, the most dangerous monsters are those cloaked in the guise of normalcy, walking undetected among us.

12

Tamara Samsonova: The Granny Ripper; an unlikely murderer

If you were asked to imagine a serial killer, you would probably think of someone young, someone strong, fit, agile and able. Any preconceived ideas you might harbour about what kind of person is capable of murder will be shattered by the horrifying case of sixty-eight-year-old Tamara Samsonova. Small and fragile in appearance, this infamous pensioner epitomises the idea that looks can be deceiving and that evil can walk beside us in the most unlikely forms.

Tamara was born in 1947 in the village of Uzhur, Russia. After completing high school, she attended the Moscow State Linguistic University before moving to St Petersburg after graduating in the late 1960s, and it was here that she met Alexi Samsonova, whom she married in 1971.

The couple moved into a house at 4 Dimitrov Street, a new-build at the time, and Tamara began working for the Intourist travel agency, mainly at the Grand Hotel Europe – a stunning hotel which was famous for its iconic building. Tamara enjoyed her work, meeting the public every single day and living a seemingly normal life; she was educated, had a good job and appeared to have settled down with a partner she loved deeply.

In 2000, however, Tamara's husband suddenly went missing. Reporting his disappearance, she said he had possibly run away with another woman. Tamara and Alexi had been married almost thirty years by this point and, although the police didn't find him, they believed her story. After all, she was a respectable woman who had been married for three decades. They probably felt sorry for her that she had been treated so badly by a man she had given half her life to.

By 2001, Tamara claimed she was lonely, having been deserted by her husband, and being unused to living alone. In order to remedy her feelings of isolation, and to make money, she decided to rent out a room in her apartment; Alexi had been gone for some time and she told her neighbours that she did not think he was going to return. In spite of her need for company, however, Tamara proved difficult to live with; many who knew her described her as strict and volatile. Her neighbours said she would often bang on the radiators and swear at them, completely unprovoked. Unsurprisingly, this meant conflicts arose between Tamara and her tenants, with many only living with her short term.

Volodya began living with Tamara in the summer of 2001, and was her first lodger. By the end of the year, he had seemingly left. Tamara would tell neighbours there had been arguments and that he had been difficult to live with. The young man had not been known by the other tenants in her building, so they accepted her story, even as Tamara became more difficult, volatile and aggressive. They probably put her erratic behaviour down to her husband's desertion, assuming it would have been a hard blow to recover from.

Another young man, Sergei Potanin, would similarly become a lodger of Tamara's. However, like Alexi and Volodya before him, in 2003, Tamara said he'd left abruptly. No one knew where he had gone, and his departure was quite sudden but, because he wasn't from the area, it was assumed he had returned to his hometown. No one had become close to the young man, so no one ever thought to follow up. In the years that followed, neighbours would notice a plethora of young people briefly frequenting Tamara's apartment, then disappearing from sight, but she simply reiterated the fact that she was difficult to live with.

By March of 2015, Tamara's apartment was undergoing renovations, so she had to find somewhere to stay temporarily while the work was going on. A mutual friend fatefully asked seventy-nine-year-old Valentina Nikolaevna Ulanova, who lived on the same street, if Tamara could lodge with her. It was agreed that she could as it would prove mutually beneficial, with Tamara acting as a caregiver to Valentina, helping her with housework and cooking for her. The arrangement continued for months, and Tamara began to enjoy living in the apartment, so much so that she wanted to stay beyond the renovations on her own apartment being completed and way past the point which they had agreed. Of course, Tamara was headstrong and used to getting her own way so, when Valentina asked her to leave outright, Tamara stubbornly refused.

Naturally, their relationship fell apart as Tamara began to show her true colours, continually arguing with Valentina and destroying the home that had once been her haven. In fact, it was after one of these arguments, concerning some unwashed dishes, that Tamara decided she was going to kill Valentina, the woman who had offered her shelter when she most needed it.

On 23 July 2015, she convinced a pharmacist to sell her a drug – phenazepam – which is usually only available on prescription; a long-acting benzodiazepine which can be used for anxiety, when overdosed it can act as a sedative or even put the patient into a coma. It would prove fatal in the hands of this volatile woman, yet she was given it by a pharmacist who was clearly duped by the frail- and vulnerable-looking deceiver.

Claiming she wanted to treat Valentina and charming her with her apparently good intentions, Tamara bought her an Olivier salad, one of her favourite meals. She then drugged the food with the phenazepam, rendering Valentina unconscious after she had eaten it. Tamara then proceeded to coldly and callously dismember her body using a hand saw; it would later transpire that she had borrowed the saw from an unsuspecting neighbour. Poor Valentina was still alive when the dissection of her body began. Cutting up and getting rid of the body reportedly took her two hours: not long for an inexperienced murderer, particularly for an older woman, which suggests that this was not her first experience of hacking apart a body. After the horrendous ordeal, Tamara calmly disposed of the body parts – some of which she transported in bin bags.

Later, CCTV footage from the apartment building would show Tamara, wearing a blue raincoat, making seven trips to dispose of Valentina's body parts. She had the audacity to dump the torso by a pond on Dimitrov Street, then carried the hips and legs to the nearest back garden where she dumped them.

On 26 July 2015, the harrowing discovery of a body, with the head and limbs removed, wrapped in a shower curtain, was made by an unfortunate neighbour in some flowers, near a pond in St Petersburg. It had been there for a few days without attracting any attention, but local dogs had begun to show an interest in the gruesome package. This alerted the public, and eventually the police, to the grisly remains.

On 27 July 2015, the body parts were identified as Valentina after police interviewed neighbours who lived in the same apartment block. When they knocked on Valentina's door, Tamara answered; police very quickly discovered blood traces in the bathroom, and that the shower curtain had been torn down. Tamara was arrested on the spot.

Considering her stubbornness and volatility, it is surprising that Tamara was very cooperative, instantly confessing to the murder, telling police that she had put the full pack of phenazepam – fifty tablets – into Valentina's Olivier salad. She asserted that her victim had 'liked it very much'. Tamara continued to tell them that, when she had woken up at 2 a.m. that morning, she had found Valentina lying on the kitchen floor and cut her body into pieces, removing her head and limbs and sawing her torso in half. She heartlessly complained, 'It was hard for me to carry her to the bathroom; she was fat and heavy. I did everything at the kitchen where she was lying.'

The gruesome story continued as she explained that she had cut off Valentina's head and hands and boiled them in a large saucepan. Some believe that she did this to make it difficult to identify the victim; however, the Russian media would later dub her 'Baba Yaga', after she would claim to have eaten the lungs of her victims. Whatever the truth, CCTV showed Tamara carrying a large saucepan down the stairs of the apartments, and out of the door. Unfortunately, Valentina's head, which was disposed of with the saucepan, was never found, nor were her internal organs. One of Valentina's neighbours commented that she believed that Tamara had thrown the saucepan containing the head into the communal rubbish, which would have been collected, so would now be almost impossible to locate.

Tamara told police that she had panicked when Valentina had wanted her to go back home; she claimed she had got used to having company and did not want to return to an empty apartment. She thought that if she killed Valentina, she could live 'in peace for another five months, until her relatives turn up, or somebody else'. Her motive clearly lacked thought: staying in Valentina's home after her murder would have left Tamara alone again anyway.

Later, Detective Mikhail Timoshatov would tell the media, 'Tamara Samsonova says that at first she made her friend sleep – and then cut her into pieces.'

Once they realised what this apparently innocuous old woman was capable of, the police began to search her flat, making the grim discovery of Tamara's horrifying diaries, which were written in Russian, English and German (which highlights her education and the potential she chose to waste). Harrowingly, entries in this diary have linked her to eleven other murders, spanning at least the previous fifteen years. She is still being investigated in relation to fourteen murders in total, although the Investigative Committee of

Russia has not given any further details. Tragically, the bodies of the victims she claimed to have killed in her diary have never been found.

One of her diary entries regarding her first lodger read, 'I killed my tenant Volodya, cut him to pieces in the bathroom with a knife, put the pieces of his body in plastic bags, and threw them away in the different parts of Frunzensky district.' Her diary also referenced a tattoo which was found on Volodya's body.

In addition to the chilling confessions of murder, the diaries also contained boring details of her day-to-day life, things one would expect to find in any typical older woman's diary, including 'slept badly', 'take medicine', and 'I woke at 5 a.m. I am drinking coffee. Then I do work around the house.' Her seemingly mundane existence certainly jars with the confessions to heinous murders and dismemberments.

The full extent of the horrors which the diary contains has not been made available to the public. However, it is speculated that she confessed to removing and eating body parts of her victims, with the police alleging that she had a particular liking for lungs. When authorities were asked whether or not she was a cannibal, they replied, 'It is not excluded.'

On 29 July 2015, Tamara attended the Frunze District Court of St Petersburg where it was determined that she should be held in custody. When this was announced, Tamara smiled and clapped her hands, and when the judge stated, 'I am asked to arrest you, what do you think?' Tamara replied, 'You decide your honour, after all, I am guilty, and I deserve a punishment.' When the judge asked her to address the court, she said, 'It's stuffy here, can I go out?' She also divulged that she had been prepared for court for the last decade saying, 'It was all done deliberately . . . This is no way to live. With this last murder I closed the chapter.'

Unsurprisingly, the case of the old-lady ripper cannibal attracted media attention, with journalists attending her court hearing. Tamara reprimanded them, saying, 'I knew you would come. It's such a disgrace for me, all the city will know.' In a contradictory move, she then blew a kiss to the reporters.

Tamara Samsonova soon became known as the Granny Ripper in the media, with one article reporting that she had become obsessed with a notorious Soviet murderer, Andrei Chikatilo, aka the Red Ripper, who murdered, sexually assaulted and ate parts of his victims.

Tamara's diaries were discovered alongside books about black magic and astrology. Another neighbour, Maria, told reporters, 'It was obvious Tamara was a bit strange. For example, she would go out barefoot and in a dressing gown, even in winter. She liked to go out and buy food at night,' and, 'She thought people came into her flat when she was out and cut up her clothes.' She also acknowledged that she had lent Tamara a hand saw around a decade earlier, but that she had never received it back.

Samsonova undoubtedly had a history of mental illness and initially told police that she was an actress, then claimed she was a graduate of the Vaganova Academy of Russian Ballet. Forced to undergo a psychiatric assessment, it was determined that she had paranoid schizophrenia and was therefore not considered competent enough to stand trial. Unsurprisingly, it was deemed that she was a danger to society, as well as to herself.

What makes a woman who has lived for decades as a loving

wife and typical neighbour turn into a cold-blooded killer? While detailed psychological evaluations of Samsonova are not publicly available, her behaviour and the nature of her crimes suggest possible personality disorders. Traits such as a lack of empathy, grandiosity and manipulativeness could be indicative of antisocial personality disorder. One plausible explanation of her heinous actions is a late-life onset of mental illness. Conditions such as schizophrenia or psychotic disorders, if undiagnosed and untreated, can manifest in extreme ways. The disorganised nature of her crimes, along with her disjointed diary entries, might reflect underlying psychotic breaks from reality. Ageing is often accompanied by cognitive decline, which can impair judgement and increase impulsivity. In rare cases, this could exacerbate latent psychopathic tendencies, leading to a loss of control and the emergence of violent behaviours.

At the end of 2015, Tamara was sent to a specialised hospital in Kazan to receive compulsory psychiatric treatment. She will be under the constant supervision of doctors and be monitored for the rest of her life.

Samsonova has subsequently been implicated in the murder of another one of her tenants, a forty-four-year-old man who is believed to have been killed on 6 September 2003. At the time, a torso with the arms, legs and head missing was found on the street. After Tamara's arrest, evidence including a business card which belonged to the victim was discovered in her apartment. It is believed that Tamara killed him and dismembered his body. Though it hasn't been proven, it is also suspected that she is responsible for the disappearance of her husband, Alexi Samsonova. No one knows where he is, and it is very likely that he was her first victim. The investigation into the full extent of her murders is still ongoing.

Tamara Samsonova's life and crimes present a complex tapestry, intricately woven with elements of psychological disturbance, a startling late-life emergence of violent criminal behaviour, and an array of societal and individual factors that allowed her to evade capture for nearly two decades. Her case stands as a dark beacon in the annals of criminal psychology, challenging our understanding of serial killers, particularly those emerging in their later years. Details about her early life are sparse, but what is known does not immediately suggest a predisposition to violent crime. This lack of early indicators is not uncommon in late-onset criminals, complicating efforts to understand their motivations.

Tamara's later confessions and behaviour in custody hinted at possible underlying psychiatric conditions. There were suggestions of schizophrenia, but without a detailed psychological evaluation, any diagnosis remains speculative. Mental illness alone does not lead to criminal behaviour, but in rare cases, it can contribute to the emergence of violent tendencies, particularly if untreated.

Samsonova's ability to evade capture for so long can be partly attributed to societal stereotypes. Elderly women are rarely perceived as capable of heinous crimes, and this allowed her to blend seamlessly into her environment. This underestimation, combined with a lack of overtly suspicious behaviour, created a perfect smokescreen. Furthermore, the dismemberment and disposal of her victims' bodies in such a calculated manner suggests a level of premeditation and cunning that was belied by her outward persona. Her ability to evade suspicion can also be attributed to societal biases. Elderly women are rarely perceived as threats, so Samsonova could operate under the radar. This societal blind spot towards elderly criminals, especially women, is a critical factor in understanding how she could commit such crimes unnoticed.

What was the trigger for her criminal behaviour? Was it a latent predisposition activated by specific life events, psychological deterioration, or perhaps a combination of both?

Her diary entries, often rambling and disjointed, provide a window into her troubled mind but do not offer a clear motive. They do, however, suggest a deep-seated anger and a possible enjoyment of power and control, common traits in serial killers. The gruesome nature of her crimes, including dismemberment, indicates a level of detachment from societal norms and human empathy that is chillingly profound.

Tamara Samsonova's case stands as a stark reminder of the complexities underlying criminal psychology. It challenges our perceptions of who can be a criminal, particularly in terms of age and gender. The lack of early-life indicators in her case suggests that we may need to expand our understanding of what can trigger violent criminal behaviour, especially in later life stages. Her story is a patchwork of enigmas and horror, a psychological puzzle that remains only partially solved. As we strive to understand the darkest aspects of the human psyche, Samsonova's life story serves as a cautionary tale about underestimating the potential for evil, regardless of age or appearance.

13

Juana Barraza: The Mataviejitas

The case of Mexico's most prolific serial killer is a disturbing one indeed. It was one that was aided by an incompetent and misogynistic police force, ensuring that the 'Mataviejitas', or Little Old Lady Killer, would remain free to commit their reign of terror, killing forty-nine of the most vulnerable people in society, elderly women, over the course of a decade.

In 1998, the body of María Amparo González was found in her home in Mexico City. She had been robbed and strangled to death. Although María's cruel killing would mark the beginning of a pattern of brutal murders, it would not be recognised as the work of a ruthless and incredibly organised serial killer until far too late.

Later that same year, the body of Concepción Carranza would be discovered, murdered in the same way as María. In 1999, two more elderly women would meet a similar fate; both Regina Jiménez Peña and Consuelo Ortiz González would be found strangled with their own possessions.

Horrifyingly, however, no links would be made. After all, the elderly, particularly elderly women, were highly respected in Mexican culture, so the idea of someone targeting them specifically seemed unfathomable. It was erroneously believed that even the most brutal criminals respected the elderly.

However, the killings continued into 2001 with the murders of Victoria Alicia Domíngues y Solís and Margarita Margoliz Kenigsberg. It now seemed obvious that Mexico City had a ruthless killer walking silently among its inhabitants and preying upon its weakest and most vulnerable.

In spite of the already prolific nature of the killings, the police were struggling with the case that the press had dubbed 'El Mataviejitas', presuming the killer to be a man. Although there was much press speculation, authorities were determined not to make their knowledge of a serial killer public, leaving the potential victims even more vulnerable to this predator. The meticulous murderer left virtually no evidence and the distraught families of the victims aided their escape by cleaning their loved ones' homes, so that photographic evidence could not be taken from the crime scenes. It was also clear that the victims had no relationship to their killer; their motivation simply seemed to be robbery, making it even harder to find their perpetrator.

Realising they were out of their depth, the authorities set up a task force and requested help from police forces in other countries. French police had previously dealt with a serial killer dubbed 'The Monster of Montmartre', who had strangled at least twenty-one women to death after following them home and torturing them until they gave up their life savings to him. An officer who had worked on that case flew to Mexico to help train the task force who felt out of their depth, organising a homicide investigation course and specifically sharing techniques on how to catch a serial killer.

In 2002, the strangled body of María Del Carme Juana Montalvo Ruiz was discovered and, later that same year, on 25 November, the badly beaten and strangled body of sixty-four-year-old María de la Luz González Anaya would be found in her apartment. Described by neighbours as vulnerable and depressed, it seemed the killer had gained María's trust and been welcomed into her home. Now authorities had to publicly admit they had a serial killer on their hands and district attorney Bernardo Bátiz assured the public that he would find the killer. He said that grandmothers were sanctified and respected in Mexican culture, even by criminals, and that he would catch this monstrous perpetrator before he finished his term in office.

By now public fear and resentment had begun to escalate but, along with this, so did the crimes committed by the Little Old Lady Killer. In 2003, the monster would take twelve more innocent lives. On 2 March, eighty-four-year-old Guillermina León Oropeza would be discovered strangled. On 25 July, eighty-six-year-old María Guadalupe Aguilar Cortina would be found similarly murdered. On 9 October, the body of eighty-seven-year-old María Guadalupe de la Vega Morales was discovered, strangled to death and tied up with fractured arms. On 24 October, seventy-eight-year-old María del Carme Muñoz Cote de Galván was discovered strangled with a stethoscope. On 4 November, eighty-five-year-old Lucrecia Elsa Calvo Marroquín was found strangled with her curtain cord and just over two weeks later, eighty-five-year-old Natalie Torres Castro's strangled body was discovered. On 28 November, seventy-six-year-old Alicia Cota Ducoing would be discovered

similarly strangled. That year, five more elderly women –
María Guadalupe González Juanbelz, Gloria Enedina Rizo
Ramírez, María Eugenia Guzmán Noguez, María Guadalupe
Aguilar Cortina and Luz Estela Viveros Padilla would be dis-
covered brutally killed in the same manner.

Finally, police had enough witness evidence and testimonials to create a profile of their suspect. They believed their
perpetrator was between forty-five and forty-eight years old,
that they were broad and strong, with large hands and short
hair. They were certain the killer dressed as a nurse or carer
to gain the trust of their victims. In fact, ironically, a recent
government welfare policy, started by the governor of Mexico
in order to provide financial aid to the elderly to help preserve
their dignity, seemed to be playing into the hands of this
ruthless predator, allowing them to be invited into victims'
homes as a friend who would help them to improve their
quality of life.

In spite of this knowledge, police were still reluctant to
make this public. Rather, the 'Mataviejitas' had become
a weapon in the fight between Mexico's federal government and the capital's city council; they were controlled by
opposing political parties, and each claimed the other's incompetence was responsible for the killer still being at large.

Finally, however, in December 2003, police released two
sketches of their suspect – one masculine version and one
feminine – and placed them in the windows of all squad
cars. These sketches were also printed in local papers in the
hope that someone would recognise the perpetrator. Surely
it would not be long before this cunning chameleon, living
among the people of Mexico and murdering those it should
have most respected, would be brought to justice.

Matilde Sánchez Gallegos was a well-respected nurse who was loved by her colleagues. On 4 January 2004, she was seen by two police officers as they queued at a bank. She matched their killer's description and appeared to be avoiding eye contact; they thought they had finally found their killer. They immediately detained her, prematurely informing news outlets that they had found their culprit, so desperate were they to solve the case and prove their own competency.

Matilde was put in a line-up behind a two-way mirror, but none of the eyewitnesses identified her. By now her co-workers were aware of the accusations aimed at their colleague and were determined she would not be scapegoated for these foul crimes. With no evidence other than her similarity to the police sketch, the police released her without charge fifteen hours later. This wrongful arrest was a major source of embarrassment to the authorities, who were then forced to publicly apologise to the innocent woman. The police were no nearer to finding the monster that was terrorising their city.

Now even more desperate for help, they accepted FBI support for a police force that was out of its depth. Similarly to the way the French had helped, the FBI tutored officers on how meticulous and premeditated serial killers work in stages; that they would select their victim by observing and stalking them to ensure they were alone and vulnerable; that they would seduce their victim by befriending them, making them tea and offering their victims help because, in spite of the fact that everyone was aware of this killer by now, they were still being invited into their victims' homes by being charismatic enough to fool their prey. The execution stage came next, where they strangled their victims using their own possessions, like scarves, curtain cords or stockings, and the final stage was the taking of a trophy to remember their victim by. This would usually be an item of jewellery.

Armed with this new and helpful information, police arrested their second suspect, Araceli Vázquez, in 2004. After she had been caught scamming the elderly with the promise of financial aid, police found property of previous victims at her home. One item in particular, a watch which still had its label on, was recognised by the daughter of one of the victims. Her mother, Margarita Aceves Quezada, had been applying for a senior's card at the time of her murder and a social worker had apparently paid her a visit. Although Vázquez quickly admitted to the burglaries, she vehemently denied murder. However, like Matilde before her, she was paraded in front of more than seventy news outlets, dressed up in a white coat, and made to hold a wig that did not even belong to her. Vázquez did not match the killer's description, nor was she muscular and strong, yet she was charged with several counts of robbery and two of murder, in spite of the fact that the reign of terror continued while she was incarcerated. Although many questioned whether they had the right perpetrator, she remains in prison today.

The third suspect for these heinous crimes was also arrested in 2004. Jorge Mario Tablas Silva was reported to police by the family of the sixty-six-year-old victim, María Eugenia Guzmán Noguez. Jorge had pretended to be a nurse, promising to get her a financial aid card, in order to establish a relationship with her. Searching his home, police found items implicating him, including a blond wig, a stethoscope and a Bible in which passages about extermination and death had been highlighted.

Deciding he was a copycat of Vázquez, despite no real

evidence linking him to the murders, police first decided he was responsible for four of the killings, then seven, then nine. Although he too vehemently denied his involvement in the murders and strongly maintained his innocence, he was sentenced to almost seventy years in prison and died a convicted murderer. Despite both Vázquez and Tablas Silva's incarceration, the killings continued. Surely this should have been evidence enough of their innocence.

Although police now had two people imprisoned for the Little Old Lady murders, women continued to be brutally killed. In fact, the murders escalated, killings now taking place just weeks apart. Unsurprisingly, public faith in the authorities was at an all-time low, as people feared for the safety of their loved ones, and the district attorney's job was on the line. A media frenzy ensued.

Public unrest was growing more and more, as people, particularly women, began to realise how little money was spent solving femicides, which were increasing in general alongside the Little Old Lady killings, but being given little attention. Violent crimes against women were rife in the poorer nearby town of Cuidad Juárez, with little media or public attention. Murdered women in that region made up of more than ten per cent of crimes recorded and, harrowingly, ninety-eight per cent of Mexico's femicide cases remain unsolved today.

Despite the news reports of murdered elderly women, seventy-year-old teacher María Dolores Martínez Benavides felt happy and safe in her apartment, even though she lived alone. There was a doorman for her building and she had neighbours who knew her close by. Tragically, however, she was unaware that a predator had infiltrated her haven. Shockingly the 'Mataviejitas' had ingratiated themselves with

María's doorman, whom they regularly sat and chatted with, often asking about the neighbours who lived in the building, cleverly discovering which of them was the most vulnerable and lived alone.

In 2004, the cunning chameleon befriended María, learning about her life and her daily routine, before strangling her to death with her own telephone cord in her apartment on 24 October. So much strength was used in this heinous murder that María's neck was broken. Unfortunate María would not be the only woman to be murdered that year, during which sixteen more women would fall victim to the predator.

Police were now certain that the killer had to be male because no woman would be capable of exerting such force. Their new theory was that a transgender sex worker was the likely culprit. A series of violent raids began targeting sex workers, and more than a hundred were arrested and booked, yet there was no evidence to suggest their killer was transgender, other than the strength they exerted. Perhaps this drastic move was simply a reflection of authorities' desperation to find a killer who was continuously walking among their people choosing their next victim, while seemingly hidden from view.

As 2005 dawned, almost forty women were dead and, although two people were serving prison sentences for their murders, the police were no nearer to finding the real perpetrator. Many of the murders had occurred near parks, which led them to believe the killer had befriended these women in those locations and offered to help them get home. It was then realised that all the victims' homes were connected to main roads with fast escape routes, and that this was likely the reason the innocent victims were chosen.

Eleven more women would lose their lives in 2005. These were Julia Vera Duplán, María Elisa Pérez Moreno, Ana María Velázquez Díaz, Celia Villaliz Morales, María Guadalupe Núñez Almanza, Emma Armenta Aguayo, Emma Reyes Peña, Dolores Concepción Silva Calva, Guadalupe Oliveira Contreras, María de los Ángeles Repper Hernández and the upper-class mother of Luis Rafael Moreno, a well-known criminal psychologist in Mexico, eighty-two-year-old María del Carme Camilla González, who would fall victim to the Mataviejitas on 28 September. Her killing led to the creation of a special project known as 'Operation Parks and Gardens' where officers would patrol areas where victims might be stalked, even going to the extreme of paying potential victims to act as bait. All police cars continued to display posters of the killer's sketched profile and used their sirens to make their presence felt. Though this still proved unsuccessful in catching their killer, the murders seemed to stop and police developed an optimistic theory that the killer could have died by suicide. They even fingerprinted bodies in mortuaries, to see if their prints matched any found at the killer's crime scenes.

The murder of eighty-two-year-old Ana María de Los Reyes Alfaro proved this theory wrong in the most brutal way. On 25 January 2006, her neighbour, Joel López, returned to his apartment after being kept late at work. On stopping by to check on his neighbour, he discovered the door left open. Entering, he was filled with a sense of foreboding, and discovered the apartment had been ransacked. Continuing to the living room, he made the horrifying discovery of Ana's dead body, before coming face to face with her killer.

Later, Joel would testify that the woman in a red coat

calmly looked him in the eyes before walking out of the door and down the street. Coming to his senses and realising there was a chance that the killer might escape justice, Joel chased her and alerted nearby police officers. Thankfully, though she put up a fight, this cold and arrogant killer was apprehended before she could make it to the subway. Joel and the police involved in apprehending the most sought-after killer Mexico had ever known were hailed heroes, although Joel refutes this, claiming that a hero would have saved the woman he had come to love dearly. The police officers were rewarded with 100,000 pesos and an apartment each, so grateful were authorities to finally have their perpetrator.

The authorities were shocked to discover their cruel and callous killer of vulnerable elderly women was a woman herself. In her possession she had two shopping bags containing financial aid cards, a wrestling business card and a receipt for a wrestling-ring rental. She also had a blood-pressure gauge, jewellery, a prayer card and a key chain with the inscription 'The Lady of Silence, professional wrestler, wrestling world champion'.

It turned out that their elusive murderer was Juana Barraza Samperio. She immediately confessed to Ana's murder, while denying any involvement in the others. Sceptical, police took her prints and found they matched those found in at least ten previous murder scenes. Later, she even willingly re-enacted how she had murdered Ana on one of the investigators, using stockings they gave her and signing them. Both the signature knot and her own written signature would prove vital as evidence when she faced trial.

Within hours of her arrest, Barraza was paraded in front of the media, where she posed alongside a plasticine model of her face that had been created using police sketches. For Barraza, like those wrongly accused before her, there was no presumption of innocence. Emilio Álvarez Icaza, a human rights ombudsman for Mexico City, stated, 'The media became the great judge.'

Born on 27 December 1957 in Mexico, Juana Barraza's story began with profound betrayal and abuse, abandonment and exploitation. Her alcoholic mother, a figure who should have been a source of protection and love, reportedly traded thirteen-year-old Juana to a man for three beers, subjecting her to sexual abuse by a paedophile who would repeatedly rape her. Harrowingly, she would become pregnant with his son. This ultimate betrayal by her mother laid the foundations of a deep-seated resentment towards older women: a festering wound that would later manifest in her string of violent acts.

In her adult life, Juana found an outlet in the world of wrestling, adopting the persona of 'La Dama del Silencio', or 'The Lady of Silence'. In the ring, she imagined that she would be powerful, in control: a stark contrast to the powerlessness of her youth. Wrestling became a symbolic battlefield where she could exert control and strength, traits she was denied in her formative years. But even this area of her life involved lies. While she claimed to be a professional in the ring, in truth, Juana Barraza's association with wrestling was not as a professional wrestler, but rather as an aspirant and fan.

Barraza's fascination with wrestling, particularly her admiration for the theatrical and powerful figures in the wrestling world, is a notable aspect of her personal history. This interest in a domain characterised by physical dominance and dramatic personas can be seen as a symbolic escape from her troubled past and a reflection of her desire for a different identity.

Juana Barraza's darker impulses surfaced with a vengeance in the early 2000s and she embarked on her killing spree. These acts were not just murders; they were symbolic acts of revenge, echoing the resentment and anger she harboured against her mother and, by extension, all older women.

Barraza never learned to read or write and, after her mother died of cirrhosis, she moved to Mexico City. She had four children, the eldest of which died at the age of twenty-four, when he was attacked by muggers. Unsuspecting neighbours in the largely middle-class area where she lived would later describe her children as friendly and her as pleasant. Her hairdresser would remark that she had a new look every couple of weeks, but that she had never thought anything of it. In her living room, police found an eighty-centimetre photograph of her posing as a wrestler. Although she was illiterate, articles about the 'Mataviejitas' were strewn around the room. She also had an altar to her god, Santa Muerte, who she would later claim protected her.

It transpired that Barraza's wrestling community saw her as a sweetheart, someone who would treat them to expensive meals. She enjoyed a form of wrestling called lucha libre, which involved choreographed fights, with fighters being *tecnicos* (good guys) or *rudos* (villains). She had been interviewed just a week before her capture and had described herself as '*rudos* to the core'. She would later tell police that she chose the wrestling name 'La Dama del Silencio' because she was quiet and kept herself to herself.

It transpired that she had to quit wrestling because of a back injury from lifting 100-kilogram weights and, although she had never wrestled in the ring, she provided the media with the perfectly sensational story they desired. The truth was, although she dreamed of becoming a famous wrestler, she had never entered the ring to fight. The costume and stage name were one of many lies she lived, and when the chance of becoming a wrestler was truly taken from her, a new outlet for her frustrations emerged; murdering women she identified with her mother.

Barraza went to trial in the spring of 2008. The evidence was presented to a single judge, with the prosecution alleging that she had been responsible for more than forty deaths and citing her resentment towards her mother as motive. Although her defence team claimed she was mentally unfit to stand trial, psychological analysis proved otherwise and, on 31 March 2008, she was found guilty on only sixteen charges of murder and aggravated burglary, meaning at least thirty-two murders remain officially unsolved to this day.

Barraza was sentenced to 759 years in prison, a purely political sentence given to appease an angry public and also reflecting the fact that women who kill, in Mexico and around the world, often get longer sentences than men be-cause some cultures cast them as more evil by nature.

The previous suspect in Barraza's case, Araceli Vázquez, has served nineteen years in El Reclusorio Oriente – a violent, maximum-security prison – and remains there, convicted of some of the 'Little Old Lady killings' despite Barraza's guilt. She has more than twenty years left to serve, even though there is no evidence against her, and witness sketches did not match her features. Since being imprisoned, her son has been killed in a robbery and her husband has moved on. She has not received a single visit in the last six years. When the attorney general who was in the position at the time of her sentencing was asked about her case, he abdicated responsibility, saying the current attorney general needed to resolve the issue. Many people now acknowledge that culprits were 'manufactured' by a desperate and ineffectual justice system.

In marked contrast to Vázquez's plight, Barraza has reached celebrity status since her incarceration, with songs and poems written about her, and documentaries being made. Children even dress as her for Halloween. Although she will end her days in Santa Martha Acatitla prison, her life there is more than bearable. She works as a gym instructor and cooks and sells food to other inmates on Tuesdays. It has even been claimed that she charges ten thousand pesos for interviews.

In 2015, Barraza married seventy-four-year-old Miguel Ángel Quiróz, a violent offender housed in the male side of the same prison, who had courted her through letters, though they had not met in person. The marriage, widely covered in the media, failed when they did meet. In her own words, 'Once we saw each other, the love vanished.' She divorced her husband in 2016, having spent only forty minutes in his presence.

The case of Juana Barraza presents a harrowing and perplexing narrative, weaving together elements of tragedy, betrayal and deeply ingrained psychological turmoil. Barraza's psychological profile is a complex collision of trauma, resentment and a desperate need for control. The abuse and betrayal she suffered in her childhood likely played a pivotal role in shaping her pathological hatred towards elderly women.

A toxic blend of emotional scarring and a distorted perception of justice drove Barraza to commit heinous acts as a twisted form of retribution. Her wrestling persona, a figure of strength and control, contrasted sharply with the reality of her crimes, which were acts of dominance over the most vulnerable.

Juana Barraza's reign of terror came to an end with her capture in 2006, an event that prompted widespread media attention and introspection in Mexican society. Her case raised unsettling questions about the nature of evil and the capacity of a seemingly ordinary individual to commit such extraordinary crimes. It highlighted the often-overlooked plight of the elderly and deep-seated issues of abuse and neglect in society.

This case remains a disturbing reminder of how past traumas can warp the human psyche, leading to acts of unimaginable cruelty. Her story is a sombre narrative about the consequences of abuse and the dangerous potential for its scars to manifest in violent and tragic ways. Juana Barraza's life and crimes serve as a dark testament to the complex interplay of psychological damage, societal factors and the individual choices that lead down the path of infamy and destruction.

14

Aileen Carol Wuornos:
Vulnerability to vengeance

In the annals of crime history, there are few stories of women who repeatedly kill. Sometimes, however, a killer is created through a lived experience that would be intolerable and unimaginable for most people, going through things that would warp and desecrate even the most stable of minds. The horrifying story of Aileen Carol Wuornos, who was dubbed America's 'first' female serial killer, is one such case and is certainly not a simple one to tell. In fact, her life was the epitome of a horror story from her conception to her execution by lethal injection on 9 October 2002, when she was just forty-six years old.

A large body of work has evolved around this twisted tale which has been retold in an array of documentaries and films, the most famous of which is 2003's *Monster*, starring Charlize Theron. There are documentaries, books, academic studies, podcasts and even songs about Wuornos' life and criminal activity, and Nick Broomfield's first documentary about her, *The Selling of a Serial Killer*, conveys the mercenary exploitation of Wuornos by those she knew, including three of the officers involved in her case.

Her life was marred by adversity, anguish and a series of events that, when pieced together, offer a deeper understanding of the woman behind the notoriety. The journey of her life underscores the profound impact of early-life experiences on an individual's development, both psychologically and behaviourally.

So, when delving into her tragic story, one must ask if the term 'serial killer' is too simplistic to describe this convicted and executed murderer. Is Aileen Carol Wuornos, the woman who became known as the 'man-hating lesbian prostitute who tarnished the reputation of her victims', a victim in her own right who was cruelly failed by a system that could have saved her?

Wuornos' horror story really did begin at conception. She was born on 29 February 1956, in Rochester, Michigan. Wuornos' mother, Diane, married her father, eighteen-year-old Leo Pittman, on 3 June 1954, and her young life had horrors of its own. Diane was only fourteen years old, still a child herself, when she married an eighteen-year-old man, and one cannot help but wonder how this could have been allowed to pass. Their first child, Keith, was born on 14 March 1955, when Diane was just fifteen, followed by their second child, Aileen, less than a year later.

Diane had already filed for divorce from her husband by the time Aileen was born. It turned out that Wuornos' father was a paedophile: an alcoholic sex offender who was later sentenced to life imprisonment for raping a seven-year-old girl.

He was diagnosed with schizophrenia and died by suicide in prison by hanging himself on 30 January 1969.

Although Wuornos never met her father, she clearly came from a damaged and unstable background and her early years reflected the chaos of her parents' existence. Her mother, far too young and completely unsuited to the task of nurturing two young lives, was incapable of loving her unfortunate babies. An alcoholic, and perhaps overwhelmed by the responsibilities of parenthood, she abandoned both children in January 1960, when Aileen was just three years old. She was left in the incapable hands of their maternal grandparents, Lauri and Britta Wuornos, who were also alcoholics. Wuornos' view of this early betrayal certainly impacted and sullied future relationships; she would later tell film director Nick Broomfield, 'We never knew her ... she had me and left, she can go to hell. I don't even know her.'

Life with the Wuornos grandparents was anything but nurturing. Reports and later testimonials by Aileen herself indicated that she was subjected to both physical and sexual abuse. Incestuous relationships, particularly one with her brother Keith, further marked Aileen's introduction to sexuality and intimacy, pushing her understanding of these concepts into dark, convoluted territories.

In spite of them both being abusive alcoholics, her grandparents were allowed to legally adopt poor Aileen and her brother on 18 March 1960. It was in this cold and cruel environment that Aileen learned that men could not be trusted and that adults let you down. The unfortunate girl never stood a chance. Her grandfather was emotionally and physically abusive, tarnishing her early view of herself by branding her a 'whore' while regularly beating her, as well as sexually assaulting her. A childhood friend would later recount witnessing one such horrific ordeal and another would later describe her grandfather as 'a bastard who beat the hell out of her'. Her grandmother did absolutely nothing to help her, completely ignoring her husband's physical, emotional and sexual abuse. In fact, she was also emotionally abusive towards Aileen. Aileen became the victim of family and friends in her developing years and was raped repeatedly.

By the age of nine, this damage was manifesting itself in her aberrant behaviours. She was trading blow jobs for cigarettes and stealing from family and friends. It was also around this time that she was involved in an accident playing with fire, setting her family home on fire, which left her face and hands severely burned. Unsurprisingly, she had an explosive temper as a child, and this made it difficult for her to maintain friendships. She would repeatedly end up fighting with other children and alienating them. She set the girls' bathroom at school on fire at the age of thirteen and also set a field on fire at the age of fourteen.

By the age of eleven, she began having sex for money, drugs and food, exchanging what she had come to believe was affection with men and boys in the neighbourhood when she was still a child. Her warped view of relationships would fester and taint both her future ones and her evolving view of men.

At junior high school Aileen was found to have hearing and visual problems that were contributing to her poor adjustment. Her IQ was tested and found to be eighty-one, which was only just above borderline impaired or delayed, and school officials tried to persuade her grandparents to allow her to receive counselling for her behavioural problems. Her grandmother refused to give permission for this intervention, and they unsuccessfully tried to improve her behaviour by using a mild tranquilliser. Devastatingly, her early cries for help were all but ignored by those who could have made a difference. For Aileen, the adult world was one that hurt or failed her from the very beginning. This would become a pattern she would experience throughout her life and would undoubtedly impact her view of herself as she matured into adulthood.

By her pre-teen years, Aileen continued trading sexual favours for commodities. This exploitative environment set the stage for her tumultuous teenage and adult years, during which she faced homelessness, further sexual exploitation, and a spiral into criminal activities.

In 1970, when she was fourteen, vulnerable Aileen became pregnant, claiming a friend of her grandfather's had brutally raped her. Neighbours, who clearly knew about Aileen's abuse, concurred that her pregnancy was the result of her rape by an older man, yet they had done nothing to prevent this happening or to protect young Aileen. Feeling she had no one to turn to and fearing her grandparents' reaction, she kept the pregnancy a secret for six months. Upon learning of the pregnancy, they sent her to a home for unwed mothers where she gave birth to a baby boy on 23 March 1971, whom she was cruelly forced to give up for adoption. It is not surprising that she kept her pregnancy a secret, as she knew how her grandparents would react and, again, any chance to help this troubled teenager was unforgivably ignored.

Aileen's early years foreshadowed her later life. She was continually and indefensibly failed by the adults she found herself in the care of and, just a few months after the birth of her son, she dropped out of school. At fifteen, her grandfather threw her out of her home, and she ended up living in the nearby woods. Left with little other choice, and used to having her body used and abused, she began supporting herself through sex work.

In that same year, while Aileen was living rough, her grandmother died from her long-term alcoholism. She returned home for the funeral and, shortly after, was found living in the woods by the police and placed in a girls' training school for several months. After her release, she briefly returned to her grandfather's home. This didn't last long, though, and he threw her out after just a few weeks. Given little choice, she again reverted to sex work to survive.

In the following years, while still an adolescent, she was reportedly raped on multiple occasions, at least twelve times and, unsurprisingly, her criminal activity started young: on 27 May 1974, when she was just eighteen, she was arrested in Jefferson County, Colorado, for a DUI offence, disorderly conduct and firing a .22 calibre pistol from a moving vehicle. She was later charged with 'bail jumping'.

By the age of twenty, Aileen Wuornos was living in Florida, having managed to hitch-hike there. Here, she met and married sixty-nine-year-old yacht club president Lewis Gratz Fell. Their marriage was a whirlwind; its announcement was even printed in the local paper's society pages. Unsurprisingly, however, it ended after only sixty days. Their relationship had been violent from the beginning and came to its inevitable and early end when she was accused of attacking her husband with his own cane. He ended up filing a restraining order against her and, like every other relationship in her life, theirs broke down painfully and she found herself alone again.

With little other choice, Wuornos returned to Michigan

where her behaviour became more and more erratic. She was arrested on 14 July 1976, after throwing a snooker ball at a bartender's head, and was charged with assault and disturbing the peace, briefly being sent to jail.

In that same year, her brother Keith died from oesophageal cancer. Wuornos received ten thousand dollars from his life insurance and, unused to having money, she spent it in just two months, frittering it away on luxuries. She bought a car and wrote it off shortly afterwards.

During this same period her grandfather died by suicide, and Wuornos had now lost everyone she had considered family. By the age of twenty-two, in 1978, Aileen was losing her struggle with her mental health and, like her grandfather before her, made a very real attempt to take her own life by shooting herself in the stomach. She was hospitalised for two weeks, then discharged. A week later she overdosed on tranquillisers. One cannot but wonder, given these very obvious cries for help, why Wuornos was denied the psychological help she clearly needed. Between the ages of fourteen and twenty-two, she attempted suicide six times.

On 20 May 1981, Wuornos was arrested in Edgewater, Florida for the armed robbery of a convenience store. She had stolen just thirty-five dollars and two packets of cigarettes and was sentenced to two years in prison for it. After her release, her criminal activity really began to escalate. On 1 May 1984, she was arrested for trying to use forged cheques at a bank in Key West. On 30 November 1985, she was named as a suspect in the theft of a revolver and ammunition in Pasco County. On 4 January 1986, she was arrested for car theft, resisting arrest and obstruction of justice for claiming to be her aunt when asked for ID by the police. Police later found a .38 calibre revolver and a box of ammunition in her stolen car. On 22 June 1986, when she was thirty, she was arrested in Volusia County after a man accused her of threatening him with a gun and demanding two hundred dollars. Police discovered a .22 pistol under her passenger seat.

In the same year she met, and made the fatal decision to move in with, twenty-four-year-old motel maid Tyria Moore. This was the first and only meaningful relationship in Wuornos' life, although it was the second she'd had with a woman. She would later assert, 'It was love beyond imaginable. Earthly words cannot describe how I felt about Tyria.' In fact, she still claimed to be in love with her on the day of her execution.

Wuornos was determined that her relationship with Moore would succeed, unlike the others she had experienced in her life, so she supported the two of them with her earnings as a sex worker. This relationship certainly exacerbated her criminal behaviour, as it appeared she would do anything to keep Moore in the style she had become accustomed to. Undoubtedly, Moore played a pivotal role in Wuornos' escalating criminality.

Just a year after they met, they were both detained for questioning about an incident involving assault and battery with a beer bottle, and eight months later, on 12 March 1988, Wuornos accused a bus driver of assault, citing Moore as the witness.

As their relationship continued, so did Wuornos' deviant behaviour, and this would reach a crescendo in 1989, when Wuornos would begin a killing spree that would take the lives of seven men and see her life ended by lethal injection. All her victims were male motorists between the ages of forty and sixty-five, all were white and had been robbed and shot.

Wuornos' first murder was of fifty-one-year-old Clearwater electronics store owner Richard Charles Mallory. Wuornos claimed he beat, raped and sodomised her after driving her to a remote area and hiring her as a sex worker. Murdered on 30 November 1989, his body was found on 13 December. He had been shot several times in the chest. Items belonging to him were later found at a local pawn shop and the receipt for these contained Wuornos' thumbprint. Other stolen items were then also traced back to Wuornos, including a camera and a key. Many believe that this rape, which she would later to go on to describe at trial, was the catalyst for her killing spree. She would describe his attack in court, saying he had sadistically smeared rubbing alcohol into her rectum, vagina and nose before raping her and intended to rub it in her eyes as 'a grand finale'. Although Mallory had previously spent ten years in prison for rape, his previous offences would not be mentioned in court, ensuring Wuornos' accusations would not be taken seriously by a jury.

David Andrew Spears, a forty-seven-year-old construction worker in Winter Garden, was declared missing on 19 May 1990. His naked body was found on 1 June, in Citrus County. Wuornos had shot him six times in the torso with a .22 pistol.

Only five days later, the body of Charles Edmund Carskaddon, a forty-year-old part-time rodeo worker, was found in Pasco County in a secluded area. He had been shot eight times in the chest and stomach with a .22 calibre weapon. Wuornos wrapped his body in an electric blanket, and it was badly decomposed by the time it was found. Witnesses would later testify to seeing Wuornos in his car, and it was also discovered that she had pawned one of his guns.

Peter Abraham Siems, a sixty-five-year-old merchant seaman, was her next victim. He left his home in Central Florida for New Jersey and was not heard from again. The police found his car on 4 July 1990, in Orange Springs, Florida. Both Moore and Wuornos were seen leaving it and Wuornos' handprint was later discovered on the door handle, but tragically his body was never found.

Just twenty-seven days later, on 31 July 1990, Troy Eugene Burress, a fifty-year-old sausage salesman from Ocala, was reported missing. Killed by two gun shots, his body was found on 4 August 1990, in a wooded area along State Road 19 in Marion County.

Just over a month after this discovery, Charles Richard 'Dick' Humphreys, a fifty-six-year-old US Air Force major and former chief of police and child abuse investigator, was murdered by Wuornos. She later claimed he had grabbed her arm and said, 'How would you like to suck my dick and I won't do anything, but you're not getting any money for it. If you suck my dick ... you can go scot-free.' His fully clothed body was found on 11 September 1990, in Marion County. He'd been shot seven times in the head and torso; his car would later be found in Suwannee County.

Her final victim was discovered on 19 November 1990 in Dixie County. Walter Jeno Antonio, a sixty-two-year-old trucker and security guard, as well as a reserve police officer, had been shot four times in the back and head. His car was located five days later in Brevard County.

There is no doubt that Wuornos' upbringing, steeped in trauma, contributed to her fractured psyche. Children and adolescents exposed to continuous trauma often develop reactive attachment disorder, which makes it challenging for them to form healthy emotional attachments. This condition can manifest in various ways, including impulsiveness, aggression and a consistent pattern of mistrust towards others. Coupled with the potential genetic predisposition to mental health disorders, considering her father's schizophrenia, her psychological make-up was a potent mix of environmental and genetic factors. The sexual exploitation she experienced at a tender age likely distorted her perceptions of power dynamics, self-worth and relationships, making her see violent acts as both a means of survival and a form of empowerment.

The repercussions of her childhood trauma were evident in her adult life. Wuornos became a drifter, engaging in sex work as a means of survival. Her string of violent crimes against men can be interpreted as the culmination of years of suppressed rage and trauma, and a desperate need to assert control in situations where she felt vulnerable, mirroring her experiences from childhood. Although her stories regarding the murders would be inconsistent, she claimed each and every murder was an act of self-defence. Later, psychologist Melissa Farley, who was involved in her case, would state: 'Aileen was terrorised by violent johns, and eventually lashed out in a crazed defence, just like men do in wars when they are also afraid of getting killed or tortured.'

Whatever her motivations, police knew they had a dangerous killer of men on the loose, who had to be stopped. Initially they were looking for two female perpetrators. In a stroke of luck for authorities, on 4 July 1990, Wuornos and Moore abandoned Peter Siems' car after a road traffic accident in which Moore had been driving. A witness, Rhonda

Bailey, provided a description of the two women involved and a media campaign was launched to find them. Belongings of Siems were subsequently discovered in a pawn shop and Wuornos' fingerprint was found on the receipt. Because she had a record, her details were on the police database, and she was arrested on 9 January 1991 at a biker bar in Volusia County. Police cited an outstanding warrant in the name of Lori Grody as the reason. Moore was located in Pennsylvania the next day. Although she was a suspected killer – seen driving and leaving a murdered man's car by a witness, being in possession of the property of another victim and being located by a witness with Wuornos at the time of Humphrey's murder – she was not charged and instead made a state witness, as she agreed to get a confession from Wuornos in exchange for immunity from prosecution. Moore returned to Florida with police where they housed her in a motel. She made various calls to Wuornos that were knowingly recorded by police, asking her to help clear her name. In an act of love, Wuornos reassured her, 'I'm not going to let you go to jail.'

She would later listen to the recorded calls and weep in court as she finally understood the depth of betrayal from the woman she had loved and protected, who gave seventy-five minutes of testimony against her. She would naively assert, 'I'm gonna miss her for the rest of my life.' Unbelievably, Moore and three officers involved in her case would later exploit her in an attempt to make movie rights packages and book deals selling their story, leading to the resignation of three detectives on her case. Far too late Wuornos recognised that Tyria, and others, were 'using [her] monetarily'.

On 16 January 1991, just three days after those recorded calls, Wuornos confessed to all of the murders, claiming the men had tried to rape her and that she killed them in self-defence. Wuornos did not understand her rights when she was arrested, and her confessions were inconsistent. This undoubtedly played into the hands of the prosecution. Tragically for Wuornos, her determination to clear the name of the woman she loved, rather than herself, sealed her fate. She even told her public defender to be quiet, telling interrogators, 'I took a life, I am willing to give up my life because I killed people. I deserve to die.'

On 14 January 1992, Wuornos went to trial for the murder of Richard Charles Mallory. Although previous convictions are normally inadmissible in criminal trials, under Florida's Williams Rule, the prosecution was allowed to introduce evidence related to her other crimes to show a pattern of illegal activity. Added to this, and against her attorney's advice, Wuornos also made the mistake of testifying at trial. Although she repeated the claim of self-defence, she became agitated during cross-examination and she was consistently told not to answer questions, invoking her Fifth Amendment right against self-incrimination twenty-five times! She was the only defence witness, and on 27 January 1992, damned by Moore's testimony, Wuornos was convicted of Mallory's murder. At her sentencing, psychiatrists for the defence testified that Wuornos was mentally unstable, and they diagnosed her with borderline personality disorder and antisocial personality disorder. This was ignored and, four days later, she was sentenced to death with a 12:0 verdict.

Wuornos' defence made efforts after the trial to introduce pertinent evidence that Mallory was previously convicted for rape in Maryland and served a sentence in a maximum-security correctional facility providing remediation to sex offenders. Records obtained from the correctional institution showed that from 1958 to 1962 Mallory was committed for treatment and observation resulting from a criminal charge of assault with intent to rape. These records also reflected eight years of overall treatment from the facility, and in a note on his file from 1961, 'it was observed of Mr. Mallory that he possessed strong sociopathic trends'. In spite of this, the judge refused to allow the records to be admitted in court as evidence and denied Wuornos' request for a retrial.

On 31 March 1992, despite her earlier claims that two of her victims 'raped [her] and five tried', and her alleged belief that, 'they were gonna rape [her], kill [her], strangle [her]', Wuornos pleaded no contest to the murders of Charles Richard Humphreys, Troy Eugene Burress, and David Andrew Spears. She claimed she wanted to 'get right with God' and, in her statement to the court, she said, 'I wanted to confess to you that Richard Mallory did violently rape me as I've told you; but these others did not. [They] only began to start to.'

On 15 May, Wuornos was given three more death sentences and in June, she pleaded guilty to the murder of Charles Edmund Carskaddon. In November, she received her fifth death sentence. In February 1993, Wuornos pleaded guilty to the murder of Walter Jeno Antonio and was sentenced to death again. No charges were brought against her for the murder of Peter Abraham Siems, as his body was never found. She was given a total of six death sentences in all and, in her own words, the question had to be asked, 'How many times you gonna kill me?'

Throughout her trial and incarceration, Wuornos continued to be used and let down by those who should have helped her. Her case is a catalogue of missed opportunities and failures that ended in seeing someone who was of unsound mind executed. Standing trial only once, for the Mallory murder, she pleaded *no contest* or *guilty* to the subsequent murders while represented by her private attorney, Steve Glazer. The state's capital collateral office, representing Wuornos later, told a judge in support of an argument for new trials that 'her attorney did a rotten job of defending her in Pasco and other counties ... and that she deserved new trials.' Center for Constitutional Rights attorney Joseph Hobson asserted, 'Essentially she had no representation.' Glazer had negotiated cash deals with media outlets for interviews. He was also filmed smoking marijuana en route to advise Wuornos in prison. Her case was his first death-penalty case and he admitted to arranging an interview with Nick Broomfield for ten thousand dollars, taking a quarter of that for himself. However, it was under Wuornos' specific instruction that he entered a guilty plea. Prosecutor Phil Van Allen stated, 'It was clear Wuornos was on a mission of self-destruction.'

Perhaps the most surreal example of the exploitation of Wuornos during her incarceration was her adoption by an evangelical Christian, Arlene Pralle, who befriended her claiming she had a dream where Jesus told her to write to Wuornos. In the end it transpired that Pralle was using her to fund her failing farm and that she was also receiving a cut of the payments Glazer had arranged for interviews with Wuornos, including one with Broomfield which gave her a cut of ten thousand dollars. Wuornos would later tell Broomfield that both Pralle and Glazer had given her advice on how she could take her own life in prison. Later she would tragically acknowledge, 'She adopted me to bury me ... I think their motive was just to make money.'

From 1994 to her execution in 2002, Wuornos tried unsuccessfully to argue that her original counsel failed to provide effective representation: they had not used Mallory's previous rape conviction, which would have aided her case, nor had they brought in witnesses who could have testified to her claims of childhood abuse. Many childhood friends and neighbours asserted that they were contacted by the media, but never by her defence team, and they would later substantiate Wuornos' claims of abuse in a number of documentaries. She also argued that her mental health had not been evaluated effectively before she stood trial.

Wuornos told several inconsistent stories about the killings, and these aided the prosecution. She claimed initially that all seven men had either raped or attempted to rape her while she was undertaking sex work. She later recanted the claim of self-defence, citing robbery and a desire to leave no witnesses as the reason for murder. During an interview with Broomfield, when Wuornos thought the cameras were off, she told him that all of the killings had, in fact, been in self-defence, but that she could not stand being on death row, where she had been for ten years at that point, and wanted to die. Broomfield concluded that Wuornos was 'mad' after his interviews with her.

As her years on death row continued, her mental health declined further and it seems that, in the end, death seemed preferable for a woman whose life had been intolerable from birth. She fired her lawyers, dropped all appeals and rejected witnesses that might have helped her in an act that deliberately sabotaged any form of defence. In fact, she determinedly stated, 'You have to kill Aileen Wuornos because she'll kill again.' In the end, she simply wanted to be executed and, tragically yet predictably, this is the only wish that ever came true for Wuornos, the killer who was also a victim.

Feminist and psychologist Phyllis Chesler's book *Requiem for a Female Serial Killer* emphasised the horrors of Wuornos' life: 'She had been raped and beaten so many times that, by now, if she was at all human, she'd have to be permanently drunk or out of her mind.' In a letter written to Chesler from her prison cell, Wuornos stated: 'I am a female who has been raped and the male dominant world is laughing. They've succeeded in putting me in the chair to prove that men can and will do as they want to us women of America.'

When she thought she was off camera, she told Broomfield, 'They're too corrupt, they stick together, they'll only fuck me some more.'

In fact, Julie Bindel, an investigative journalist and campaigner, asserts that Wuornos perfectly fit the role of victim of a serial killer, acknowledging that news coverage completely omitted any mention of her tormented mental state. Instead, she was depicted as a sexual deviant who seduced and murdered innocent men, as a lesbian who used men to her advantage.

Even Florida state governor Jeb Bush used her case to his advantage while running for re-election. Although he granted a stay of execution on 30 September 2002, to assess whether Wuornos was competent to be executed, he stated, 'I hope to have these competency issues resolved fairly but promptly.' It took only fifteen minutes for a psychiatric assessment to deem her competent for execution. This was despite a number of her sacked attorneys writing to the

Supreme Court to express their belief that she absolutely was not competent. Even the day before her execution, Wuornos was exhibiting signs of paranoia and instability, claiming that prison guards were poisoning her food and that she had to wash it before consuming it. Raag Singhal, the attorney appointed to represent her after she complained about conditions on death row, argued, 'She's got to rely on someone to stand up for her, even though she doesn't want that person standing up for her.' He also poignantly asserted, 'I don't think there is any societal goal that is reached by executing someone who might be mentally ill.'

Aileen Carol Wuornos was executed on 9 October 2002, in spite of misgivings from many who met and knew her. Indisputably, she was a danger to society and needed to be incarcerated to protect both herself and those she met. She was a convicted murderer and had to face justice; however, whatever story you believe about her murders, one cannot help but wonder at the motivation for her six death sentences, without any recognition of her intolerable life experiences and unstable mental health. After all, even a sadistic and heinous killer like Ted Bundy was offered life imprisonment instead of execution.

This then has to beg the question: did the fact that Wuornos was a woman who not only killed men, but tarnished their reputations, mean that she was treated more harshly in a system dominated by men than a man facing a similar sentence? Should rehabilitation and treatment not have been offered to this very damaged and neglected individual – a woman who was let down continuously by a system that failed her from her very conception and could have saved her long before she trod the path of her own destruction?

Sometimes the signs that things aren't right are there after all, if you look closely enough at what's happening next door. Could the creation of this female serial killer have been prevented if she had been helped by those neighbours that watched and witnessed, yet remained silent?

15

Joanna Dennehy: Deadly charms

What makes a girl, who was described as so sweet butter wouldn't melt in her mouth by her mother and those who loved her, leave home at the tender age of sixteen and turn into a heartless, thrill-seeking killer? Any assumption that women are not capable of mindless cruelty simply by way of them being female is shattered by the case of Joanna Christine Dennehy, who epitomises the fact that appearances may be deceptive.

Our tale begins in an ordinary English town, but the protagonist of this story is anything but ordinary. Dennehy, a figure of contrasts, was known for her charismatic charm and manipulative prowess. These traits, often found in psychopathic personalities, were the veils behind which lurked a deeply troubled and violent nature.

Unlike many who kill, there were no childhood traumas that could possibly foreshadow the dark path Dennehy chose to take. She came from a stable, loving home in Redbourn,

Hertfordshire and her family of four was a typical one. Her mum, Kathy, worked in a local shop and her dad, Kevin, was a security guard. She had an older sister, Maria, and growing up the girls were extremely close; they shared bunk beds and were so bonded to one another that they invented their own secret language. Young Dennehy was described as sensitive and caring by her family, to the degree that if she stood on a worm and it died, she would cry.

In school, Dennehy consistently attained good grades. Her parents hoped she would go to university to study and become a lawyer. They had even paid for extra tuition to this end. Her teachers remembered her as polite and 'a nice girl' and also knew her as a 'bookworm'. She loved netball and hockey and, at least to many who thought they knew her, appeared to be a normal teenager from a loving home.

It transpired that beneath this veneer of normality, the girl many described as 'smart, pretty and kind' was not who she seemed. In fact, a very different character was trying to emerge: a character that showed itself to some friends long before her murder spree began, and who were probably not as shocked as her family to discover the monster hiding beneath.

Dennehy's primary school best friend Vicky Greenwood's recollections of her are different from those of her family. She asserts that by the age of fourteen, a dark side was beginning to emerge; she was smoking and drinking, sometimes even taking alcohol into school. By the age of fifteen she was playing truant and hanging around with older boys. She had also started making boys she considered 'geeky' do her homework for her. Vicky remembers her as being manipulative from a very young age; if friends did not conform to her standards, there would be consequences.

Another friend, Marika, who initially considered herself close to Dennehy at high school, found out what it was like to get on the wrong side of her. Out of the blue, Dennehy started bullying her. She threatened she would 'get her' on the way home from school and Marika felt so unsettled by this threat that she walked longer routes home for fear of bumping into her. Marika was frightened of what teenage Dennehy would do to her and suspected her capacity for evil long before her true potential for it was known publicly. Chillingly, Dennehy also told Marika that she would be better off dead and said that she could help her kill herself.

One cannot help but wonder why this cruel behaviour wasn't noticed and dealt with before it escalated, and Dennehy ran away. How were her parents and sister so oblivious to her true nature? It certainly highlights what a good actress Dennehy was. Her chameleon-like nature certainly fooled those she loved. These were the early signs of her emerging psychopathy, and these early behaviours give us some insight into the monster she became and foreshadowed the darker paths she chose to take.

The catalyst that triggered Dennehy's massive decline seems to be her decision to leave home, which shocked her family. Any stability in her life was eradicated by this bad decision. In August 1998 at the age of sixteen, she left her loving family, only returning occasionally when she needed money. She ran away with twenty-one-year-old John Treanor. She was only fifteen years old when she met him and, although he claims there was no sexual relationship before she was sixteen, he was a man, and she was still a child.

Her story is a stark reminder of the complex interplay between nature and nurture. While some aspects of her psychopathy might have been innate, it is conceivable that her life experiences played a role in sharpening these tendencies. The traumas and turmoil of her teenage life, often cited in discussions about serial killers, might have been the dark soil in which the seeds of her future actions were sown. It is possible that, though self-inflicted, these traumas and adverse life experiences played a part in her journey towards violence. Serial killers often have backgrounds marked by traumatic experiences, and though these do not excuse their actions, they can contribute to the development of destructive behaviours and attitudes.

Treanor still asserts that he loved Dennehy and he was certainly willing to endure difficult times in order to be with her. Initially they lived in tents, as they had little money and no one to support them. Treanor struggled with their chaotic existence but, although Dennehy was used to the comfort of a secure and loving home, she is said to have thrived in this world of chaos.

Unsurprisingly, her family were frantic when she left them; they loved their daughter and sister and could not imagine what had caused her to abandon them so coldly and cruelly. There was a brief reconciliation when they discovered her and Treanor living on wasteland. Sadly, however, the damage had already been done; the drugs and drinking and her determination to be with the man she had left them for made her leave again.

The pair rented a room in a shared house and Dennehy became pregnant at the tender age of sixteen. She did not want children and Treanor claims everything changed once their first child was born. Dennehy would regularly get stoned and take drugs and, from the moment her baby was born, she seemed incapable of displaying love towards her. She even used her firstborn to bribe her parents, telling them that if they wanted to see their grandchild, they would have to pay for the privilege.

Treanor was devastated that Dennehy had no motherly instinct. Instead, she would drink, take drugs and have sex with other men. She could not cope with emotional closeness, and rather than persevere with her intimate relationships, she numbed herself with alcohol. Although she was with him for five years and had a child with him, as her deviant behaviour escalated, Treanor could not cope and left her, taking their child with him. He knew life with her was dangerous and needed to protect his baby.

Their break-up did not last long, however, and it appears that Dennehy's magnetic pull was a seductive force that Treanor could not resist. Taking her back, their small family moved to Wisbech where Dennehy began working on a farm. Here, she found herself pregnant again and, unsurprisingly, her response to this second baby was no better than it was to the first. If anything, it exacerbated her instability.

Dennehy's erratic behaviour escalated along with motherhood, and she would disappear for weeks at a time, returning with black eyes and bruises. Treanor later described her as having turned into the devil. She even etched a tattoo under her right eye herself. Treanor would recount one occasion when she went out drinking in the middle of the night and sent a man round to beat him up, totally unprovoked. Her children were in the house during this horrific attack, and her eldest, Shianne, remembers the feelings of terror she experienced to this day.

Around the same time as Dennehy's aberrant behaviour

escalated, her older sister, who was in the armed forces, finished her tour of Helmand Province in Afghanistan. She loved her younger sibling and could not comprehend what had gone so wrong as to cause this chasm within her once close-knit family, so she traced her to an address in Cambridgeshire. Determined to stay where she was and continue in her chaotic existence, however, Dennehy rejected her, saying she wanted nothing to do with her or her parents. As her erratic behaviour continued, she began self-harming and even confided in Treanor that she felt like she could kill someone. This coincided with increasingly violent behaviour towards Treanor and she began carrying a dagger in her boot. In 2009, concerned for his family's safety, he moved out and took the children with him. Again, one cannot help but wonder why he did not seek help for her. It could have made a difference.

Dennehy's behaviour continued to deteriorate after her abandonment, and she drifted around East Anglia, stealing and using sex work to feed her drug habit. She served some time in prison for theft and drug offences, where she received some help for her deteriorating mental health. She had also been given a twelve-month community order for assault and owning a dangerous dog in 2012.

In February of that same year, she spent a few days in Peterborough City Hospital and was diagnosed with anti-social personality disorder that manifested itself in anger, aggression, impulsivity and irresponsibility, and obsessive compulsive disorder.

At this point she was on probation and under supervision. Frustratingly, however, the probation service failed her and, more importantly, her victims. Dennehy was described by her probation officers as having 'a sadistic lust for blood'. Although she was under the supervision of Cambridgeshire and Peterborough probation services, she missed a number of appointments. Sadly, her offender manager lacked experience; they had appraised her and come to the conclusion that she had 'the potential to cause serious harm ... but was unlikely to do so ... unless there was significant change in her circumstances'. There were many missed opportunities to put Dennehy on a better track.

The role of mental health in Dennehy's decline cannot be overlooked and it is conceivable that her untreated or undiagnosed mental health issues could have influenced her violent tendencies. Dennehy's journey into darkness was also marked by a profound lack of empathy, a characteristic void that often lies at the heart of a serial killer's psyche. This absence of empathy was not just a deficit but a chasm that allowed her to commit her heinous acts without the burden of conscience or remorse.

The psychological canvas of Joanna Dennehy shows a particular form of psychopathy. Unlike the cold, calculating demeanour often associated with serial killers, Dennehy displayed traits of 'impulsive psychopathy'. Her actions were spontaneous, driven by a terrifying need for thrill and control. This type of psychopathy is characterised by reckless disregard for the safety of self and others, a trait chillingly manifested in her crimes.

Freed from any obligations or responsibilities as a mother, Dennehy moved into a bedsit that she rented on the outskirts of Peterborough, and it was here that she fatefully met John Chapman. From the moment he met her, John seemed to recognise Dennehy's instability. Their neighbours, Michelle

Bowles and Toni Ann Roberts, claimed he was frightened of her and referred to her as a 'crazy woman'. Soon after her arrival, their landlord, Kevin Lee, would start using Dennehy to intimidate tenants into paying their rent. In this role, she certainly intimidated John Chapman and exacerbated the feelings of fear he had for her.

Of course, Dennehy was already known to the police and probationary services because of her previous sentence and, although Kevin Lee was warned he was playing a deadly game using Dennehy to do his dirty work, his infatuation with her overwhelmed him and would be his undoing. His wife would later claim he was being coerced by Dennehy, but she could certainly charm men and her seduction of Lee ensured she got what she wanted; although he employed her, she controlled him. In fact, she would later be described as 'extremely seductive' and other neighbours would fall under her dangerous spell, including Robert Moore, who she manipulated to carry out her dirty work. John Chapman was possibly the only man who could resist her apparent charms. Sadly, however, this immunity would not be enough to protect him from this monstrous psychopath and, although he seemed safe from her charms on meeting her, that would change as Joanna's confidence in her new status evolved.

As our narrative delves deeper, we encounter the grim theatre of her crimes – a spree that sent shockwaves through the heart of England. Dennehy's victims, chosen without motive for the most part, became unwilling actors in her macabre play. The randomness of her attacks, a departure from the more patterned approach of many serial killers, added a layer of terror to her rampage. She and her accomplice Gary Stretch modelled themselves on the infamous duo Bonnie and Clyde and set out with the goal of murdering nine men. Although she would later attempt to kill two more men, she failed and fortunately fell way short of her intended number.

Keeping his distance from Dennehy, John could see her evil potential from the very beginning. Sadly, this was not true of her first victim, thirty-one-year-old Lukasz Slaboszewski, who had come to the UK to begin a new life in 2005. Dennehy met and seduced him, and within days he was dead. Tragically, just before she murdered him, he had texted his friend describing his life as 'beautiful' because he had Dennehy as his girlfriend. Tragically it turned out he was just a pawn in her macabre game. Luring him to her flat in Peterborough, solely to kill him, she stabbed him through the heart. Then she callously put his body in a wheelie bin while she decided how to dispose of it.

She was thrilled by this first kill; she even showed the body in the bin to a fourteen-year-old girl she had befriended. She then borrowed money from Kevin Lee and bought a car for the sole purpose of disposing of the body. She travelled by taxi with Stretch, whom she had met and befriended not long after moving to Peterborough, to pick it up. Then the two of them found a suitable place to dump Lukasz's body. The site they chose was Thorney Dyke, a place near to where Stretch used to live and where he had chillingly claimed you could hide a body and it would never be found. From the moment he met her, seven-foot-three Stretch was infatuated with Dennehy, even though she allegedly 'made it clear' she 'wasn't the sort of person one should pursue'. Although he would pay for his obsession with her and never be free of her beguiling spell, at least he would live to tell the tale.

Her next victim was the neighbour who had previously

shared his fears about Dennehy: fifty-six-year-old John Chapman. She murdered him about a week later, probably in the early hours of Friday 29 March. She callously stabbed him to death in his own bedsit. John, a Falklands veteran, had bravely served his country and had been in the Royal Navy, but had become an alcoholic after discharge. Dennehy exploited this weakness. She, Stretch and fellow tenant Leslie Layton drank with him just days before his murder.

Dennehy had previously threatened that she would get John out of the house by any means. An eviction notice had already been served, and Lee was still using Dennehy to intimidate tenants. Lee could have had no idea of the means by which she planned to rid them of John, or of the thrill she would get from murdering another man for kicks. Enjoying her feeling of power, she callously stabbed him to death – once in the neck, severing the carotid artery, and five times in the chest, puncturing the heart twice. She used so much force that his breastbone was penetrated right through.

There were no defensive injuries found on his brutalised body, and his blood alcohol level was four times the limit for driving. He was probably asleep at the time of his murder. No doubt Dennehy got a sadistic kick from stabbing a defenceless victim over and over again.

Shockingly, when Leslie Layton discovered what Dennehy had done, rather than calling for help, he took a picture of John's butchered body (evidence he later tried to delete, but police forensics found it). Layton also assisted in the disposal of John's body; Dennehy, Stretch and Layton dumped him in the ditch at Thorney Dyke where the body of Lukasz Slaboszewski still lay.

Her next victim was her landlord, forty-eight-year-old

Kevin Lee, whom she was having an affair with and working for. She clearly felt nothing for him, in spite of their affair. Lee was a much-loved husband and father who wanted to help Dennehy and fell under her spell, becoming infatuated with her. In order to ensnare him, Dennehy claimed she had been abused as a child and that, because of her abuse, she had killed her own father and spent years in prison.

Of course, this was a web of deceit woven simply to manipulate Lee. His belief in her tragic tale would captivate him and be the undoing of this naive man. Kevin believed her tale of woe and befriended her, giving her a both a home and a job. In fact, they became so close, she even confessed her first murder to him. She would later tell another tenant, Georgina Page, that she had to kill Kevin because he had seen Lukasz's body.

So, she lured him to 11 Rolleston Garth, a property he owned in the Dogsthorpe area of the city, to kill him, promising him that she was going to dress him up and rape him. (He confided this to best friend David Church before meeting her.) Kevin had previously told David of their sexual encounters, and they were always extreme. Instead of the promised sex, callous Dennehy stabbed Kevin five times in the chest, penetrating both lungs and his heart. Unlike John before him, he fought for his life and had defensive wounds to show for it. Yet this did not deter the monster from achieving her end game, and Lee was overpowered by this heinous killer.

She then called in Gary Stretch to help with the clean-up operation. The pair were seen by a number of witnesses as they coldly went about their foul business and, later that same evening, Dennehy, Stretch and Layton set fire to Kevin Lee's Ford Mondeo after dumping his body at Newborough, another remote rural area. Dennehy had dressed his body in a black sequinned dress. He was deliberately dumped with his buttocks exposed as a final act of humiliation. Her callousness towards his wife and children in leaving him in this way highlighted her absolute lack of remorse or human empathy.

Kevin's disappearance sparked a murder hunt. His wife reported him missing and his burnt-out car was found in the Peterborough countryside. His body was found by a dog walker. Police instantly knew they had a deeply disturbed killer, but even they could not imagine the extent of her psychopathy or of her bizarre ability to cast a spell over others and manipulate them into doing her bidding. It would have been impossible for Dennehy to hide the bodies of her victims without the help of accomplices and, unbelievably, she had three: thirty-six-year-old Layton, fifty-five-year-old Moore and forty-seven-year-old Stretch. Although Layton at least had the decency to appear upset to friends Toni Ann Roberts and Michelle Bowles, he did not go to the police and consistently lied to them, claiming he had no idea what had happened to John Chapman.

Moore was so besotted with Dennehy, he was prepared to do anything for her, even if that meant jeopardising his own freedom.

Stretch, her third and main accomplice, was always willing and able to do her bidding. But his part in the murders would extend way beyond transporting bodies and helping her evade police. They shared a classic case of *folie à deux*, a shared psychosis, where they experienced a world in which even the most extraordinary ideas and behaviours are seen as permissible. David Wilson, professor of criminology at Birmingham

City University, said that in these cases, it is normally the woman who follows the dominant male partner. Unusually, however, Dennehy was the dominant partner, and infatuated Stretch willingly 'accommodated her world view'.

On Monday 1 April, Dennehy and Stretch would boast about the three murders to another tenant, Georgina Page. Watching footage of the massive nationwide hunt for them, Dennehy would callously laugh about having dressed Kevin Lee up and lubricated his backside, before shoving something in it to make it look like a sexual act. Dennehy told Page she knew they would get caught and go to prison for a long time. Stretch asserted that he did not care what happened to him because his children were grown up. At this point they both felt they had nothing to lose, and this made the duo more dangerous than ever. Terrified of what they would do to her, Page did not inform the police, but she did testify against them in court.

By now the police were closing in. They had mobile phone data putting both Dennehy and Stretch at the site where the bodies and the burnt-out Mondeo had been found. The assumption was that seven-foot-three, twenty-three-stone giant Stretch was their killer and, although they had got a key piece of the puzzle wrong, they realised the people that they were looking for were extremely dangerous and had to be caught immediately. Tragically they would not find them in time to spare two other innocent men and their families.

On 2 April, after returning to Peterborough and spending another night on the run at Robert Moore's home, the pair got up early and set off for Hereford, a place Stretch knew well, with malintent. He had burgled houses there looking for valuables he could sell as they had no cash. They met up with other men at a flat in Kington. One of them, Mark Lloyd, was coerced into helping them sell goods. Threatened with a gun, he would be held prisoner in their car and sit through the horror of what was come, helpless to change the outcome.

While driving through Hereford, Dennehy coldly said to Stretch, 'I want my fun!' and instructed him to find her a victim. Besotted with her, and willing to do anything to impress her, Stretch obliged, spotting a dog walker and stopping his car.

The unfortunate dog walker and Dennehy's first victim on that day was Robin Bereza, a sixty-three-year-old retired fireman. In an act of extreme yet psychopathic cowardice, Dennehy attacked him from behind, stabbing him in the back, then the right upper arm. As he turned to face her, asking her why she was hurting him, she callously told him, 'I want to hurt you, I'm going to fucking kill you.'

Robin desperately tried to fight her off, but he had been taken off guard and stood no chance against this heinous psychopath who continued the attack until another car arrived on the scene. Stretch had waited for her, watching the horrifying attack all this time. Dennehy then calmly got back into her car, smiling at the driver of the car that had arrived on the scene as she did so, leaving Robin Bereza for dead.

Miraculously, he survived, although his injuries could have been fatal. His chest wall was penetrated, causing a haemopneumothorax (when blood and air enter the space between the lungs and the chest wall) and, if he had not received medical attention quickly, and had the blood and air not been drained from his chest, he would certainly have died.

By now Dennehy was so high on adrenaline from the

attack that she asked Stretch to find her another victim. Again, Stretch chose an unfortunate dog walker; fifty-six-year-old John Rogers. Callously attacking him from behind and stabbing him repeatedly in the back, she took him completely by surprise. As he fell, she showed no mercy and continued viciously stabbing him. Mark Lloyd, who was still trapped in the car, an unwilling witness, described this attack as even more harrowing than the previous one and cried while recounting the horror of it. In court, the judge would describe John Rogers' stabbing as 'relentless and frenzied', telling Dennehy, 'you left him for dead'. After this heinous and brutal attack, she arrogantly picked up her victim's dog and left the scene. Later she would coldly inform police that she had killed Rogers.

Thankfully it would be moments later, in the car driven by Stretch, and with her final victim's stolen dog on her knee, that she would be finally captured by police. When arrested, she grossly 'flirted' with officers, saying, 'It could be worse, I could be big, fat, black and ugly.' Although she believed she had killed five men, she would display no indication of the horror of the crimes she had just committed. In fact, she was described as 'buzzing' by those who dealt with her in the aftermath of her rampage. She had clearly got a thrill from it all. In another act of cruel cowardice, when interviewed by police, her cool and detached response was simply 'no comment'. Fortunately, they did not need a confession from her as they had more than enough evidence to charge her. Unsurprisingly, her elated behaviour stopped with this realisation.

Her barrister Michael Procter would later describe Dennehy as cooperative, not at all nervous and charismatic.

He even stated that he 'felt drawn to her', which again shows the magnetic pull Dennehy had on the many people who had fallen prey to her. Although police expected a long trial where the whole story could play out as publicly as possible, to the shock of them and her legal counsel, she pleaded guilty. In her typical style, however, she did not simply plead guilty. Instead, she shouted 'Guilty!' over and over again in an act that would later be described as her last chance to be centre stage and 'a piece of dramatic theatre'. Dennehy wanted to be in control; she wanted to be known as a famous, terrifying serial killer who was not scared of the sentence she was about to face.

In the face of damning and compelling evidence, Mr Justice Spencer sentenced her to life imprisonment, saying it would have to be 'very substantially in excess of thirty years'. This was because her crimes were planned and premeditated, sexually and sadistically motivated and because she already had a criminal record.

The psychiatric report from Dr Farnham (dated 26 October 2013) stated that she suffered from a severe emotionally un-stable personality disorder, paraphilia, sadomasochism and a psychopathic disorder – that is a personality disorder char-acterised by superficial charm, a callous disregard for others, pathological lying and a diminished capacity for remorse.

The judge quite rightly said these diagnoses could not be used in partial defence and would not afford any mitigation in her case. Dennehy had showed absolutely no remorse; she had even told the judge, in a letter, that she would be lying if she claimed she did. She divulged to her psychiatrist that her thirst for murder became 'moreish'. Her final victim (who miraculously survived, but she had certainly intended to murder) had more than thirty stab wounds. She admitted killing was a kind of fetish for her.

In unravelling the enigma of Joanna Dennehy, we encounter the paradox of human nature. How can a person, capable of charm and wit, descend into such depths of brutality? This dichotomy is a key to understanding the complex nature of psychopathy, where superficial charm masks a profound moral bankruptcy. Joanna Dennehy's motivations for her heinous acts of killing are deeply rooted in a complex web of psychological, emotional and possibly experiential factors. At the forefront of her motivations was likely a profound and disturbing need for thrill and power. This is vividly illustrated in the impulsive and reckless nature of her crimes, which suggests she derived a perverse sense of gratification and empowerment from her control over life and death. The randomness of her victim selection and the boldness of her actions point towards a person in pursuit of intense excitement and dominance.

Dennehy also displayed distinct psychopathic traits, including manipulative behaviour and a glaring lack of remorse. These traits are often linked with a heightened propensity for violent behaviour. Her psychopathy, characterised by an emotional void, enabled her to inflict harm without the usual emotional restraints that inhibit most individuals. Furthermore, her charm and manipulative skills, traits commonly observed in psychopaths, may have aided her in attracting and subsequently overpowering her victims.

Another aspect of Dennehy's motivations could be a desire for recognition or notoriety. This is a characteristic observed in some serial killers who strive to establish their identity through their crimes, often leaving behind a 'signature' or taking trophies. Dennehy's seeming pride in her actions and her lack of effort to conceal her crimes might indicate a longing for acknowledgement and infamy. The dramatic spectacle of her plea in court also supports this view.

She received a whole life sentence for her murders, with concurrent sentences of life imprisonment for the two attempted murders. She also got a concurrent sentence of twelve years for preventing the burial of Lukasz Slaboszewski, John Chapman and Kevin Lee.

For their parts in her murders, Gary Stretch was sentenced to life with a minimum term of nineteen years. Leslie Layton got fourteen years as he had previous convictions and Robert Moore got three years, as his record was previously clean, and he had been infatuated with and manipulated by Dennehy.

Even after she was incarcerated in Bronzefield Prison, Dennehy's supposed charm continued in spite of being described by Jenni Richards QC, on behalf of the prison system, as 'the most dangerous woman in the prison system'. She received love letters from Gary Stretch, which he signed from 'your biggest supporter' and 'Hubby for life'. She cruelly forwarded these on to his ex, Julie Gibbons, adding her own letter, telling her she had 'no remorse' for her actions.

Years on, she is still writing to a variety of men and psychiatrists say she will never stop manipulating people. The women she has been incarcerated with are also susceptible to her charms. In 2018 she requested permission to marry her cellmate, Hayley Palmer. Palmer's family feared for her safety. Dennehy allegedly told her, 'We will tread a path so dark, so mentally and physically dangerous we will cease to know where I begin, and you end.' Palmer's family's fears proved valid when, in 2018, the two of them attempted suicide together.

In 2019 Dennehy was moved to Low Newton Prison, where it is alleged that she threatened Rose West, who had to be moved for her safety. In 2020 Dennehy was reported to be in a relationship with Emma Aitken, a woman in prison for twelve years for the murder of a man. In May 2021 there was more talk of Palmer and Dennehy marrying.

Even behind bars, Dennehy continued to court attention. Prison staff discovered a diary in which she had written the details of a 'credible' escape plan. This plan involved cutting the finger off a member of staff and using it to pass through biometric security doors.

Unquestionably, Joanna Dennehy epitomises evil. She described herself in a love letter as 'a fully committed psychopath'. Her ex, Palmer, who is now a free woman, claimed Dennehy had no regrets. In fact, she said she would regularly laugh about her heinous crimes. Sadly, this is not the case for her surviving victims or for the families of those she murdered, whose lives will never be the same again.

John Chapman's family remember him as a loving brother, brother-in-law and uncle. He had bravely served for his country.

Lukasz Slaboszewski's sister, Magda, said their whole family had been devastated by their tragic loss.

And Kevin Lee's wife and family still can't come to terms with the cruel nature of his death and the allegations Dennehy made about their husband and father. His wife still believes today that Dennehy was coercing him in some way. She said Dennehy had 'taken and ruined her family's lives'.

Robin Bereza still cannot grasp the reality of the fact that a complete stranger could commit such a heinous and unpro-voked attack. He is described as 'a shadow of his former self'. His wife's and their children's lives have been turned upside down, and it is only with their love and support that he has survived the experience at all.

John Rogers feels the same. He knows he would be dead if it wasn't for the fast actions of the medics who attended to him on that fateful day. The results of the attack affect his life every single day. He was a keen musician but can no longer play the guitar. He says the psychological trauma has been devastating and that, like Robin, without his wife, he would not have survived the ordeal.

Joanna Dennehy's path to becoming a serial killer likely emerged from a convergence of psychological disturbances, a deep-seated need for power and thrill, and potentially the impact of her later life experiences. Her case stands as a chilling reminder of the extreme manifestations of human behaviour and the dark potential that can emerge from such a detrimental confluence of factors.

It is not surprising that Dennehy's own mother cannot come to terms with what she has done. She stated, 'When I saw the footage of Jo, it was like somebody I didn't know. She's standing there being charged, smiling and laughing, that's not the kind, loving Jo that was our baby.' She also asserted, 'To me she doesn't exist anymore. I don't ever want her to come out of jail. The world is safer without her in it.'

This sentiment is also reiterated by her ex-partner and father to her two children, John Treanor, who believes Dennehy is so evil and unrepentant that she should be executed.

Her eldest child, Shianne Treanor, who has now come of age, and whose life has been affected detrimentally by her mother's infamy, stated that her mother 'deserved to die in prison', calling her crimes 'horrendous'. She also admitted that her first fear in discovering who her mother was and the extent of her crimes was, 'Will I turn into her? Will that be me?' After visiting Dennehy in prison to try and get answers from her, Shianne said, 'She apologised to me. It doesn't make it right, but I wanted the apology'. She also acknowledged that part of her mother's punishment is that she will never see her grow up.

The fact that her mother, former partner and daughter believe the world is a better place without Dennehy highlights just what a dangerous psychopath she really is. Undoubtedly, we should all feel safer in our beds knowing this heinous, unrepentant thrill-seeking monster will live out her days behind the barred windows of Low Newton Prison, County Durham.

Epilogue

As we bring this exploration of the darkest depths of humanity to its close, our hearts must be heavy with the weight of understanding and empathy for the victims of such brutal, unconscionable violence. Through these chapters delving into the twisted minds of serial killers, we have borne witness to unspeakable horrors and irrevocable losses, all while seeking answers and striving to comprehend the incomprehensible.

In the aftermath of such terror, it is paramount to emphasise that no individual, under any circumstances, deserves to become a victim of these remorseless predators. Their crimes are a perversion of humanity, leaving behind a trail of pain and suffering that defies understanding. Yet even in the face of such darkness, we must find the strength to stand tall, to protect ourselves, and to reduce the possibility of falling prey to these human monsters.

Protecting oneself from a serial killer requires alertness, awareness and a profound trust in one's instincts. It necessitates the forging of strong connections with loved ones and the cultivation of a network of support and vigilance. However, it is of utmost importance to make it clear that non-compliance is often the key to survival when faced with such a threat.

Nevertheless, we must also confront the painful reality that authorities, the institutions in place to protect us, often fail in their duty. The annals of true crime are littered with missed opportunities and oversights that have led to unnecessary loss of life, fuelling frustration and heartbreak. These instances underscore the need for vigilance, not just on a personal level, but also within our systems of law and order, ensuring that no more lives are lost to bureaucratic inertia or neglect.

We mourn those who have been lost, and we lament the failures that allowed these tragedies to unfold. Yet we must transform our grief and anger into a relentless pursuit of justice and reform, learning from the past to safeguard our future. Certainly, the change in the outdated double jeopardy rule has enabled the likes of Gary Allen and David Smith to finally face true justice.

We have laid bare the horrifying reality of serial killers, delving into their minds and exposing their methods. But amid the sorrow and the darkness, we have also uncovered the indomitable spirit of survival and the power of resilience that resides within us all.

As we turn the final page, let us not be left in despair, but rather be imbued with a fierce determination and a renewed commitment to protecting ourselves and our loved ones. We stand united against the shadows, empowered by knowledge and bolstered by our refusal to comply. In our shared journey, we have found strength, and in our collective resistance, we have discovered the enduring power of the human spirit.

As we've seen, serial killers can weave their wicked webs while hidden in plain sight. Many of them are nice neighbours, liked colleagues, even seemingly dedicated spouses and parents. The serial killer next door won't advertise themselves to you, but charm you, smile at you, maybe even befriend you. The cases we've looked at beg the question: do you ever really know who lives next door?

Thankfully, serial killers are the rarest of beasts. According to the sanctified data from the United Nations Office on Drugs and Crime, the probability of becoming entwined with a serial killer is a minuscule 0.00039 per cent.

Visualise, if you will, an endless metropolis, teeming with a million souls, each carrying their own dreams, fears and loves. In this sea of humanity, only a handful will ever know the cold embrace of such a malevolent fate. The odds wrap around you like a cloak of protection, a shield against the darkness.

But we must not forget that for some the nightmare becomes a reality, and it is crucial that we pause and turn our thoughts towards those whose lives were cruelly snatched away. The tales of horror we have navigated may have ended on these pages, but the echoes of the victims' lives resound, timeless and profound. These victims, unjustly chosen by perpetrators of the utmost malevolence, were sons and daughters, friends and lovers. Their stories, though tragically cut short, demand our attention, our remembrance.

Amid the stories of terror and the dissection of the criminal mind, we must not forget the essence of what was lost – the vibrant flames of life, extinguished too soon. In remembering them, we affirm their existence, honour their memories, and offer solace to the ones left behind, bearing the unbearable weight of loss.

Serial killers, the rarest of predators, may cast long shadows, but we must not let the darkness obscure the light of the lives they touched. We stand united, a collective consciousness, acknowledging the pain, the loss, and the unfathomable grief.

Let it be a reminder that life, in all its fleeting and fragile beauty, is to be cherished. The shadows of the past serve as a solemn reminder to hold our loved ones close, to live with purpose, and to shine our light in the darkest of times.

So, let us take this moment to remember, to honour, and to mourn. But let us also use this moment to rekindle our commitment to life, to love, and to the enduring strength of humanity. The victims' stories will not be forgotten; their lives are eternally engraved in our collective memory. In their remembrance, we find the strength to move forward, embracing life with open hearts and undying resilience.

List of Named Victims

Chapter 1

Cynthia Jaramillo

Kelli Garrett

Angelica Montano

Marie Parker

Chapter 2

Linda Slawson

Jan Whitney

Karen Sprinker

Sharon Wood (attempted)

Gloria Gene Smith (attempted)

Linda Salee

Chapter 3

Karen Spark

Lynda Ann Healy

Donna Gail Manson

Susan Elaine Rancourt

Roberta Kathleen Parks

Brenda Carol Ball

Georgann Hawkins

Janice Anne Ott

Denise Marie Naslund

Nancy Wilcox

Melissa Anne Smith

Laura Ann Aime

Carol DaRonch (attempted)

Debra Jean Kent

Caryn Eileen Campbell

Julie Cunningham

Denise Lynn Oliverson

Lynette Dawn Culver

Susan Curtis

Margaret Bowman

Lisa Levy

Kathy Kleiner

Karen Chandler

Cheryl Thomas

Kimberly Dianne Leach

Chapter 4

Ambrose Griffin

Teresa Wallin

Dan Meredith

Evelyn Miroth

Jason Miroth

David Ferreira

Chapter 5

Cindy Paulson

Celia 'Beth' van Zanten

Sandra Patterson

Megan Siobhan Emerick

'Eklutna Annie'

Joanna Messina

Sherry Morrow

Paula Goulding

Mary Kathleen Thill

Roxanne Easland

Lisa Futrell

Andrea Altiery

Sue Luna

Robin Pelkey

DeLynn Frey

Malai Larsen

Teresa Watson

Angela Feddern

Tamera Pederson

Chapter 6

Julie Harris

Debra Feldman

Bill Currier

Lorraine Currier

Samantha Koenig

Chapter 7

John Farrell

David Francis

Salney Darwood

Bill Roberts

Chapter 8

Samantha Class

Julie Hogg (victim of William Dunlop, mentioned in passing)

Alena Grlakova

Chapter 9

Sarah Crump

Amanda Walker

Linda Donaldson (suspected)

Maria Requena (suspected)

Chapter 10

Wendy Knell

Caroline Pierce

Mary Akande

Helen Akande

Azra Kemal

Chapter 11

Ruth Munroe

Malcolm McKenzie

Dorothy Osborne

Everson Theodore Gillmouth

Eugene Gamel

Leona Carpenter

Betty Mae Palmer

James Gallop

Vera Faye Martin

Dorothy Miller

Benjamin Fink

Chapter 12

Alexi Samsonova (presumed)

Sergei Potanin

Volodya

Valentina Nikolaevna Ulanova

Chapter 13

María Amparo González

Concepción Carranza

Regina Jiménez Peña

Consuelo Ortiz González

Victoria Alicia Domínguez y Sols

Margarita Margoliz Kenigsberg

María del Carme Juana Montalvo Ruiz

María de la Luz González Anaya

Manuela Torrecillas Bentabal

Guillermina León Oropeza

Alicia Cota Ducoing

María Guadalupe González Juanbelz

María Guadalupe de la Vega Morales

María del Carme Muñoz Cote de Galván

Gloria Enedina Rizo Ramírez

Lucrecia Elsa Calvo Marroquín

Natalia Torres Castro

María Eugenia Guzmán Noguez

María Guadalupe Aguilar Cortina

Luz Estela Viveros Padilla

Margarita Aceves Quezada

Alicia González Castillo

Andrea Decarte Carreto

Carme Cardona Rodea

Socorro Enedina Martínez Pajares

Guadalupe González Sánchez

Estela Cantoral Trejo

Delfina González Castillo

María Virginia Xelhuantzi Tizapán

María de los Ángeles Cortés Reynoso

Carme Alicia González Batta

Margarita Martell Vázquez

Simona Bedolla Ayala

Ana Reyna Rentería Morales

María Dolores Martínez Benavides

Margarita Arredondo Rodríguez

María Imelda Estrada Pérez

Julia Vera Duplán

María Elisa Pérez Moreno

Ana María Velázquez Díaz

Celia Villaliz Morales

María Guadalupe Núñez Almanza

Emma Armenta Aguayo

Emma Reyes Peña

Dolores Concepción Silva Calva

María del Carmen Camila González

Guadalupe Oliveria Contreras

María de los Ángeles Repper Hernández

Ana María de los Reyes Alfaro

Chapter 14

Richard Charles Mallory

David Andrew Spears

Charles Edmund Carskaddon

Peter Abraham Siems

Troy Eugene Burress

Charles Richard 'Dick' Humphreys

Walter Jeno Antonio

Chapter 15

Lukasz Slaboszewski

John Chapman

Kevin Lee

Robin Bereza

John Rogers

Acknowledgements

To my beautiful children, you changed everything, and for that I am eternally grateful. Thank you for drenching me in your love and breathing joy into every corner of my life.

To Pete, my husband, the man who adores and supports me in equal measure, thank you for never questioning my potential. Your love is never ceasing, always understanding and is genuinely unconditional in its grace.

To my beloved sister and friend Alexia, this book wouldn't have happened without your love, support, guidance and commitment. You have helped bring the vision to life on a multitude of levels and I am more grateful than you will ever know.

To my darling father Donald Stanley Taylor, the man who made me, who loved me without question and who was always there for me, until he was no longer able to be. I miss you endlessly, your friendship, your hugs, the belief you held in me. I hope somewhere in the big, beautiful beyond you are feeling these sentiments and enjoy seeing your name in print.

To all my family, both those with whom I am bonded by blood, and to those I have found on my journey through life, thank you.

Finally, to all of you who have watched my TV shows, subscribed to my YouTube and Facebook channels, listened to my podcasts and attended my True Crime theatre shows; without you none of this would have been possible. My gratitude is endless, so know that each and every one of you matters.

Sources

Chapter 1

David Parker Ray transcripts accessed via New Mexico Inspection of Public Records Act request to New Mexico police department, May 2024.

Chapter 2

Statement about Brudos is quoted in Dan de Carbonel, '36 years later, killer's death relieves victims' families', *Statesman Journal*, 29 March 2006

Chapter 4

David Wallin's statement is quoted in Luke Kenton, 'DRACULA KILLER I found my pregnant wife's disemboweled body after "Vampire of Sacramento" serial killer cut her up and drank her blood', *Sun*, 31 January 2022

Suspect description and case details quoted in Josie Klakström, 'Revisiting "the Vampire of Sacramento"', *Sacramento News & Review*, 13 August 2021

Chapter 6

Israel Keyes' suicide note, original images accessed via www. fbi.gov/image-repository/israel-keyes-writings.jpg/view

Transcripts quoted in Matt Pearce, 'Serial killer Keyes' suicide note was violent, angst-ridden poetry', *Los Angeles Times*, 6 February 2013

Chapter 7

Page 128 statement of Maudsley's childhood quoted in Andrew Robinson & Connor Dunn, 'Sadistic life and crimes of Robert Maudsley living in glass box under "Monster Mansion" HMP Wakefield', *YorkshireLive*, 28 March 2022

Pages 130–132 statement of Maudsley's criminal intentions accessed via www.blackkalendar.nl/c/1508/Robert%20 Maudsley
National Archives J 202/103, J 291/249, J 82/4134, J 267/548

Page 134, Robert Maudsley's statement is quoted in Tony Thompson, 'The caged misery of Britain's real "Hannibal the Cannibal"', *Guardian*, 27 April 2003

Page 135, Robert Maudsley's statement is quoted in Ryan Merrifield, 'Calls for twisted serial killer "Hannibal the cannibal" to be removed from glass dungeon', *Mirror*, 26 February 2024

Page 136, Robert Maudsley's letters quoted in Sian Hewitt & Lily Morl, 'Broadmoor Hospital killer Robert Maudsley 'to die in underground glass box' after appeal for freedom rejected', *BerkshireLive*, 27 December 2021

Chapter 8

Probation officer Rosemary Park's statement about Gary Allen accessed via www.judiciary.uk/wp-content/uploads/2022/07/R-v-Gary-Allen-Sentence-Note.pdf

Page 146 threat by Gary Allen quoted in Danielle Hoe, 'How a chance meeting at a bus stop led to the brutal murder of beloved Rotherham mum Alena Grlakova', *YorkshireLive*, 17 June 2021

Page 157 statement by Gary Allen quoted in Pritti Mistry, 'Gary Allen: The killer who nearly got away with murder', *BBC News*, 17 June 2021

Statement by Sophia Class quoted in Philip Whiteside, 'Gary Allen: Double-murderer convicted of killing women 21 years apart may be behind unsolved violent crimes, say police', *Sky News*, 18 June 2021

Chapter 9

Steven Williams and Mr Justice Bryan statements accessed via www.judiciary.uk/wp-content/uploads/2023/05/Sentencing-Remarks-R-v-David-Smith.pdf

Sarah's family statement quoted in 'Killer guilty of murder 30 years after he was cleared', *Shropshire Star*, 24 May 2023

Chapter 10

Unnamed mother quoted in Tom Pettifor, 'Morgue Monster "Like an animal"', *Mirror*, 16 December 2021

Nevres Kemal quoted in Daniel Keane, 'David Fuller: Mother of woman whose body was raped in mortuary by murderer speaks out', *Yahoo News*, 5 November 2021

Bill Knell quoted in Tom Symonds, 'The double murderer who sexually abused the dead for decades', *BBC News*, 4 November 2021

Chapter 12

Pages 211 and 212 Tamara Samsonova statement quoted in Will Stewart, 'Serial killer cannibal 'Granny Ripper' reenacts how she cut off head of final victim then boiled it in a saucepan to shocked police', *Mail Online*, 4 September 2015

Page 213 Tamara Samsonova statement and Mikhail Timoshatov quoted in Will Stewart, 'Did she EAT her victims?: Serial killer "Granny Ripper" who kept diary of 11 people she decapitated may be a cannibal', *Mail Online*, 5 August 2015

Maria Krivenko quoted in Anna Pukas, 'Gruesome granny: Russian pensioner confesses killing 11 victims', *Express*, 18 August 2015

Emilio Alvarez quoted in Jo Tuckman, 'The lady killer', *Guardian*, 19 May 2006

Chapter 14

Pages 237, 238 and 246 statements from *Aileen Wuornos: The Selling of a Serial Killer*, Nick Broomfield, 1992

Page 242 statement by Aileen Wuornos quoted in Jamie King, *Serial Killers: Shocking True Stories of the World's Most Barbaric Murderers*, Octopus Publishing Group, 8 February 2024

Page 244 statement by Aileen Wuornos accessed via https://library.law.fsu.edu/Digital-Collections/flsupct/dockets/81498/81498ans.pdf

Melissa Farley's comment is quoted in Julie Bindel, 'Aileen Wuornos was no monster', *UnHerd*, 12 November 2020

Emma Kenny is a psychologist, TV presenter, writer and expert media commentator, and is now recognised as one of the UK's leading TV psychological experts. She is perhaps best known for her role as resident therapist and agony aunt on ITV's *This Morning*, where she provides expert advice on a whole range of sensitive issues. Emma has also emerged as a fan favourite for her presenting roles on true crime programmes, most notably *Britain's Darkest Taboos* on the Crime & Investigation Channel. Her YouTube True Crime series is becoming one of the most watched on the platform and her live theatre tour continues to sell out around the UK. *The Serial Killer Next Door* is her first book. She lives in Bury with her family.